PRAGMATIC HISTORICISM

PRAGMATIC HISTORICISM

A Theology for the Twenty-First Century

SHEILA GREEVE DAVANEY

State University
of New York
Press

Published by
State University of New York Press, Albany

Production by Susan Geraghty
Marketing by Anne M. Valentine

Printed in the United States of America

For information, address State University of New York
Press, State University Plaza, Albany, N.Y., 12246

Library of Congress Cataloging-in-Publication Data

Davaney, Sheila Greeve.
    Pragmatic historicism : a theology for the twenty-first century / by Sheila Greeve Davaney.
       p. cm.
    Includes bibliographical references and index.
    ISBN 0-7914-4693-x (alk. paper) — ISBN 0-7914-4694-8 (pbk. : alk. paper)
       1. History (Theology). 2. Historicism. 3. Pragmatism. 4. Theology. I. Title.

BR115.H5 D28 2000
230'.046—dc21

99-057803

10 9 8 7 6 5 4 3 2 1

For
Larry and
Peter, Emily, Renée, and Megan

who sustain and challenge me and
make me laugh

CONTENTS

PREFACE

Books are written for many purposes. This one had its origins in the sense that theology on the current North American scene has made, in recent decades, important shifts reflective of and responsive to the widespread historicist sensibilities of our age. For many years theologians engaged in intense self-scrutiny concerning the possibility of theology when theology's traditional sources—reason, revelation in the natural world and through human artifacts such as scripture, and experience—have all progressively been challenged. What could theology be in an age when our sources have been relativized, our subject matter, religion, socially marginalized, and our own intellectual discipline increasingly interpreted as unsuited for the academy within which the questions and content of knowledge are determined? Yet while many thinkers have concluded that theology has come to an end, at least as a legitimate intellectual pursuit, others have boldly reconceived theology's task and purposes in light of the historicist turn that has so broadly characterized our moment. The impetus of this book was, in part, the desire to get a handle on these developments, to chart in a systematic way the outlines of theology as a historicist enterprise.

But if this general purpose has propelled this work, more personal reasons have really been its driving force. Those reasons have to do primarily with the desire to create an identifiable locale for myself and like-minded thinkers on the theological spectrum, on the theological map of our day. As the introduction to this volume will reiterate, one of the ways we organize a sense of our time and place is to draw and assume particular portrayals or maps of our intellectual, cultural, social, and political landscape. Maps highlight different landmarks, tell us how to get to different places, and utilize varying identification schemes. Depending upon the intellectual maps we employ, different questions emerge as important, some positions seem central and others peripheral and, indeed, depending upon the boundaries we draw, certain options are included in the landscape while others fade into uncharted wilderness beyond recognized boundaries.

There certainly has taken shape today a map of the theological terrain that is historicist in character. In particular two theological perspectives, postliberalism and revisionist theology, both deeply responsive to the historicist temper of our times, have taken center place on our theological landscape. Many contemporary depictions of present-day theology portray these approaches to theology as exhausting the legitimate options for theology in our historical moment.

Each of these approaches raises significant questions about the implications of an intensified historical consciousness for theology and has developed distinctive responses in an historicist mode. They offer theological options that should command our attention. Nonetheless, the kinds of theology envisioned in these perspectives have seemed, as the analysis of this book will try to demonstrate, to be expressions of a partial and finally fainthearted historicism. As I have sought my own place on the theological landscape, both postliberalism and revisionist theology have, in the end, appeared to me as inadequate locations to carry out theology at the beginning of a new millennium.

This book is my effort to identify an alternative historicist perspective on the theological scene. That alternative approach I have termed pragmatic historicism. It is a mode of theological reflection that I will argue combines an expansive historicism with a clear pragmatism. Elements of this form of theology can be found in a number of theologians working today. But pragmatic historicism has not yet been designated as a definite trajectory with a clear identity. A good part of this work is addressed to the identification and, in a sense, the creation of this trajectory as a viable option for current theology. Hence, I will bring together a number of people, some of whom have been previously linked together and others who have pursued their work under a variety of rubrics and from disparate locations. By juxtaposing their ideas I do not intend to claim that they all agree on every issue but that when taken together they represent a distinctive way of envisioning theology in a historicist mode.

But my purposes exceed the detailing and critical analysis of other persons' positions. I also seek to encourage the development of pragmatic historicism in very particular directions, especially in directions that are responsive to insights about the embodied, material, and political character of historical existence and to the pluralistic context within and external to our distinctive historical strands of inheritance. This, then, is also a constructive effort, emergent out of my engagement with the thinkers I seek to enlist as fellow pragmatic historicists.

The theologians I am recruiting, so to speak, as pragmatic historicists identify themselves primarily as Christian theologians. I, too, have been trained as a Christian theologian and have worked most extensively in relation to the Christian tradition. Thus, in a significant way, this work is an argument for the appropriateness of pragmatic historicism as a mode of Christian theology and will therefore often illustrate its claims by reference to this tradition. But it assumes that theologians who relate to other traditions might also follow the dictates of the approach proposed here, thereby constructing, say, a Buddhist pragmatic historicism or a Jewish pragmatic historicism. Hence, though pragmatic historicism, as articulated herein, has emerged out of a particular lineage of Christian and, indeed, modern western thought, its application is not confined to these locales.

Moreover, this work will be seen to argue that while theologians are located thinkers, situated within traditions, those locations are not always so neatly confined to single traditions but take shape out of and at the juncture of multiple, overlapping, and sometimes tension-filled influences. There is a real sense, thus, in which to state that this book is a work in Christian theology is inadequate. It not only seeks to propose an approach appropriate for other settings but also to push toward a kind of theology that emerges at the intersection of traditions. Hence, throughout this book there is an interplay of theology as Christian theology, as theology formulated in light of other traditions, and as theology not confined to one given tradition.

Chapter 1 sets forth my version of the historical setting in which we find ourselves. It details those earlier historical developments that have brought us to this time and the general assumptions that are now framing so much of the intellectual, including theological discussion today. As such it is a prolegomenon to the analysis and argument that follows.

Chapter 2 examines postliberalism and revisionist theology as two central historicist modes of reflection. The analysis suggests that while both perspectives draw our attention to the importance of the past for historical existence and for theology that purports to be relevant to that existence, neither offers an adequate interpretation of historical traditions and hence result in problematic renderings of how we should relate to our inheritances. In particular, it is asserted that postliberalism explicitly and revisionism more obliquely continue ahistorical and essentialist assumptions about the past. Thus while often postliberalism and revisionist theology are opposed to one another, this work will contend that they both set forth untenable views of the traditioned character of life.

Chapter 3 marks the explicit turn to pragmatic historicism. In this chapter I begin to identify those thinkers I will suggest fit into the pragmatic historicist approach for which I am contending. These theologians include, but are not limited to, persons such as Gordon Kaufman, William Dean, Sallie McFague, Delwin Brown, and Linell Cady. Others whose work would resonate with much that is set forth here include Rebecca Chopp, Victor Anderson, Francis Schüssler Fiorenza, Robert Neville, Nancy Frankenberry, and John B. Cobb, Jr. There are also other thinkers, more clearly identified with other disciplines, who would also, if space permitted, be valuable contributors to this work. These include Hilary Putnam, Charlene Haddock Seigfried, Nancy Fraser, Henry Levinson, David L. Hall, and Giles Gunn. Given, however, the constraints of this project, the purposes of this chapter are more limited. It is the task of chapter 3 to explore how pragmatic historicists understand the relation between theology and other intellectual disciplines. In particular, its seeks to detail the historicist rendering of reality and human existence that permeates much of the work of pragmatic historicist theologians as they forge their positions in interaction with these other disciplines.

Chapter 4 turns explicitly to theology. It sets forth the view of theology that emerges when historicity is taken as the central organizing rubric. Moreover, it turns our attention to the questions of how theology should construe the two dimensions of historical existence—our constitution by the past and our present context, and our agential capacity to create historical reality. How to interpret the interrelation of our traditionedness and human agency becomes an important angle of analysis as various pragmatic historicists are examined. This chapter also sets before the reader my own version of theology in historicist perspective, urging particular attention to the multitraditioned character of human existence and to the nondiscursive ways in which that existence is constituted.

If chapter 2 examined theological roads not taken chapter 5 turns to the work of pragmatist fellow travelers who are not theologians. This section explores the pragmatist positions developed by Richard Rorty, Jeffrey Stout, and Cornel West. It has as a specific interest not only how each thinker resonates with the views espoused in this book but also how these thinkers interpret religion and theology. On these issues, as on others, it is clear that while there is much support to be gained here, there are also important ways in which theological historicists and pragmatists offer views quite distinct from their more philosophical fellow pragmatists.

And finally chapter 6 turns to the question of where and how we should test our theological claims. In particular, this part of the book is concerned with the public character of our justificatory practices and the pragmatic nature of our claims to legitimacy. In a historicist age what can public mean? How are we to evaluate and assess competing proposals that take shape in disparate historical locales? Are our judgments simply local or are we compelled to engage broader communities and voices as we formulate and judge our theological visions of reality? It is to questions such as these that the final chapter of this work turns.

As in any intellectual enterprise an individual's work is reflective of the contributions and influences of far more than the author. I am grateful for the theological struggles and efforts of all the thinkers I analyze in this book. I have learned much not only from those with whom I agree but also those positions that I finally judge inadequate. I am also grateful for the responses these ideas have received as I have tried them out in various settings. Preliminary versions of several parts of the manuscript were given as the Cole Lectures at Vanderbilt University, the McFadden Lectures at Brite Divinity School, as lectures delivered at Phillips Theological School, and as papers at faculty colloquia at my own institution, Iliff School of Theology. The responses, including criticisms, I received were both enlightening and encouraging.

I am especially grateful to the band of thinkers I have labeled pragmatic historicists. Many of these thinkers have read this work and given support and guidance to this project. Gordon Kaufman, Linell Cady, and William Dean (who, in the midst of my writing this book, became my colleague) all read the manuscript with extreme care. Their insights and critical acuity have been extremely influential on its final form even as I found their questions daunting. My cohorts at the Highlands Institute of American Religious Thought honored me and this movement with a seminar focussed upon the manuscript. Delwin Brown, Victor Anderson, Nancy Frankenberry, and Wesley Robbins all wrote papers on the text, shaping its final outcome in significant ways. Of all the people who have worked with me on this project my colleague and friend Delwin Brown deserves particular mention. Every part of this book reflects his influence, in particular his relentless insistence that we are traditioned creatures with histories to which we must attend. That this book has come to fruition is in good part the result of Del's friendship, love for theological argumentation, and willingness to encourage me even when he thought I was wrong.

Most importantly all these thinkers have ventured their own theological proposals. In so doing, I believe, they have not turned their gaze away from the implications of being historical beings but have courageously and boldly sought to redefine theology in light of our historicity. For that courage and for their friendship, both intellectual and personal, I am indebted.

I want to thank, as well, my doctoral assistant Meredith Underwood, who corrected various drafts of the manuscript and who prepared the index. Gene Crytzer, my late secretary, worked on many versions of the text, helping to bring it to fruition. My current assistant, Maggi Mahan, has contributed greatly to getting the manuscript in publishing order.

And finally, I want to acknowledge my family, my husband and colleague Larry Graham, and our children Peter and Emily Davaney-Graham, Megan Graham, and Renée Adams. Their love and support made the completion of this project possible. But more significantly, they remind me daily that it is for the purposes of life that we carry out the theological task.

ACKNOWLEDGMENTS

Portions of these articles have been reproduced in this volume:

"Judging Theologies: Truth in an Historicist Perspective." Copyright 1997. From *Pragmatism, Neo-Pragmatism, and Religion*, ed. Charley D. Hardwick and Donald E. Crosby. Reproduced by permission of Peter Lang Publishing, Inc.

"Mapping Theologies: An Historicist Guide to Contemporary Theology." Copyright 1996. From *Changing Conversations*, ed. Dwight Hopkins and Sheila Davaney. Reproduced by permission of Taylor & Francis/Routledge, Inc.

"Human Historicity, Cosmic Creativity and the Theological Imagination: Reflections on the Work of Gordon D. Kaufman." *Religious Studies Review*, vol. 20, no. 3. Copyright July 1994. Reproduced by permission of *Religious Studies Review*.

"Directions in Historicism: Language, Experience and Pragmatic Adjudication." *Zygon: Journal of Religion and Science*, vol. 26, no. 2. Copyright June 1991. Reproduced by permission of *Zygon: Journal of Religion and Science*.

CHAPTER 1

Histories and Contexts

PRELIMINARY REMARKS

It has become axiomatic in the late twentieth century to acknowledge that human beings are neither residents of everywhere nor nowhere but are situated within particular locales demarcated by distinctive languages, worldviews, political and economic structures, and social, religious, and ethical configurations. Moreover, this acknowledgment of the localized character of experience and knowledge has contained the recognition that our current context is the product of the vagaries of complex and varied historical processes that have preceded our era and of our own contemporary responses to and transformations of these processes. Human historicity, thus, entails both being constituted by our past and context and being agential contributors to new historical realities.

This book is about the present-day theological setting and the theological alternatives that have been taking shape in recent years. In particular, it is a volume about those theological trajectories that have emerged precisely out of this consciousness that we are historical beings, situated in particular contexts, products of specific historical lineages, and constructors of new possibilities, and from the attempt to think through what historicity entails for how we understand theology, its status and tasks. But in order to understand how we construe historicity today and what it implies for theology, we must, in good historicist fashion, understand something of how we got here; we must grasp something of the historical developments that have brought us to our late-twentieth-century situation. This opening chapter has as its purpose the tracing of these historical influences both as they have positively funded the stances we hold today and as that which we now repudiate and seek to move beyond.

The attainment of such historical knowledge and insight has not, however, proven to be an easy matter. For as our awareness of the importance of historical understanding has grown, so has the cognizance of the complexities, ambiguities, and even contradictions of the historical events and developments to which we are heir. The history we must sort out and comprehend no longer appears, as for many it once did, as singular, linear, and driven by an indefatigable telos. Instead, we confront our historical lineage today as plural, convoluted, and multidimensional, "with no single theme and no controlling plot."[1] Moreover, not only does history appear comprised of multiple, interacting processes—sociopolitical, economic, intellectual, religious, cultural, and so on—but these processes now can be seen more clearly to be both shaped by and the effective vehicles for the deployment of power. And, as the analysis of such deployment of power has become more central in a variety of historical interpretations, groups, and perspectives negatively affected by these arrangements and thereby often excised from earlier historical accounts are now increasingly visible and challenging prior renderings of the past.

But our understanding of the importance of history has not only been chastened by the complexities of the past and by the history of negative effects that has attended it. We, as we enter a new century, continue to be confronted by not only the ambiguous quality of history but by events of such enormous negative proportion that they seem lacking in all meaning or appear to have endless meanings and hence are without comprehensibility or closure. These events of holocaust and genocide, nuclear warfare and environmental destruction, too, are part of the history we must face and trace, products not of some extrahistorical reality breaking into the human plane but of the varied processes that have produced the rest of contemporary reality. Events of such magnitude also are part of the lineage that has brought us forth, reminding us that contemporary theological efforts are carried out not only in the face of positive historical potential but also before the horrors that human beings have wrought in history.[2]

Running through the recognition that we are products of historical processes that we both inherit and transform and that, therefore, we are thoroughly situated beings located within particular strands of history, has been the further insight that such history never comes to us in any self-evident or uncontrovertible manner. How we conceive of the past, delineate its processes, and evaluate its effects are always matters of interpretation that are infused with our understandings of the present and fraught with values, power, and commitments; how we read the past has a great deal to do with what purposes we pursue in the present. Thus, the pictures we draw of who we are today and of our current situation, and the renderings we offer of how we got here are profoundly interconnected and neither construals of the present nor those of the past are neutral or value-free.

While the difficulties of making sense out of the chaos of the past and discerning order in the confusion of the present are immense, such tasks are, nonetheless, imperative for thought and action. Hence, we employ what historian Peter Novick calls "regulative fictions" to organize periods of time, distinguish and systematize issues and events, and thematize trends and movements.[3] These are always artificial to some extent and, by virtue of generalizing and abstracting from the welter of concrete details of lived history, impose upon time and events an order they do not clearly have. Yet by so doing they allow us to define our historical location and to formulate the responses and initiatives that are possible at this particular time and place.

Currently, one of the most prominent regulative fictions western thinkers are utilizing to interpret our contemporary situation is to understand our own time in radical contrast, indeed opposition, to the preceding era that we call "modernity," a period that stretches from the Enlightenment through most of the twentieth century. Many western thinkers have, thus, come to characterize our historical moment as postmodern. What postmodernity entails varies from thinker to thinker with no common definition except that it is the "not modern." Increasingly a more nuanced rendering of modernity as culturally and cognitively pluralistic is emerging, replacing the monomythic interpretations of the modern period that tended to reduce the whole age to the Enlightenment and its assumptions and practices. Nonetheless there has continued a widespread tendency to define the present moment as a repudiation of the modern epoch. The analysis set forth in this chapter will suggest a less "pure" reading of our historical lineage and of its relation to our current situation.[4] It will reflect contentions made later in the book that we are inescapably shaped by our past, even when we reject it, and that past is not singular or univocal but always plural, consisting of multiple, diverse, and even conflicting elements. By calling for this impure rendering of our historical inheritance, this chapter will suggest that our present situation continues, albeit in a transformed manner, a number of the developments that preceded our era and simultaneously scrutinizes, challenges, and rejects other assumptions and projects of modernity. We are both constituted by our pasts and ever the transformers of that inheritance.

What follows in this chapter is a brief, and obviously selective, version of the infinitely more complex historical happenings that compose the seventeenth, eighteenth, nineteenth, and twentieth centuries in Europe and North America.[5] It focuses on those developments that have had continuing impact upon western, especially Christian, North American theology, and most pertinently upon reflection about the nature of theological discourse. And in particular it is concerned with those developments that have influenced, either positively or negatively, the historicist theologians dealt with in this book. Other theological trajectories might well have differing historical lineages, including nonwestern ones, and other kinds of relationships to the period in western culture that has preceded our own. Certainly non-Christian theologies have their distinctive historical narratives and relation to this period. Thus this section traces the background of a particular set of historicist theologies, not that of all theologies, even all Christian theologies, abroad in the contemporary world. Moreover, this chapter, because of the limits of space and the training and skills of the author, deals mostly with intellectual developments and less fully with the political, economic, and cultural lineages that immediately predate our own age. As many of the arguments that will take shape in this book suggest this focus is ultimately inadequate in itself and requires supplementation by more detailed analysis of the historical context within which these intellectual claims and arguments emerged; for finally, no intellectual positions stand alone, fully comprehensible outside of their concrete setting. The purpose of this chapter is not to provide such a detailed depiction but a more self-consciously limited one of highlighting, in a more or less panoramic sweep, those elements of modernity that form the most prominent backdrop for the theological trajectories engaged in this volume, especially those currents that have contributed to making "historicity" a central issue and, thus, "historicism" a viable, even inescapable, perspective. As such it seeks to set the stage for what follows while fully aware of the need for other types of analysis to supplement these efforts.

PLURALISTIC MODERNITY

One of the ways of demarcating historical periods is to interpret them as significant cultural, political, economic, and intellectual shifts that are responses to both crises in which previous order and consensus have broken down and significant changes in which new modes of existence or historical directions have emerged. Modernity has frequently been depicted as that seismographic set of changes that grew out of the demise of the medieval world and the developments commenced during the Renaissance and Reformation. Numerous elements contributed to these shifts: the dissolution of a Catholic Europe and with it the breakdown of ecclesiastical authority; the advent of Protestantism and the religious conflicts of the sixteenth and seventeenth centuries; the rise of modern science and the scientific method; the emergence of national states and centralized governments; technological advances; widespread exploration and global colonization, including the ongoing conquest of the Americas; alterations in commercial patterns and economic organization; even the reorganization of the family.

The results of such developments were profound. On the one hand, the breakdown of authority and of societal consensus, especially in the arena of religious conflict, indicated increasingly the need for public norms and criteria, not tied to particular traditions, that could be utilized to resolve conflicts among groups and individuals representing different perspectives, be they religious or political. On the other hand, advances in science, especially in mathematics, suggested that precise forms of knowledge, accepted broadly, could be formulated and demonstrated to be true. Thus, while old forms of authority and adjudication fell asunder, resulting in widespread cultural crises, concurrently new possibilities for secure knowledge and clear norms gained ascendancy.

The quest for a new certitude, now based on reason, not authority, found its fullest expression in the Enlightenment, generally taken to commence with René Descartes in the seventeenth century and culminating with Immanuel Kant in the late eighteenth and early nineteenth centuries. Its two main strands, rationalism, deriving from Descartes and his followers, and British empiricism, defined by Locke and those who followed him, identified the location for securing sure knowledge differently, the rationalists in the innate ideas of the mind and the empiricists in sense experience. Yet, despite offering conflicting arguments for where rational reflection should begin and what yielded indubitable grounds for further claims to knowledge, both the rationalists and empiricists evidenced an overwhelming confidence in reason's capacities and a conviction that it was human reason that led to liberation from superstition and the dismantling of stifling authoritarian structures, whether religious, political, or economic.

This confidence in reason's capacities did not stand in isolation but was part of an interlocking set of ideas that took compelling shape during the Enlightenment. Such complementary notions included the scientific-inspired conviction that the world was harmoniously ordered and that this natural order was accessible to human reason and knowledge and, hence, open to manipulation for human ends. Moreover, there was a strong confidence that human history was also capable of rational organization and direction and, hence, that progress, deliberately pursued, laid within the grasp of an enlightened humanity. Modern notions of the autonomous individual also took definitive shape during this era and with them the sense that humans should not capitulate to unexamined authority but should heed the rational or natural rules to be discovered within each human. And not only were human beings taken to be rational, capable of knowing the world and themselves and of directing history's future course, but increasingly, following John Locke, humans were understood to possess self-evident rights and it was upon such natural unabridgeable rights that the modern political order was to be established.

Hence, rationality, with its liberating impulses, was to govern all arenas of human activity and reflection. Theoretical rigor and clear and precise argument were the goals in scientific, philosophical, political, and even moral reflection. All that continued to embody earlier forms of so-called superstition or unreflective acceptance of authority was to be critically scrutinized and jettisoned. Ambiguity in thought or language and hence subsequent obscurity were ruled problematic. Religion, an obvious prime candidate for critical examination, was either denounced or made rationally acceptable in the forms of deism or a Lockean-type natural religion with its highest expression in a reasonable Christianity. Political and social philosophy also embodied the convictions of the Enlightenment with thinkers such as Montesquieu, Rousseau, and Diderot developing ideas that would impact later events such as the French Revolution. Even poetry, especially during the eighteenth century, sought, according to sociologist Donald Levine, scientific precision and became "plain" and "straightforward," devoid of allusions and ambiguities.[6]

If reason was interpreted as the vehicle or means by which all else was critically scrutinized, it was not unexamined itself. David Hume and Immanuel Kant were the clearest examples of critical consciousness making reason its own object of analysis. Hume's skepticism concerning knowledge of causal relations in the physical world, knowledge of God, and knowledge of the self exemplified both the encompassing range of critical consciousness and the limitations of reason. Kant, taking seriously Hume's critique of reason, sought to articulate fully its scope and outer boundaries. Combining the insights of both rationalism and empiricism, Kant argued that knowledge entails not only sensations but most importantly the active contribution of the mind that orders these sensations according to innate and universal forms or patterns of knowing. Moreover, knowledge was limited to the sphere of humanly ordered sensation and the categories or forms that were assumed to be necessary to the ordering of such sensory data. Thus *knowledge* of God and of any nonsensory realm became, in this schema, impossible.

The repercussions of Kantian philosophy reverberated throughout modernity and have influenced numerous disciplines, not the least theology. From the perspective of contemporary historicism, much of Kantian thought has had a deleterious effect, leading western thought in misguided directions. The Kantian dualistic portrayal of a reality divided between a phenomenal realm accessible to human knowledge and a noumenal sphere of things-in-themselves that escapes reason, the reduction of religion to morality and of God to a moral adjunct or alternatively a regulative ideal and the universal character of the categories of reason all have contributed to a dehistoricized view of reason. Importantly, for us, Kant's interpretation of religion and God removed them from arenas of empirical and historically defined knowledge and argument. Thus, Kant figures largely in the criticisms of the modern period offered by present-day historicists, more notably in historicists' depictions of modernity as that which should be rejected than as part of the lineage continued today.

Despite the anti-Kantian rhetoric of many present-day historicists, it is the contention of this rendering of our historical lineage that Kant has also played a substantively positive role in influencing both the historicism that emerged in the nineteenth century and the historicism of our current scene. In particular, Kant's insistence upon the active character of human knowing and his critical tracing of the *limits* and *scope* of reason and knowing have left a rich inheritance that continues in the thought of significant historicists engaged in this work. While the ahistorical categories structuring the knowing process have given way to interpretations of reason that are less universal and more contingent and localized, the recognition that the human knower is not only a passive recipient but an active participant in the construction of knowledge contributed immeasurably to the eventual historicizing of knowledge itself. And, while many thinkers, especially theologians, have resisted the Kantian reduction of religion to morality, it has become almost axiomatic that human reason cannot justify theological claims concerning God's existence or character in the manner that pre-Kantian thinkers assumed was possible, at least not the existence or character of a God assumed to transcend the natural and human spheres.

Kant represents, in significant ways, both the high point and the closure of Enlightenment modernity. For while the nineteenth century certainly saw the continuation of many of these concerns and the extension of the Kantian project, it also witnessed the intensification of the sense of historicity that was incipiently found in Kant's own work and that had been incubating in the thought of other seventeenth- and eighteenth-century thinkers and that would eventually question reason's universality, neutrality, and capacity for objectivity.

Numerous developments in the nineteenth century and into the early twentieth century embodied this growth of historical consciousness. These included the flourishing of biblical scholarship, the emergence, with thinkers such as Dilthey, Schleiermacher, and Ranke, of hermeneutics as philosophically and theologically important, the increase of interest in nonwestern religious traditions, the expansion of the emerging social sciences, the Hegelian historicizing of reason and Geist, and the Darwinian historicizing of the natural order in the theory of evolution. Moreover, the masters of suspicion—Marx, Nietzsche, Feuerbach, and Freud—all made their appearance, linking knowledge and claims to truth not to a neutral rationality functioning publicly and without distortion but to often hidden economic and psychological processes and operations of power. While all of these developments contributed to the simultaneous erosion of early modernity and the growth of historical consciousness, I will highlight those lines of thought that had the most significant influence upon theology as it has taken shape in the twentieth century.

Perhaps most significantly for theology there emerged during this period what is termed Romantic modernity or the counter-tradition to the Enlightenment. Disenchanted by the prioritizing of a reason that seemed to exclude the Spirit, nature, except as that which was to be utilized, and history, the Romantics stood in protest against the ruling tenets of the Enlightenment. Manifested in art, literature, poetry, music, philosophy, and theology, Romanticism emphasized the immediate, the aesthetic, the feeling dimensions of experience and the dynamic processes of life. Romanticism, moreover, embodied a turn toward nature in which the natural world was not viewed as merely a valueless realm suitable only for human manipulation, but as a dynamic, alive context, characterized by both beauty and tragedy, wherein humans have their home. Thus against the intellectualism of the Enlightenment, Romanticism proclaimed the truths of particular histories, nature, and the immediacies of experience.

Friedrich Schleiermacher was the most important theological exemplar of this counter-Enlightenment tradition. Schleiermacher accepted the Kantian strictures on reason in relation to God, acknowledging that rational argumentation failed to establish either God's existence or a clear knowledge of God's nature. However, he rejected the Kantian relegation of religion to morality and of God to the adjunct status of a postulate of moral reason. Instead he embraced two central tenets of Romanticism—the centrality and immediacy of feeling and the historicity of human existence—and out of these Schleiermacher fashioned what has come to be known as modern liberal theology. According to Schleiermacher, all experience entails a dual form of consciousness: The one consists of a consciousness of other finite creatures like ourselves characterized by the recognition that humans are both shapers and creators of that world and beings dependent upon and created by it. The other form of consciousness, never existing in isolation from the first but always a dimension of finite experience, consists in the immediate awareness of our absolute dependence upon that which is not finite for our very existence at all. This latter—the feeling of absolute dependence—is the source of religious feeling and awareness and it is by extrapolation from this immediate, indeed apparently preconceptual and prelinguistic, "unstructured by thought" mode of experience that humans come to speak of God at all.[7] As reason was universal, common to all humans for Enlightenment thinkers, so for Schleiermacher this immediate form of consciousness was also universal, a dimension of every human experience, shared by all human beings, exhibiting a common singular character. But while the feeling of absolute dependence was universal in scope and character, it also came, Schleiermacher argued, to express itself in particular historical communities, beliefs, and rituals that were unique to their time and place. Hence, religion, born in the foundational affective dimensions of life, issued forth in concrete, distinctive, nonuniversal forms of historical existence. Schleiermacher, thus, found a way to affirm the historicity of human existence, including its religious expressions, while maintaining a universal, affective dimension of experience and at the same time maintain the strictures placed upon claims about God and religious experience by critical reason.

As the effects of Kantian thought were far-reaching, so, too, were those of Schleiermachian liberalism, most especially for theological reflection. Though Schleiermacher rejected Kant's relocation of religion to the moral arena, he himself carried out a parallel move by locating religious feeling, at least in origin, in the sphere of the affective, and then construing that sphere in noncognitive and nonlinguistic terms. Thus, religious feeling and the theology that purported to reflect upon it, were removed from the scrutiny of critical consciousness and rendered no longer accountable to the canons of scientific inquiry and explanation. In a world increasingly dominated, even in the Romantic era, by the model of scientific knowledge, Schleiermacher appeared to provide a safe haven for religion and for claims about God, assuring them a secure place in the modern world.

Schleiermacher's work, thus, sought a way to honor historicity while maintaining universality. However, it did so at great cost. Increasingly, religion and theology were marginalized, relegated to the private and subjective dimensions of life, away from what would come to be known as the public sphere. Such "protective strategies," as Wayne Proudfoot designates the theological maneuvers carried out by Schleiermacher and the liberal theology that followed him, may have momentarily protected religion but eventuated in the twentieth-century world, and now into the twenty-first century, in making religion and theology culturally extraneous.[8] While they continue to influence society, they do so with no clear or legitimate public role to play. While safe from the criticism of scientific reason, religion has, thereby, also forfeited a legitimized public function in culture.

Not only did many theologians follow the protective strategies suggested by Schleiermacher, they often *failed* to embrace his interest in

concrete, particular communities of faith. Thus Schleiermachian universalism won out in much liberal theology over against the historicist tendencies also present in his thought. Schleiermacher's heritage, like
Kant's, therefore comes to us in an ambiguous fashion, representing
emphases that historicists strongly repudiate today while simultaneously
turning to paths that Schleiermacher himself proposed.

While Schleiermacher turned to the depths of human subjectivity and
to the historical realm as the sphere in which humans give concrete
expression to that depth, Georg Wilhelm Friedrich Hegel set forth the
most ambitious philosophical system of the century, arguing that history
itself was the arena within which the divine and the absolute came to self-
consciousness and realization. History, in Hegel's schema, thus took on
a significance heretofore not imagined; it no longer stood in complete
opposition to Geist but was the very province of its self-actualization. So,
too, human subjectivity could no longer be understood except in reference to its dynamic becoming in history. Though many twentieth-century
thinkers have questioned Hegel's historicism as illusory, deterministic,
infected with untenable assumptions about historical progress, and
finally as unable to accept and contend with otherness, nonetheless, he
moved philosophical and theological thought toward the serious consideration of history as the central reality of human concern and reflection.

If central theologians such as Schleiermacher carried out maneuvers
that removed religion from the critical scrutiny of science and philosophers like Hegel developed architectonic visions of religion as a moment
in the process of divine self-actualization, there were thinkers from the
sixteenth century onward and with ever greater intensity in the nineteenth century who proffered "naturalistic" interpretations of religion.[9]
These interpretations sought to explain religion according to the canons
by which all other cultural phenomena were analyzed and explained.
From Jean Bodin in the sixteenth century to the towering nineteenth-
and early-twentieth-century figures of Müller, Durkheim, Troeltsch,
Marx, Feuerbach, and Freud, increasingly religion was something to be
examined, not protected or located in grand metaphysical schemes. Its
origins, supposed essence, functions, and forms were all open to investigation and religion more and more appeared to be a cultural phenomenon that could be made to yield to critical inquiry. Moreover, the
understanding of religion seemed to require less and less that its investi-
gators be believers or participants but that they be equipped with appropriate explanatory methods and theories; thus understanding and belief
were severed. And Christianity, treated by so many as superior whether
by virtue of a purported ahistorical uniqueness or evolutionary development, more and more came to be seen as one among the plurality of
religions in the world.[10]

Of all these developments, Ernst Troeltsch's legacy has been of particular importance for contemporary theology. Bridging the nineteenth and twentieth centuries, Troeltsch focused attention upon the spreading canons of historical inquiry, the historical character of religious traditions and the resultant problematizing of apologetic practices that had asserted the superiority and absoluteness of certain religions on nonhistorical or pseudohistorical grounds. While early Troeltsch sought to identify norms *within* history by which religious traditions could be compared and judged, by the end of his life even these efforts seemed illegitimate. In their place, Troeltsch emphasized the discrete particularity of traditions, linking them to specific cultural locations and heritages. And, opening the specter of relativism that has haunted historicism ever since, Troeltsch questioned whether judgments indeed could be made across religious traditions and suggested that all such considerations were finally intrasystematic affairs, a question of what was valid "for us."

This brief sketch clearly indicates that pre- and early-twentieth-century modernity was no monolithic affair, but was, in the words of philosopher Thelma Lavine, "cognitively pluralistic" as well as religiously, politically, and culturally diverse. For there was not only Kantian rationality or Lockean empiricism but also Romanticism and Hegelianism; there was not only "reasonable Christianity" but religion of the heart, of Lutheran pietism and Wesleyan Methodism; there was the poetry of the eighteenth century of Pope, Addison, and Johnson and of the nineteenth-century Romantics, Wordsworth, Coleridge, and Keats. It was also the era of Napoleonic adventurism in the name of a French universalism and Bismarckian nationalism in the name of the distinctive and "local" character of Germanic culture. For many such as Lavine, the contrasts within modernity are so great that the period must really be characterized as divided within itself. Thus on one side there is found an emphasis upon scientific rationality, the conviction that sure and indubitable grounds can be ascertained upon which universal claims to knowledge and truth could be built, the elevation of the autonomous individual as the site of knowledge and value, a belief in indefatigable progress, the repudiation of traditional authorities, and the demystification of religion. On the other side is found a celebration of history and the natural, the conviction that insight exceeds the rational, an appreciation of the aesthetic and the affective, a growing sense of the historicity of human existence and knowledge, and an identification of religion with the realm of feeling. Thus Lavine accordingly claims that "[m]odernity is the conflict and confluence of two diametrically opposed cognitive styles, each subverting, demystifying and delegitimizing the other's conception of human nature, truth, morality and politics and the appropriate methodology for knowing them."[11]

But while it is the case that conflicting strands can be identified within modernity, it is also true that many thinkers espoused elements of various perspectives at the same time. That is, thinkers of these centuries did not always reside neatly within only one trajectory of modernism but commingled various strands. Thus, Schleiermacher did not repudiate Kantian rationality in any wholesale sense but instead sought to delineate a distinctive space for religious experience. Or again, Schleiermacher certainly did not deny all forms of universalism but relocated them in the noncognitive realm, a realm that provided as indubitable grounds for claims as did any rationalist arguments. And Romantic modernity, no less than the Enlightenment, evidenced a disdain for unexamined acceptance of authority. Thus the search for secure foundations, the universalism of the Enlightenment, and the rejection of authority, while greatly transmuted, were not merely foregone by theological liberalism.

Importantly, it must also be stated that while much of what is designated theological liberalism is understood to descend from Schleiermacher and his Continental followers, there also developed a strand of North American theological liberalism that evidenced a somewhat different relationship to the Enlightenment and sought to reconcile religious and theological assertions with the positions of modern knowledge, especially the sciences and historical inquiry. In the United States, both liberal religious leaders and academics attempted to demonstrate that commitment to Christianity and fidelity to the modern world were not incongruent with or dependent upon, as Schleiermacher's reconciliation of the two appeared to be, the subjectivizing and privatizing of religious experience. There, therefore, appeared, in the nineteenth and early twentieth centuries an ethically oriented liberalism, including the "social gospel movement," more akin to Ritschl's mode of liberalism than to Schleiermacher's, and a sociohistorical method, associated with the early Chicago School, that utilized the insights and methods of the social sciences and historical fields of inquiry to analyze religious experience and life.

Of special importance to our project is the work of the early Chicago School. For it is not only from and in reaction to Continental developments that the contemporary historicist theologians we will focus upon, including Gordon Kaufman, William Dean, and Delwin Brown, have fashioned their work but also from this American strand of theological reflection and argument. Working out of sociohistorical methods and advocating a self-conscious historicism North American scholars of religion such as Shailer Mathews and Shirley Jackson Case set a strong direction for religious thought that deviated considerably from their European counterparts. They treated religion, Christianity included, as a social and cultural phenomenon that developed over time. They tended to reject notions of some unchanging core or essence that was thought to characterize all religions or even a core that was present within a particular religious tradition that gave it identity and continuity. They argued that religious ideas and doctrines and practices cannot be understood outside of their historical context but only in relation to "the social setting in which they have been used."[12] And they stood in opposition to forms of authoritarian theology that thought they had uncovered timeless truth or located unquestioned authority in the past. Instead, as Shirley Jackson Case so bluntly put it, the historicist thinker would "make no pretensions at uncovering either in the past or the present a quantum of dogma absolutely valid for all time."[13]

Parallel to these developments in religious and theological studies in the United States was the articulation of a distinctively American philosophical trajectory. With roots all the way back to Emerson and Edwards, thinkers such as Charles Sanders Peirce, William James, and John Dewey presented positions that were the forerunners of contemporary historicism and pragmatism. This American philosophy stressed an openness to science and the scientific method, a strong sense of history, a spirit of experimentation, a pragmatic interpretation of truth, a belief, especially in James, that reality exceeds the linguistic and the conscious and, especially in Dewey, a confidence in and loyalty to democratic processes. Just as we will see that contemporary historicists of the sort advocated for in this work resonate with persons such as Shirley Jackson Case and Shailer Mathews so we will hear echoes of James and Dewey in the pragmatic historicism of today as well as responses, criticisms, and continuations of Continental philosophy and theology.

This is all to say that our intellectual lineages are often, like our biological ones, quite mixed. Many contemporary western historicists, including especially the postliberal theologians we will discuss in the next chapter, have set forth their own positions in relation to the developments of European modern thought discussed above. Others, including some of the pragmatic historicists treated in this book, have claimed a more exclusively American background. But the analysis that follows suggests that for many theologians our inheritances are more pluralistic. In particular, the position that will take shape and be advanced in this book freely acknowledges that it comes from a complex lineage and has been influenced both by European predecessors and by these early Chicago thinkers and their philosophical counter-parts. Thus the reader will hear strains of Continental thought in contemporary theology from Kant's insistence on the knower as active to Marx's concern for power and Durkheim's assertion of the social function of religion, and Troeltsch's loyalty to the canons of critical inquiry. There will equally important be echoes of the earlier American contribution to historicist thought. The turn to the social sciences, the move away from essential-ism, the dynamic notions of religious change, the critical stance toward religious beliefs and practices and inherited philosophies, and the com-mitment to ongoing reconstruction and democratic conversation all will emerge again in the form of pragmatic historicism that centers this work.

Thus while contemporary historicism certainly distances itself from certain elements of the modern project we must acknowledge that modernity itself was plural and important dimensions of it have ani-mated and continue to be represented on the current scene. Moreover, thinkers today, as one suspects thinkers always did, have garnered from differing perspectives bits and pieces out of which to conceive a con-temporary vision. We cannot so easily cut perspectives off from each other. Thus even as we acknowledge, along with philosophers such as Thelma Lavine, the dimensions of modernity that stood in tension with one another, we must simultaneously recognize that sometimes thinkers creatively appropriate varied and even seemingly contradictory elements to fund new positions not heretofore considered.[14]

DIRECTIONS IN AND CHALLENGES TO TWENTIETH-CENTURY THEOLOGY

By the early twentieth century varied forms of liberal theology dom-inated in both Europe and the United States, with European Christian theology working out of modes of Schleiermachian thought and, at least in certain circles of American religious thought, theologians in the United States articulating a more firmly sociohistorical perspective. However, both these forms of liberalism were to lose their hold as the twentieth century unfolded. The theological liberalism that grew out of the Schleiermachian trajectory came under severe attack from Barthian neo-orthodoxy and as that critique gained ground in the United States the American form of theological liberalism was also eclipsed. The lib-eralism of the Chicago School with its belief in science and reason, its focus on social forms of Christianity, and its attention to experience all were called into question by neo-orthodoxy's advance just as surely was Schleiermachian liberalism. Moreover, the pragmatic philosophy that resonated with and supported theological liberalism also lost ground as logical positivism ascended to dominance. According to some accounts this Barthian assault on theological liberalism was a temporary inter-ruption or detour in modern theology. However, this reading of neo-orthodoxy misses the fact that Barth and his fellow thinkers undercut any easy turn to experience as decisively as Kant repudiated the theological uses of reason and critical historical studies problematized the return to the past. As such, neo-orthodoxy is significant not only because it undermined directly the varied forms of Schleiermachian theological liberalism and indirectly American liberalism but also because it set the problematic with which much of contemporary theology has had to struggle, that is, what can theology have to say after reason, tradition, and experience have all been called into question as reliable guides to truth and what substantive visions can be articulated when traditional sources have been eroded.

Barth and his compatriots carried out their undermining of earlier sources for theological claims, especially the liberal appeal to experience, through several maneuvers. They concurred with the Kantian limitation of knowledge to the human realm, thus denying reason's capacity to know God. However, they simultaneously rejected the Schleiermachian turn to a noncognitive religious experience, asserting that such experience did not yield legitimate knowledge of God but was only the reflection of humanity. Hence, according to Barth, neither in the depths of experience nor by virtue of the reaches of reason was knowledge of the divine to be ascertained. Yet Barth did not conclude that thereby human beings were condemned to ignorance concerning God. Instead, he argued that God makes Godself known in an act of radical revelation in Jesus Christ and that in this revelation the true natures of God, the human self, and the world are disclosed. Barth, on the one hand, undermined all human attempts to make true claims about God, indeed about human nature and the world, be they located in experience or rationality. But, at the same time, he offered a new foundation, located not in a fallible human reason or experience, but in the self-disclosing act of an omnipotent and transcendent deity. It was God, in Godself, who funded and insured legitimate claims to knowledge.

Liberal theologies, both in their Schleiermachian form and in the American mode, were deeply damaged by the onslaught of neo-orthodoxy with its simultaneously negative evaluation of human capacities and its triumphant belief in an omnipotent but gracious and self-revealing God. As the twentieth century unfolded not to an era of peaceful progress and clear advancement but to "the pity of war" (Wilfred Owen) and to atrocities unimagined before this century, neo-orthodoxy appeared as both an insightful diagnosis of a dangerously hubristic modernity gone awry *and* a new, chastened hope, grounded not in the delusions of a sinful humanity, but in the love and power of God.

But, if neo-orthodoxy appeared at first as the antidote for the presumed failures of modernity, its own fatal weaknesses gradually grew more apparent. For revelation, grounded solely in God's decision, proved elusive. It became difficult to discern who was the recipient of such revelation or how to conceive of a revelation totally distinct from other forms of human knowing. And an utterly transcendent God, while presumed gracious, increasingly appeared remote and irrelevant. Moreover, the sweepingly negative evaluation of human capacities appeared to many to be a prescription for quietism and noninvolvement in the world. And finally, the neo-orthodox concentration upon Jesus Christ as the central site of revelation and the resultant assumption that Christianity was, though a sinful religion, the location of true faith, became less and less compelling in light of historical studies and the growing awareness of other, equally ancient and profound religious traditions.

Thus by the 1960s, neo-orthodoxy's hold on theology had greatly weakened. However, its critique of liberalism remained. Its demise, therefore, did not signal a ready return to the options of the earlier centuries. Instead, especially in the United States, the discipline of theology entered an uneasy and conflicted period reflecting widespread doubts about theology's task and object. In turn, reason, experience, and now revelation had each been deposed as reliable grounds for theological claims. Whether talk about God or religious experience or theology made sense, at least to growing numbers of intellectuals, was no longer clear at all.

One radical reaction to the decline of neo-orthodoxy was the death of God movement. Thinkers such as Thomas J. J. Altizer and William Hamilton assailed traditional and neo-orthodox notions of God, declaring them either morally reprehensible (Hamilton) or ontologically suspect (Altizer). Thus the idea of an omnipotent, all-ruling God was rejected as detrimental to human freedom and responsibility. And the Barthian independent and utterly distinct deity was proclaimed dead, emptied of transcendence and reinterpreted, at least by Altizer, as fully incarnate in the finite world.

While the death of God movement was certainly a cultural event and though the work of Altizer is having a renewed impact upon theological reflection, especially upon today's deconstructionists, for the most part theologians did not pursue that direction. Instead, North American theology took several different courses. In the United States, process theologians, who had never succumbed to the lure of neo-orthodoxy, continued their constructive endeavors, working out of perspectives more American than Continental, still committed to the liberal belief that theology should and could coexist with other contemporary forms of knowledge. Others, primarily theologians Gordon Kaufman, David Tracy, and Edward Farley, led the discipline in an intense reexamination of its nature and task. Fascination, indeed obsession, with questions of method consumed much of the attention of theologians during the 1970s and 1980s. Though such methodological fixation issued forth neither in consensus concerning the nature and task of theology nor in clarity about what direction substantive theological work should go, it has been these reflections that have set the immediate stage for contemporary historicist theology and determined the parameters within which contemporary proposals have been ventured.

But although this methodological work has been extremely important there have been other elements, as well, in our immediate past that have shaped the milieu within which contemporary theology has emerged. Significantly, while the dominant theological perspectives spent much energy on method and wondering what theology might consist in today, other theologians found a good deal to say. In particular, there arose in the late 1960–1970s voices of those who had heretofore been absent from the theological scene—African Americans, women, Latin Americans, and representatives of other oppressed groups or geographical locations. These thinkers and activists, including most prominently James Cone, Mary Daly, Rosemary Ruether, and Gustavo Gutiérrez, argued that so-called mainstream theology had attended almost exclusively to the issues emerging from the affluent and powerful forms of modernity while being blind to the realities of oppression, imperialism, poverty, and patriarchy that modernity had produced or abetted. Moreover, liberation, black, and feminist theologians indicted the dominant white male theology as complicit in such oppression, not only by virtue of ignoring it, but by often providing religious and theological sanction for it. Liberation thinkers explicitly claimed their perspectives were grounded not in the debates unleashed by the Enlightenment or nineteenth-century liberalism but in the concrete historical struggles for liberation of the poor, women, and persons of color. Thus, Gutiérrez could state that liberation theology focused on the question of the nonperson in the modern world, not on that of the nonbeliever, and that it emerged out of and issued forth from the concrete realities of contemporary struggles.

The insistence on the part of liberationist theologians that not all contemporary theology emerges out of the same concerns or commitments is an important historicist reminder of the concrete and particular location of all thought, including theology. But as this chapter has insisted, historical lineages are complex and contemporary theological options have developed not out of singular lines of inheritance but in response to many. Thus while many liberation, African American and feminist theologians proclaimed their distance from the dominant modes of theologizing, they nonetheless altered the entire theological scene in profound ways. For they introduced, in a manner previously unheard of in theology, the issue of power and how it was deployed throughout reli-

gious worldviews and theological symbol systems. The seeming innocence of theology, for everyone, was over. Moreover, they opened the
way for multiple other perspectives, of Asians and Africans and Native
Americans and gays and lesbians, to begin to articulate their understanding of the nature, task, and criteria of late-twentieth-century and
now early-twenty-first-century theology. And while the issues that
emerged from modernity's rise and its current, not too clear, state have
continued to vex contemporary theologians—liberationists no less than
others—they have now been joined permanently by the challenge of
those who seek not only viable intellectual stances but pursue just and
equitable social, political, and economic systems. And finally, just as
was the case in nineteenth-century Europe, there are increasingly theologians whose work and identity cannot be clearly separated into one
of these categories rather than another but who are the product of and
whose theological proposals have emerged from the multiple developments that confront us. Thus there are thinkers dealt with in this volume, such as myself or Cornel West, who trace our constructive stance
not only to feminist or black thought but also to American pragmatism
and sociohistorical perspectives as well as the influences of Continental
thought.[15]

The importance of liberation perspectives has not only been their
intellectual challenge but that those challenges self-consciously emerged
out of and in solidarity with particular communities of the dispossessed
and concrete struggles for transformation. This self-conscious location
has pushed theology's awareness of historicity, contextuality, and of the
political and social roles all theologies play. Moreover, as part of
broader social and political movements, liberation theologies have functioned as theological indicators of widespread social change and
upheaval. Not only have they pointed us to the internal dynamics of theology, they have been theology's access to developments beyond the
academy and church. In particular, they represent an intense and prevalent repudiation of western social, political, sometimes economic, religious, and intellectual ideals. Both in its capitalist and now apparently
in its socialist forms, western culture is under attack and in many areas
of the world, its influence is being contested, even as its impact continues. Moreover, even within western contexts, representatives of
oppressed groups have increasingly located the sources of their oppression within the western cultural tradition and especially within its modern manifestations. Thus, western theologies today, insofar as they
embody or respond to liberationist concerns, now must work within a
more global context that brings to bear nontheological factors and that
evidences a conflicted attitude toward the western tradition.

If liberationist perspectives in theology are part of wider cultural developments, so, too, are other challenges especially to the legacy of Enlightenment modernity that have appeared recently.[16] While these challenges do not necessarily coincide with liberationist commitments, they, too, represent repudiations of certain elements of our modern heritage. In particular, across many disciplines from literary criticism to philosophy of science, from political theory to anthropology, and within nonacademic and even popular culture, the understanding of reason espoused by the Enlightenment has been thoroughly criticized and, by many, rejected. Assumptions of neutrality, of the capacity to ascertain sure and indubitable foundations, of reason's transcendental character and universal nature, shorn of historical particularity all seem problematic today. Moreover, the accompanying notions of the self as autonomous, independent of tradition and transparent to itself, are equally under attack. And language, once presumed to be capable of adequately representing reality, now appears multivalent, obscure, and infused with ideological commitments. As Peter Hodgson has stated, relativizing reason born in the Enlightenment is now itself relativized.[17]

While the assault on Enlightenment reason is epidemic and its defenders are few, there is little consensus about what this critical stance toward Enlightenment modernity signifies. For some it is the clearest embodiment of a decisive cultural and intellectual shift from at least Enlightenment modernity to a postmodern era. For others, especially certain religious and theological thinkers, it signals the end not only to Enlightenment pretensions but also to the expectations of nineteenth-century liberalism. And for others, in contrast, it is the extension and radicalization of historical consciousness as it developed in the nineteenth century and into the twentieth century.

Theologians, no less than other thinkers, have offered varied, indeed disparate, responses to this cognitive crisis, ranging from postmodern deconstructionism to postliberalism to a critical revisionism to, as I will argue, a pragmatic historicism. Yet, whatever the theological response, it is clear that for contemporary theology to have credence within contemporary western culture, it must attend not only to the challenges of liberation perspectives but also to the sweeping intellectual indictment of the early modern era while forthrightly acknowledging the ways in which that heritage continues to shape us. Both acknowledgment of the problems with the early modern period and of its continued relevance in such things as the assumption of human rights and ongoing commitments to democratic reforms are required if theologians are to understand our situation.

These developments signal, in complementary and sometimes disparate ways, challenges to modernity and hence indicate significant moves *away* from at least Enlightenment assumptions and projects. But if they embody drifts away from the Enlightenment, they are moves *toward* new assumptions and projects, especially historicist ones. From Altizer's incarnational theology, to Kaufman's antisupernaturalism, to liberationists' commitment to concrete struggles and the tracing of historical causes and effects to postmodernists' assertions of the local, temporal, and culturally specific character of subjectivity and knowledge, there has been a decisive turn to the historical and to thinking about humanity and the broader context through the lens of historical consciousness. While there are great differences among all these perspectives, they share to some extent not only the negative assessment of certain aspects of our inheritance, but a common historicist direction that is broadly influencing the tenor of our times.

These political, socioeconomic, and intellectual shifts have been part of broad cultural developments that have both impacted theology and been contributed to, albeit in mostly insignificant ways, by theologians and religious thinkers. There have also been concurrent developments that have been specifically religious and have, therefore, been peculiarly important to theology. And these, too, share the historicist tendencies of the broader cultural and intellectual shifts examined above. One such development has been the growth in awareness of the religiously plural nature of modern society. The world has always been religiously diverse but we have today a far greater sensitivity to religious pluralism and, especially for members of western societies, a recognition that pluralism is not a world away but constitutes, in an ever greater fashion, the fabric of western culture itself.

For western Christians, these realities hold particular significance for other religions, most markedly Islam, are growing rapidly both in the West and beyond. Meanwhile, Christianity, tied in modernity to the fortunes of western culture, has been challenged as the West's power and influence have declined. Though Christianity continues to grow, its major areas of sustained increase have been outside of the West and signal a decisive shift within Christianity as it becomes ever less of a European and North American religion but an internally pluralistic tradition no longer dominated by western conceptualities or ideological interests. And, even within the West, Christianity has become increasingly polyglot and multiple, with little cohesion. Moreover, all this is taking place while western Christians of various perspectives demonstrate, despite conservative resurgences, a good deal of alienation from their religious traditions and a seeming inability, especially in the United States, to conceive of how these traditions can contribute to the moral and public spheres. Hence, western Christian theologians are confronted simultaneously with the realities of religious pluralism, which mock traditional Christian claims to superiority, and with the contemporary challenge of how Christianity itself might understand its role in the twenty-first century. In light of these profound shifts today in our religious topography, Christian theology must not only respond to the various shifts and challenges detailed above but must also confront the need to interpret anew the meaning of radical religious pluralism while simultaneously reconstruing how Christianity itself is to be understood both in relation to its past and to contemporary culture.

There are two other prominent shifts or crises that are also part of the unique character of our age and delineate the boundaries within which current-day theology operates. The first affects equally all present and future inhabitants of the planet earth and that is the reality that we live under the two-pronged threat of nuclear war or accident and ecological deterioration and disaster. Theologians Gordon Kaufman and Sallie McFague have forcefully pointed to these realities, arguing that such nuclear consciousness and the growing awareness of ecological destruction shape, in heretofore unknown ways, the context within which we do theology. For they contend no other humans have confronted, even in their most apocalyptic dreams, the possibility of such comprehensive ruin wherein not only all life but the potential for future life would be destroyed. If theology today is to make sense at all, McFague and Kaufman assert, it must critically analyze its role in the creation of such destructive possibilities and must advocate substantive claims that counter all that contributes to our current precarious situation. Without altering our course, the outcome for the earth and its inhabitants, human and nonhuman alike, is bleak and hence all else is for naught.[18]

The final crisis I wish to point to is a peculiarly western one and that is the loss of the sense of sure progress that has long marked Western thought and has been present, if battered, throughout modernity. Theologians Langdon Gilkey and Peter Hodgson have referred to this loss as the collapse of salvation history.[19] The belief in history as a salvific process, lured by an indefatigable telos, has had different forms, including traditional Jewish and Christian ones, Enlightenment and liberal bourgeois accounts, nationalistic and Marxist-Leninist versions. But in each form it has evidenced the conviction that history was the arena in which humanity might pursue its destiny and within which evil was to be progressively overcome. Yet today confidence in such a vision seems quite unrealistic as we court nuclear and ecological disaster and confront, ill-prepared, the collapse of or the challenge to the great modern systems of economic and political power. Moreover, science and technology that once promised so much appear, while still dominant, nonetheless as increasingly powerless against the realities of population explosion, disease, famine, and ecological despoliation, or as complicit in the mechanization, militarization, and impersonalization of contemporary life. Accompanying these is the pervasive sense that life has lost the meaning previously endowed by religion or culture with no genuine substitute to revitalize it. Finally, our era has brought an intensified awareness of radical evil, of Holocaust, and ethnic cleansing, and with such consciouness the certainty of history's progressive character has been muted forever. Hence, the current situation renders earlier notions of salvation history untenable. And while the crises or shifts being outlined often are ones that affect all of humanity, western thought, for its part, must confront them, shorn of its previous confidence, and must develop new understandings of history, now shaped by a profound sense of contingency and fallibility, in which loss, disintegration, and the possibility of ultimate destruction are as prominent as visions of hope and progress.

EMERGENT HISTORICISM

As I stated earlier, eras are often defined by the crises that confront them and the transformative shifts that mark their responses to these changes in the historical situation. By any measure, contemporary western culture is facing pervasive challenges; novel, even revolutionary alterations are evident in the political, socioeconomic, religious, intellectual, and even biological and natural realms. And, while clarity about such matters is difficult under any circumstance and nearly impossible within the whirlwind of radical transition, it appears that the transformations we are experiencing indicate a decisive move away from, at least part of, the legacy of early modernity and an intensification, though in transmuted form, of other directions that first took shape in the era that preceded our own.

While such moves appear underway, these changes cannot be delineated easily, utilizing one rubric or interpretive category. They do not all exhibit a common character, indeed, some appear in tension with one another, for example, the cognitive relativism implied, for some, by the breakdown of the Enlightenment ideal of reason versus the continuing claims to universalism permeating many liberation movements. Still, if there were one theme or strand that runs throughout many of the shifts depicted in this chapter and that might be said to express the temper of our times, it is the profound and pervasive sense of the historicity of human existence.

The remainder of this book will seek to explore how historicity is conceived theologically and what it portends for the theological task in the twenty-first century. The full detailing of this will take place as the volume unfolds. But it is desirable to state, in preliminary form, several interlocking assumptions about historicity. These are both suggested by a number of the developments that we have been tracing and will emerge in a fuller form in the specific analysis offered in this work. Thus, as most of this chapter has offered a sweeping view of our recent past so that we might better understand the dynamics to which we are responding, so the following statement sets forth in anticipation the outline of the historicist orientation that will guide the rest of the volume. Some of these claims will already be clear from what has been detailed thus far, but others will represent the explicit developments that are emerging as theologians and other thinkers grapple with our current situation. Hence, as we have been claiming, contemporary historicist theology is both the product of what has gone before but also a distinctive and novel development taking shape today.

Epistemologically contemporary historicism has clearly set itself apart from the quest for sure and universal knowledge and aligned itself with the growing conviction that all knowledge is localized, relative to its time and place, shaped by its history, infused by interests and interpretive in character, and part of a historical strand of other interpretations. Humans have no access to the world in an unmediated manner nor any way to compare an uninterpreted reality with our various accounts of it and thereby ascertain whose version of reality is the true one. Hence, for historicists, attempts to achieve sure and certain knowledge, applicable for all times and places, and predicated upon unquestionable foundations appear misguided and illusory.

Ontologically, contemporary historicism is increasingly portraying the larger reality within which humanity is situated and with which humans continually interact as both fluid and forceful, altered by human action and presence but determining human prospects as well. Moreover, both the efficacy and receptivity of each, humans and our encompassing reality, occurs in and through a rich spectrum ranging from the rational, logical, and mechanical to the murkier realms of the intuitive, the affective, and the aesthetic. Humans are not simply cognitive agents manipulating a passive material reality; we are also bodies and our environments are also affective. The interaction, thus, between humans and these environments, throughout the full range of efficacies and meanings, is dynamic and constantly affecting both us and our world.

Precisely because it is malleable, fluid, and dynamic, reality is not of a piece, it is not the same everywhere. Neither, for the same reasons, are humans. Thus, anthropologically, there is emerging the notion of the historicized subject. According to historicism, human existence is embedded in the matrix of particular, concrete histories; there is no humanity in "general," but only specific individuals and communities.

water & food & oxygen, nest & sleep

a sense of community requires some form of language

most all human bodies req means of expulsion

But while specific human life, as historical, is also social and interconnected. Moreover, its interconnections occur not only at the natural and biological levels but also in the interactions of economic, political, and psychological processes and across the full range of the intellectual, affective, and material vectors of human life. To affirm the fully social character of the human, however, is not to detract from the diversity of historicized existence. It is instead to insist that our varied forms of human life influence and are influenced by each other and by the larger environment and that through and by virtue of these interactions particularity emerges.

Permeating these anthropological, ontological, and epistemological shifts toward historicism is the general recognition that humans are preeminently linguistic and cultural beings dependent upon language as a primary, though certainly not exclusive, means of engaging and interpreting the world. Historicism does not deny the enormous power of the noncognitive in the lives of creatures such as ourselves who have bodies and quite literally feel our way through life; indeed much that historicism has to offer contemporary discussions today follows from its increased recognition of the embodiedness and material embeddedness of historicized existence. But it remains the case that language is one of the most prominent and powerful dimensions of existence through which we form and are formed by the world around us, both human and nonhuman. Our language, like all other dimensions of human existence, is not universal, static, or neutral. Language, too, is the product of particular historical processes and carries the particularities of time and place. The linguistic worlds we inhabit are not impartial and transparent; they are the bearers of the powers, ideological commitments, and the specific values that operate, consciously and unconsciously, in human life. To acknowledge the centrality of our linguistic formations is not to reduce life to language; it is to affirm the distinctive role that language plays in our varied worlds of feeling, thinking, and acting.

These historicist responses to the cognitive crises of the present era are echoed in relation to the other historical changes outlined in this chapter. The radical political and socioeconomic shifts have given rise to assertions that history is composed of contingent, unstable, and dynamic processes that are interrelated, and that issue forth in unpredictable and novel occurrences. In these scenarios, history always includes the legacy of effects that impinges upon the present, but no longer is there a sense that such effects bring about necessary or able-to-be-anticipated present reality. Thus, while the growing sense of historicity entails the recognition of the importance of historical and material conditions, it simultaneously also points to the contingency of existence, and to the open and fortuitous character of history itself.

The current nuclear threat and the recognition that if humans do not destroy ourselves in a nuclear war or accident, we may well do it by the progressive death of the biological and natural foundations for life, have also led to a heightened sense of historicity. In particular, the ecological and nuclear situations have demonstrated, as perhaps nothing else has quite so dramatically, that humans are part of the web of historical and natural existence and that we both depend upon that web for life itself and also shape it, for good or evil. The dualisms that were so prevalent in modernity—distinctions between phenomenal and noumenal, body and spirit, and human and nature—are less and less tenable as we confront a situation that demands that we acknowledge our embeddedness in the natural realm and affirm our responsibility for enhancing that sphere if life is to continue and flourish. Human history brought us to this juncture and it is human action and decision that will, at least in part, decide both ours and nature's fate.

Finally, the two shifts that have had a particularly religious character have also elicited responses marked by a sensitivity to historicity. First, the recognition of pluralism, especially in its religious forms, has led theologians, among others, to acknowledge the particularity of traditions and progressively to forego attempts to reduce various religious or cultural traditions to some common denominator. It is now less and less viable to see such traditions as historically particular expressions of a common essence or of a universal experience. The Schleiermachian solution to the tension between universality and historical particularity—a common human experience, prelinguistic in constitution, and a diverse, localized, and historically unique articulation of this experience—has not held as claims to prelinguistic experience have been challenged and the distinctive character of historical traditions has become clearer. Moreover, it has become evident that the standards or norms for deciding such questions are always situated within particular historical locations and do not represent neutral standards common to all and impartially applied. With this recognition, the other prevalent response to pluralism prior to the present, which stated that one religion was truer than all others or that a certain culture was superior to others, has also been undermined. Judgment, it appears, is always historically relative. Neither the attempt to reduce the multiplicity of traditions to a common essence nor the repudiating of the value of the many in the name of the superiority of one, invariably our own, tradition, is finding compelling support among historicists in our era. Instead, as the historicity of human existence has been affirmed, so, too, has there increased the acknowledgment of its plural forms, irreducible to one another and with no easy way to adjudicate among them. While, I will argue, judgment and adjudication are not impossible, they like much else today will need to find a historicist form.

The loss of belief in history as a salvific process, be it secular or religious, is in many ways the embodiment of our historicist consciousness. For in place of a sure sense of progress, we now have a pervasive sense that while history is our home, indeed our only home, it has no clear direction, no telos to bring it safely to its destination. While the future is open, it is just as surely uncertain containing no promise of fulfillment, rest, or victory. And the past, far from being a legacy of unrelenting progress, now appears marked by tragedy, loss, and ambiguity. Thus, as we increasingly assume that it is the historical arena, broadly conceived to include nature, that circumscribes human existence, we do so at a time when confidence in the future is diminished though our sense of human accountability for it has grown; if the historical is our only context, it is a context which we do not control but for which we are, in good part, responsible.

CURRENT HISTORICIST THEOLOGICAL OPTIONS

As this chapter has demonstrated, our contemporary world is undergoing fundamental historical changes. While these transitions are affecting all members of our progressively interconnected world, they present western culture with a particular set of challenges. For indeed many of the shifts are the result of the decline of western culture and its presuppositions. Hence, western culture, as it responds to these crises and challenges, is, in effect, remaking itself, setting the direction for its future development.

It has been a further contention of this chapter that while no single explanatory category will suffice for describing our age, the notion of historicity can be seen to be a pervasive and illuminating theme that runs throughout much contemporary analysis. Though thinkers disagree about whether we are witnessing the demise of modernity, in part or as a whole, and what might be emerging in its place, nonetheless there are broadly shared, across many disciplines, fundamental assumptions concerning the historical nature of human existence. Thus, one way, though certainly not the only one, to explicate our current options is to explore how the category of historicity is given expression and what repercussions result from the development of this as a central motif.[20]

Currently there are a number of theological perspectives, especially but not exclusively Christian, that are conceiving of themselves as distinctive alternatives to earlier theological options and that do so by embodying, at least in part, the assumptions that have been developed under the rubric of historicity. At this juncture, I would like to refer to two of these theological developments, postliberalism and revisionist theology. I will explore each in terms of the historicist assumptions set forth thus far, analyzing their interpretation of the historicist turn and its implications for theology and critically evaluating these current trends. While not exhaustive, this review will help us to delineate the theological landscape as it is taking shape today.

CHAPTER 2

Theological Roads Not Taken

PRELIMINARY REMARKS

The framing premise of this work is that the notion of historicity is currently, especially in the West, a broadly operative interpretive key for understanding humanity and our place within the cosmos. As such it is a helpful tool for accessing the various theological options that are presenting themselves today. The extended goal of this volume is to set forth one of these emerging historicist forms of theology, what I am calling pragmatic historicism. I will seek to give this approach a clear identity and to contribute my own voice to pragmatic historicism, offering critical guidance to its future direction. But in order better to perceive the significance of this option it is helpful first to present the reader with a portrayal of other historicist possibilities on the theological scene today. By demonstrating what other theologians take to be the import of recognizing our historicity and exploring the potential and limits of these approaches to theology, we will be better able to see the distinctive character of pragmatic historicism including its own problematic aspects.

This chapter will turn, therefore, to two prominent theological movements, postliberalism and revisionist theology, to further these explorations.[1] These two approaches are compelling candidates for examination for several reasons. First, they are often identified as the two central possibilities on the current theological map. A perusal of current theological journals and publishers' lists will give ample evidence that these two theological trajectories are centering much of the discussion. Indeed, the impression is often that these two approaches exhaust the options available today. The point of this book is to contend that this is not the case, that other options are presenting themselves to us. But the very prominence of postliberalism and revisionist perspectives in theology indicates that they are important perspectives to be considered in any discussion of contemporary theology on the American scene. But second, and more importantly for this work, they are each approaches that take seriously human historicity and have emerged out of the rethinking of theology in light of the presupposition that human experience and knowledge is thoroughly historical in nature. While I will argue that these two ways of conceiving theology are problematic, nonetheless, they stand as powerful portrayals of what theology in an historicist age might be; as such they have much to teach other historicist theologians and continue to be challenges to perspectives such as the one for which this volume will advocate.

With the general historicist assumptions set forth in the previous chapter as background, I will now turn to postliberalism and revisionist theology analyzing their interpretations of the historicist turn and its implications for theology and critically evaluating these options in terms of how well they embody and carry out what I take to be the mandates of a historicist approach. I will focus this analysis by examining the work of the two major thinkers who have come to represent respectively postliberalism and revisionist theology—George A. Lindbeck and David Tracy. While there are certainly other theologians who are aligned with these approaches, Lindbeck and Tracy stand out as the theologians who have given shape and content to these major trajectories in Christian theology in the North American context.

GEORGE LINDBECK AND POSTLIBERALISM

The theological perspective known as postliberalism articulates an orientation that reflects many of the historicist assumptions set forth in the previous chapter. Associated prominently with the Divinity Schools of Yale and Duke, postliberalism has been influenced by social-scientific, especially anthropological, approaches that argue for the centrality of language and culture in human life, and theological and philosophical perspectives that emphasize the "traditioned" or historical character of all human experience and knowledge. The combination of these insights has led proponents of postliberalism to develop not only a view of the human as social, historical, and linguistically constituted but of religion as a this-worldly phenomenon that functions in, contributes to, and reflects the constraints of the historical process.

The tenets of postliberalism have been most fully developed by George A. Lindbeck. In *The Nature of Doctrine: Religion and Theology in a Postliberal Age*, Lindbeck repudiates both an older, premodern cognitivist view that religious assertions were primarily propositional claims about reality, and the modern liberal, Schleiermachian-inspired view that religious claims are the expressions of more fundamental prelinguistic and immediate experiences.[2] In relation to the first, Lindbeck disavows the assumption that objective, universally valid knowledge is possible as well as the correspondence theory of truth that has often attended that assumption. Whatever we know we know from within and out of our concrete location in history. The dream of historically unencumbered knowledge, yielding certitude and available to all in the same manner, is no longer a possibility to be pursued in a historicist age.

Lindbeck joins with many other contemporary thinkers who have raised questions about propositional claims to truth, especially ones that have taken theological form. But the real target of Lindbeck's historicist attack is the liberal theological heritage that flowed from Schleiermacher and continued its influence in much of twentieth-century theology. As was stated in the previous chapter, Schleiermacher concurred with the limits Kant placed on human reason but then predicated a form of experience that was "unstructured" by thought from which religious experience and eventually belief and practice took its origins. Lindbeck calls this view experiential-expressivism. It is an approach that assumes, according to Lindbeck, that human beings have fundamentally unmediated experiences that are universal in scope and common in character that then find secondary articulation in historically particular and culturally specific forms. Proponents of this view locate, Lindbeck states, "whatever is finally important to religion in the prereflective experiential depths of the self and regard the public or outer features of religion as expressive and evocative objectifications (nondiscursive symbols) of internal meaning."[3] These outer features of religion are, thus, the culturally specific articulation of what is, in fact, a common core of experience shared by all. The task of theology then is not to make propositional claims that correspond to reality. Neither does theology attend to religious traditions that are fundamentally distinct from one another. Instead theology's task is to offer adequate renderings of the depth of human subjectivity that is common to all.

Lindbeck situates many thinkers in this theological trajectory though he acknowledges the diversity that characterizes this general approach. Thus such thinkers as Rudolph Otto and Mircea Eliade are placed here as well as more contemporary thinkers like Bernard Lonergan and, importantly for our purposes, David Tracy. And while Lindbeck recognizes that theologians such as Lonergan and Tracy also assert the public, socially mediated character of religious expression, he insists that they, nonetheless, "maintain a kind of privacy in the origins of experience and language."[4]

Lindbeck argues strenuously against the various versions of experiential-expressivism. In particular, Lindbeck contends that in positing a prelinguistic experience common to all experiential-expressivists have fundamentally misconstrued the nature of historical existence, the character of religious traditions and the task of theology. Over against these positions, Lindbeck argues for what he terms a cultural-linguistic model for interpreting religion. This position is predicated upon the assumption that human beings are thoroughly linguistic and culturally constituted creatures who depend upon their social and historical context for the resources that make experience possible at all. Humans, in this view, exist in very particularized strands of social reality and these habitations are, Lindbeck avers, "increasingly thought of as socially, linguistically, and even textually constructed."[5]

Such cultural contexts are moreover, according to Lindbeck, historical in nature. They have developed over long periods of time and embody and continue particular historical lineages that are not reducible to one another. Accordingly, to be human is not only to be constituted by culture and all that entails but also to be traditioned; human beings are, thus, the bearers of history, who live out of and carry on the past.[6]

This emphasis upon the traditioned character of life is central for Lindbeck's interpretation of religion. For Lindbeckian postliberalism, religion refers to the most encompassing and overarching interpretative schemas within which humans reside, think, act, and experience. Religions are comprehensive worldviews that express our deepest convictions about reality and about how humans should relate to such a cosmic context.[7] These overarching frameworks are historical; far from fundamentally trafficking in the suprahistorical, religions offer historically derived and tradition specific portrayals of life and its significance. Thus to be religious is not to hold some indubitable belief guaranteed by an ahistorical reason or revelation. Nor is it to have a certain immediate experience. Rather it is to live out of an interpretive story and to become a practitioner of a specific tradition's way of life.[8]

Among historicists, the view of Lindbeck and his cohorts is distinguished by the definitive and normative status they bestow on tradition and, as we will see, on the originating period of a tradition. For them, the historicized subject receives identity through the appropriation of a particular tradition, its language, convictions, values, and commitments. Without the resources, especially linguistic resources, of a tradition or culture humans could not survive and function. Following anthropologist Clifford Geertz, Lindbeck asserts "that humans are so thoroughly programmed genetically for language use that apart from acquiring a language they cannot properly develop physiologically as other animals do, but remain peculiarly immature in their sensory and physical competence."[9] To live outside of a specific tradition, structured by a particular language, symbol system, and set of practices, is, according to Lindbeck, to significantly damage one's humanity.

Moreover, and very importantly, Lindbeck and his followers do not view traditions as simply temporally linked events. A tradition is a historical line of development that embodies in an ongoing fashion a set of essential tenets. Likening such tenets to the grammatical rules that structure a language, Lindbeck asserts that these fundamental beliefs can be instantiated in diverse and creative ways but that they must be present and continually appropriated for a tradition to continue.

This appropriation or instantiation of the fundamental core of a tradition does not, for Lindbeck, entail uncreative or rote repetition of these normative tenets. Later developments do and should evidence novelty and creativity as they give expression to the authoritative depth grammar of faith; changing times demand new interpretations. And just as a language such as English can say all sorts of different things while still remaining "good" English, Christian doctrines and theological claims can make varied, even tension-filled assertions and still be valid Christian positions as long as they adhere to the normative articulations of the Christian narrative, to "the self-identical story" found in the Bible.[10] As Lindbeck puts it, "Faithfulness to such doctrines does not necessarily mean repeating them; rather, it requires, in the making of new formulations, adherence to the same directives that were involved in their first formulation."[11]

Thus, to be human is to stand within a particular encompassing interpretive tradition that is structured by beliefs or rules.[12] Moreover, these unifying elements can be traced to the origins or early periods of the tradition. It is they that provide the directives for living within and in faithfulness to a particular religious history and the norms for ascertaining what is legitimate.

When applied to Christianity this means, for Lindbeck, that Christians live out a framework "supplied by the biblical narratives."[13] But this Christian framework, while provided by the Bible, is not just self-evidently present to all who read the Bible. Instead Lindbeck contends, Christians require a theological hermeneutic—the Christological and Trinitarian rule of faith developed in early Christianity. This "classic" biblical hermeneutic allows the Bible to be read not as a collection of varied and conflicting texts but as a "canonically and narrationally unified" whole. It is through reading the Bible through such Trinitarian and Christological lenses that it becomes the basis for building communal consensus and identity.[14]

Given this view of tradition-funded existence, theology is no longer the pursuit of certain and unassailable truths or the expression of a universal religious essence. Theology becomes primarily a descriptive endeavor that seeks to delineate and make clear the normative foundations of a specific tradition.[15] It seeks to see how claims and practices operate within a particular tradition and how reality takes shape and is lived out contextually. Lindbeck, thus, claims in one of his most debated statements that "[i]ntratextual theology redescribes reality within the scriptural framework rather than translating Scripture into extrascriptural categories. It is the text, so to speak, which absorbs the world, rather than the world the text."[16]

Theology, in this view, is primarily an intrasystematic affair whose central criterion consists in faithfulness to the originating tenets of the tradition and whose reference is almost exclusively to the particular community and its history. Postliberal theology, therefore, directs its adherents back to primary communities and to the task of interiorizing particular historical modes of being. By so doing, postliberalism offers an historicism focused on the conserving and conditioned character of human existence.

Lindbeck, thus, begins with certain assumptions about the historical nature of human existence and especially about the nature of historical traditions within which humans reside and from which humans gain identity and meaning. From these assumptions he derives a particular understanding of theology and a distinctive construal of theological adequacy and truth and the norms that are to be employed in our rendering judgment concerning them. It is worth setting out in a summary form the components that are ingredient in what emerges as Lindbeck's intrasystematic view of theology and theological truth. First, as should now be clear, theological judgment takes place within a tradition, according to the norms specific to that tradition. This means that there is no appeal to broader criteria, indeed such appeal is, for Lindbeck, an impossibility. Nor are we required to defend or explain our historically situated norms and their ramifications in any wider realm than that of our fellow participants in our particular tradition. Apologetics has little or no place in postliberalism.

Second, the internal norms by which theological assertions are to be evaluated and adjudicated stem from the regulative principles or directives of a tradition. They are not given by reason, discerned in some basal experience, or hammered out in the context of prolonged discussion. They are derivative from a tradition. Third, these directives or basic grammars are located in the past, assumed to be emergent from and authoritatively expressed in the founding narratives of the tradition and, for Christianity, in the Trinitarian and Christological rule of faith developed by the early church that provides the hermeneutical key for interpreting these narratives. They do not take shape nor are they developed as a tradition develops. Instead they are the givens of a tradition that provide any particular historical strand its distinctive character.

The grammar of a tradition is, fourth, assumed to be identifiable and stable and possessing a unified character. While later theological formulations may be contested in terms of how well they conform to the grammar of faith, Lindbeck does not seem to think what constitutes that grammar in the first place is open to debate and struggle.[17] Thus he seems to envision lively conversation about what is faithful to the directives of faith but not about that to which we should be faithful. Change continually takes place but it does so as new formulations body forth the directives of the religious tradition; continuity is supplied by this core, these basic rules that "remain the same."[18]

Out of these assumptions, then, theological adequacy or truth comes to mean the faithful representation of and conformity to the normative grammar or to the regulative principles of the Christian tradition. Theological validity is determined by faithful adherence to the internal rules of the Christian tradition. Ascertaining theological truth has less, then, to do with seeing how claims "cohere with reality" than with determining how they cohere with and conform to the tradition within which they arise.

But who is in the position to render judgment about what conforms and what diverges, what is novel faithfulness and what is unfaithful deviance? Lindbeck's answer to this question also flows from his view of the nature of historical traditions. Traditions, in his view, make reference back to themselves; they give imaginative portrayals of reality but offer no way to get out of themselves in order to ascertain whether or not they correspond to some external reality. Indeed, that is not their primary purpose; religious traditions and their doctrines are thoroughly practical rather than propositional. They provide the interpretive means for getting around in life, for negotiating historical existence. And they succeed in doing so to the extent that their vision of reality is inculcated in their adherents. For Lindbeck, "just as an individual becomes human by learning a language, so she or he begins to become a new creature through hearing and interiorizing the language that speaks of Christ."[19] And it is finally, according to Lindbeck, the adept, the skillful practitioners of a tradition, "those who have effectively interiorized a religion" and who live most fully out of the tradition, who are in the best position to determine the adequacy of theological claims and developments.[20] But who are the adept, these skillful practitioners? Sometimes Lindbeck refers to the saints and prophets among us.[21] But at other times Lindbeck suggests that we seek the religiously competent not among the unorthodox as so many of our saints and prophets tend to be but in the more orthodox arenas of our traditions. As he puts it, "The linguistically competent . . . are to be sought in the mainstream, rather than in the isolated backwaters or ingrown sects uninterested in communicating widely. They must, in other words, be what in the first centuries was meant by 'catholic' or 'orthodox', and what we now generally call 'ecumenical'."[22]

While Lindbeck places most of his emphasis upon the intrasystematic definition of truth, he also nods minimally in the direction of the notion of truth as correspondence to reality, but with his own particular twist. First, he claims that while individual doctrines, as doctrines, are not propositional claims to truth but rules or guidelines for living within a tradition, nonetheless, a tradition or religion as a whole might be interpreted as one large proposition that "may as a whole correspond or not correspond to what a theist calls God's being and will."[23] But how is that gigantic proposition to be tested? Once more Lindbeck refers us back to the practice of religion; a religion interpreted as a single proposition about reality can claim validity as true to the extent that its vision is interiorized by its adherents in such a manner that their lives can be said to correspond "to the will of God." "It is a true proposition," Lindbeck tells us, "to the extent that its objectives are interiorized and exercised by groups and individuals in such a way as to conform them in some measure in the various dimensions of their existence to the ultimate reality and goodness that lies at the heart of things. It is a false proposition to the extent that this does not happen."[24] Thus, Lindbeck does not exactly jettison the notion of truth as correspondence, but relocates that correspondence in lives rather than in the relation between ideas and external objects. However, how one would know when this kind of conformity occurs remains a rather significant mystery within Lindbeck's system.

Postliberalism, in many ways, offers a strong and compelling version of historicist theology. In particular, it draws our attention to the traditioned character of life and insists on the indispensability of our historical inheritance for purposeful and meaningful existence. It further seeks to explore systematically the ramifications for theology and for theological claims to adequacy once ahistorical notions of reason and experience have been foresworn. Despite these strengths, from the perspective of pragmatic historicism for which I will soon argue, postliberalism appears very problematic. While pragmatic historicism will only unfold in future chapters, I will endeavor to indicate those problematic aspects of postliberalism and by so doing mark the points where pragmatic historicism will be seen to offer distinctive alternatives. In particular, I will focus my concerns precisely on the two general issues of the Lindbeckian theory of traditions and the implications of that theory for how theological truth and adequacy are construed.

The Lindbeckian version of historicism, as it issues forth in a theory of the traditioned character of life, is, from the perspective of pragmatic historicism, too one-sided and univocal. It fails to account for the complexity of concrete historical life in several important ways. First, while rightly contending for the traditioned character of existence, it does not acknowledge that humans, especially in our twenty-first-century world, are in fact multitraditioned, shaped by more than one strand of history, weaving together inheritances from varied historical lineages. A historicist perspective entails taking account of this multiplicity and finding a means by which to relate its various, often tension-filled components. For their part, postliberals insist that we do or should so reside within primary communities, subordinating the claims and influences of other competing traditions and communities to these central ones, "absorbing the world to the text." But for pragmatic historicists numerous persons today cannot so easily distinguish such a primary, encompassing perspective but are compelled to fashion creatively and critically the diverse traditions that impact them into some new conceptually and functionally coherent perspectives that work for today.

A related problem is that the postliberal perspective eventuates in a very isolationist stance toward other traditions. Not only are individuals seemingly enclosed within singular traditions but those traditions have little points of contact with one another in terms of what is most significant or distinct about them. Part of this flows from the postliberal repudiation of the notion that humans share core religious experiences in common. Lindbeck's cultural-linguistic approach makes the claim "that religions are the diverse objectifications of the same basic experience" unlikely or as he puts it "implausible."[25] Pragmatic historicists will be seen to share with Lindbeck and his followers this sense of implausibility and will stress the distinctive historical character of religious traditions. However, when the repudiation of the common core of experience is then linked with a view of identity formed within singular traditions and a portrayal of traditions being formed or structured by unchanging grammars or directives, then the grounds for significant engagement between traditions become unclear. Certainly Lindbeck himself does not want to rule out interreligious dialogue.[26] And a number of other postliberals are responding to the charge of isolationism and are calling for an ad hoc apologetics—unsystematic and occasional conversations with other perspectives around specific shared concerns.[27] Yet postliberals have little basis within their theory of historicity for entering into these conversations or, once there, for making them much more than show and tell. Postliberals, in the end, fail to demonstrate why communities today should or how they could genuinely interact with other communities. Postliberals offer an account of how the present relates to the past but are singularly unhelpful in regard to the relationship among contemporaries. The form of historicism articulated by pragmatic historicists will be seen to ground its sense of historicity in a profound sense of the interdependent and interconnected nature of historical existence, leading its proponents to argue against an isolationist approach and for a stance of open and critical connection among traditions.

Another issue concerning how postliberals construe historical traditions relates to their failure to include in their analysis of the relation of
past and present any rigorous exploration of or even programmatic
attention to the political, economic, social, or broader cultural location
of religious beliefs and practices. Instead, religious traditions and especially their core tenets or grammars of faith appear strangely disembodied, suspended in history but untouched by the multiple factors that
shape and are shaped by interpretive traditions. Thus postliberals primarily ask how a later belief or practice is faithful to an earlier one, not
how both are embedded in the concrete processes of history. On this
point, too, pragmatic historicism will stress an alternative direction,
insisting that religious traditions, beliefs, and practices are thoroughly
implicated in the other dynamics of culture and that our interpretations
of them and our procedures for evaluating them require systematic
attention to these dynamics.

In many ways the concerns with postliberalism's view of historicity
and historical traditions come to clearest light when we focus upon the
implications of these claims for theology and especially for how theological truth or adequacy is interpreted. It is here that we can see that
Lindbeck finally presents a very undynamic, ahistorical interpretation of
cultural-linguistic traditions. As stated above, Lindbeck argues that
within traditions many things change over time but these religious traditions also have central doctrines or "regulative principles" that are
given and invariable, providing these historical strands their distinctive
identities. While these principles or central tenets of a tradition may be
embodied over time in various, even tension-filled ways, the basic tenets,
like the grammar of a language, do not change. There is, then, a stability at the core of traditions, an unchanging grammar or rule of faith.
Theological adequacy is then judged in terms of how well a claim or
practice can be seen to embody these unchanging dimensions of faith.
The edifice of Lindbeck's view of theology or truth finally rests upon
this notion of tradition as having a stable core.

From the perspective of pragmatic historicism these assumptions
about a stable core introduce a thoroughly static, essentialist component
that renders suspect all of Lindbeck's other claims to historical consciousness. Part of the difficulty resides with how Lindbeck construes
language and part with his appeal to that analogy in the first place.
While Lindbeck's use of the language analogy is sometimes illuminating,
especially as it focuses on language as a form of social practice, it,
nonetheless, has profound problems. His portrayal of grammar as static
and stable appears to be an abstraction made at the service of theological ends. It is simply not the case that vocabularies and lexicons change
over time but grammars and their rules do not. Languages, including

their grammars, emerge over time; they do not appear, complete in all essentials, in some instantaneous moment of birth. While relative stability or continuity may eventually develop, it is never total and its form cannot be established ahead of time but can only be discerned in hindsight. Moreover, the notion that a belief, while expressed variously, remains nonetheless essentially the same is, from the perspective of a fuller historicism, a reversion to an untenable Platonism. More importantly it is a claim that is difficult to sustain in an analysis of any particular religious traditions. Real historical traditions seem not to exhibit the kind of continuity that Lindbeck posits for them.

It is, however, when we turn away from the analogy to language and instead focus our gaze upon living traditions that the limits of the postliberal project become most open to challenge from a historicist vantage point especially as these claims eventuate in the assertion that authority is located in the past. Delwin Brown has captured well the interlinking assumptions that ground Lindbeck's positing of authority in the past when he states "Lindbeck . . . assume(s) that a canon is unitary in its fundamentals, that this unity is reasonably demonstrable, that it can be conformed to, and that such conformation is necessary to preserve the authentic identity of the tradition."[28] The view being contended for in this work suggests that each of these presumptions are problematic. There is not and never has been one self-same story found in the originating narratives of the Christian tradition, nor in the early theological decisions of the church; there have been various stories, of God, Jesus, what it means to be human, and these cannot be reduced to one another or to an abstract set of rules. Even at the beginning, there was not one Christian story, agreed upon by all. Christianity's origins, like the rest of its history, are unstable and contested.

Nor is it acceptable to "rein in" the diverse and even conflicting testimonies of the Bible through appeal to the Christological and Trinitarian develpments of the early church. These are *part* of a dynamic history with which contemporary Christians must contend. They are not ahistorical, still points that "trump" all else in Christianity's history, bringing order and unity to what is far more chaotic and disparate.

Furthermore, the historical traditions of Christianity that have developed over the centuries, including those early ones, are also internally plural, appropriating and transforming earlier Christian stories, intermingling them with other traditions and creating novel understandings of reality in the process. While historical developments certainly evidence continuities with what has gone before, they are not continuities of the sort Lindbeck envisions wherein a Platonic-like unchanging form—the singular self-identical Christian story—is, to use Lindbeck's words, fused with a changing historical reality without the abiding

Christian story being affected in any way by such a fusion.[29] If we are to understand those developments at all, we must understand them as concrete and specific, not as the ephiphenomenal expression of static principles that in the end provide them with their only claim to validity.

This is to say that Lindbeck's location of authority in the narratives of the past is predicated upon the prior assumption that these narratives are stable and unified and, further, his assertion that truth or adequacy is measured by conformity to these static cores depends upon his interpretation of later theological claims as historical containers, if you will, of this self-same, never-changing story. But once the stability at the origins of Christianity is questioned and once the historical variability of Christian theological claims is recognized, then Lindbeck's version of truth as conformity begins to appear as an arbitrary assertion of authority that protects theologians and religious practitioners alike from the hard task of justifying their beliefs and practices in a historicist age. In the name of unity and purity, Lindbeck foregoes the messiness of history, reinscribing an authoritarianism that can easily dismiss all heterodoxy as illegitimate deviation from the pristine, self-identical core of Christian faith presumed the same from age to age, supposedly adequate for all.

All this leads to a reinscription of an authoritarian view that allows theology to be, as Linell Cady puts it, reduced to the citation of "designated authorities" rather than open inquiry or argumentation.[30] Because religious traditions are all-encompassing and fully historical, they are on the deepest, most significant level not open to one another. This self-enclosed character of traditions reinforces, then, the notion of truth as intrasystematic. If there are no ahistorical vantage points for ascertaining absolute truth, neither are there cross-traditioned perspectives that can confirm or challenge the claims of a tradition. Each tradition goes its own way, turning, with all legitimacy, a deaf ear if it chooses to those outside its borders. And when, in turn, these historical traditions are construed as having stable cores, truth and adequacy are not only contextual matters but now questions of conformity to a settled past. Critical engagement with that past is ruled out and the theological task becomes primarily one of determining faithfulness to an established authority.

On these points pragmatic historicism will present an alternative reading of our historicity and the nature of traditionedness. It will assert that humans do not reside so neatly within traditions and hence are forced, in a manner unaccounted for in Lindbeck's version of truth and tradition, to make their varied assumptions cohere with one another and not just with an ancient past. Moreover, pragmatic historicism will reject the notion of a settled past at all and will insist that we must not end up with a historicism strangely emptied of history. These moves will entail the repudiation of authoritarian forms of theology and a call for critical and constructive theologies in their stead.

Thus from the perspective advocated in this book, postliberalism appears to offer a partial or fainthearted historicism. It helpfully draws our attention to the past and to the ways in which individuals and communities gain identity and purpose through interaction with our traditions of inheritance. But it construes the past and our relation to it in what finally is an ahistorical manner. The result of these renderings is a reintroduction of an authoritarianism and an undermining of critical inquiry that are antithetical to the version of historicism that this volume will espouse. As such postliberalism will continue to be a conversation partner and, in particular, a powerful reminder of the importance of tradition but will also be interpreted as a problematic position in relation to which pragmatic historicism will be set forth as a more consistently historicist alternative.

DAVID TRACY AND REVISIONIST THEOLOGY

Revisionist theology is another historicist perspective in contemporary theology. It is more difficult to draw the parameters of this perspective because revisionism has come to be something of a catch-all term, often used to locate a wide variety of thinkers who do not always agree with one another on central issues. Lindbeckians have tended to see revisionists as liberals of the experiential-expressivist type, while others have designated them as the left wing, so to speak, of a general narrativist, traditioned-centered school with postliberals comprising the conservative branch. Further, the beginnings of revisionist theology predate the current more radical historicist shifts to which postliberalism is a response; it grew out of earlier methodological concerns, especially those arising from the recognition of the marginalization of theology in public life and the beginnings of the acknowledgment of the interpretive character of all human experience. And the latter concern arose not from a blanket repudiation of modern liberalism but from an extension of the hermeneutical discussions that originated in the nineteenth century. This pre-postmodern point of departure, together with revisionism's concern with the public status and role of theology and the tendency, especially in its earlier forms, to be universalistic in tone have led many to see revisionist theology more as a continuation of the modern liberal project that is less fully attuned to the historicist sensibilities of today.

This section will explore the work of David Tracy as the primary architect of revisionist theology on the contemporary scene.[31] Tracy is an important figure to examine not only because he is the most prolific revisionist thinker and the prime shaper of the revisionist argument but also because he has been the revisionist theologian who has most self-consciously sought to incorporate the insights of the more radical present-day historicism into his work. Thus, while, as we will see, Tracy's current work continues central themes of his earlier revisionist projects, he, like the postliberals, sees himself developing a position responsive to the challenges of this now radicalized sense of human historicity and hence as offering an alternative that does not, as many of his postliberal critics claim, naively continue the projects of an earlier liberalism.

The analysis to follow suggests that, in fact, Tracy has always had a determinative concern for historicity. As Tracy has stated, "We belong to history and language; they do not belong to us."[32] But it will also be the contention of this volume that both in its earlier form and even in his more recent work Tracy combines that historicist sensibility with other elements that tend to diminish the impact of the recognition of historicity on his theology.

David Tracy has developed his version of a historicist theology by arguing for theology as a hermeneutical enterprise with a method of correlation as its centerpiece. Such an approach has grown out of Tracy's construal of historicity as essentially an ongoing interpretive process whereby human identity comes into being through encounter with the other, be that other a text, person, or event. But Tracy's rendering of theology has been based on particular specifications of this interpretative mode of being. For while all of our interactions bear this hermeneutical character, Tracy has most forcefully focused upon the relation of past and present, specifically upon the relation of the contemporary situation and a tradition's "classics."[33]

Tracy's early articulation of hermeneutical theology and the method of correlation was predicated upon certain assumptions that characterized a good deal of hermeneutical theory. In particular, he espoused the notion that all human beings have existential questions emerging out of our finite existence and from the specific issues and problems of an age. But to whom or what do we turn for an answer to these concerns and questions? Tracy's reply was that we turn to the classics of our varied traditions. These classics were almost always located in the past, having gained their designation over time as "expressions of the human spirit," embodiments of humanity's responses to profound existential questions. As classics they contain both a permanence of meaning that continually commands our attention and response and an excess of meaning that gives rise to their longevity and capacity for creative appropriation.[34] The classics, for Tracy, disclose truths about reality especially as they display what Tracy poetically termed an "instinct for the essential."[35]

Tracy also defended the notion of *religious* classics. For humans do not just have existential questions; they also have questions about basic meaning and value, about the limits of life and the character of ultimate reality. Religious questions, for Tracy, are, thus, "fundamental existential questions of the meaning and truth of individual, communal and historical existence as related to, indeed as both participating in and distanced from, what is sensed as the whole of reality."[36] As such they have a unique character. They are not only disclosive about some aspect or element of reality as are other classics; they disclose something concerning the whole of reality and thereby make a particular claim for truth upon those who encounter them. According to Tracy, "explicitly religious classic expressions will involve a claim to truth as the event of a disclosure-concealment of the whole of reality *by the power of the whole*."[37] There exists, then, a correlation between religious classics, as disclosive of the whole of reality, and the uniquely religious questions of an age.

Concerning each of these kinds of classics, nonreligious and religious, notions of truth are relevant in the form of disclosure, manifestation, and realized experience of the essential. Out of the encounter of the present with the classics of a tradition some essential aspect of reality, previously concealed, is made known, at least in part. And in relation to religious classics it is not only some part of reality that is now partially unveiled but the whole of reality, ultimate reality itself. In all of Tracy's terminology there is the clear indication that some antecedent truth is there to be discovered, revealed, made known through the hermeneutical encounter. Moreover, there is the strong presumption of the authority or adequacy of those texts, persons, doctrines, events designated classics, that make them, and not other historical artifacts, appropriate locales for the disclosure of such truth.

But while Tracy, like the postliberals, pointed religious practitioners and theologians back to the classical expressions of a tradition he, even at these earlier stages in his work, argued for what he understood to be a nonauthoritarian rendering of our relation to these classics. Tracy proposed that there was a great deal of difference between truths disclosed to hearts and minds and the invocation of external norms to which we were to submit. As Tracy put it, the authoritarian response suggests that the theological task is to repeat "the shop-worn conclusions of the tradition."[38] Instead, Tracy interpreted his model as one of conversation, as a hermeneutical process in which the classics of the past are creatively correlated with the concerns of the present. Both because humans, as historical interpreters, bring a variety of factors with us as we interpret classics, and because classics harbor within them a pluralism of possible meanings there is no possibility of a simple one-to-one relation between existential question and classic answer. What can and should occur is a dynamic and transformative dialogue out of which new answers emerge for the moment. Thus classics demand our response; they lay a claim upon us but not one of conformity. They are candidates for retrieval, not external norms to which we must bow. As Tracy puts it, in his hermeneutical version of theology "The appeal of any religious classic is a nonviolent appeal to our minds, hearts and imaginations, and through them to our will. Its authoritative status is not, therefore, by the violent appeal to obedience demanded by authoritarians in all religious traditions."[39]

In recent years Tracy has both continued many of the emphases that shaped his previous efforts and modified his position through a deepened sense of historicity or, as he has self-designated it, a move to a postmodern direction. Such movement has had important implications for Tracy's position. First, Tracy is far more careful about the universalizing tendencies of his perspective suggesting now that while all humans have questions of meaning and value neither they nor their classical answers can be reduced to a common set of existential concerns and responses. Although he insists that there is enough similarity-in-difference to make conversation possible, Tracy has, nonetheless, focused his attention on otherness in a new way.

Moreover, and significantly for our purposes, Tracy seems to have altered his notion of the classic. Now Tracy has always had a fairly flexible interpretation of the classic. In *The Analogical Imagination*, Tracy used the term to refer to texts.[40] But he also referred to events, persons, even gestures, images, and symbols as classics.[41] Indeed, at times it seemed that almost anything could be a classic. In *Plurality and Ambiguity*, Tracy has now augmented this inclusive and flexible definition by pointing to the instability of the classic; whereby once it seemed that something was a classic by virtue of its permanence and excess of meaning, now things gain and lose that status for far more complex historical reasons, including reasons of power and interest.[42]

Tracy's earlier tendency to grant a presumptive positive value to tradition has been modified as well by his intensified acknowledgment of the ambiguous and mixed character of all historical reality including those designated religious classics. The past shapes the present; as Tracy quoting William Faulkner states, "the past is not dead, it is not even past."[43] But if the past still influences the present it no longer is presumed to do so in an unproblematic manner. For Tracy, "there is no such thing as an unambiguous tradition; there are no innocent readings of the classics."[44]

When we acknowledge this ambiguity our engagement with the past must be far more critical in a revisionist perspective than it is for postliberals. The result of all these movements has been demonstrated in Tracy's intensified insistence on the critical character of theology, whereby theology is not just the appropriation of the authoritative givens of a tradition but the mutually critical correlation of the present and the classics of that tradition.

This sense of ambiguity and its attendant critical stance mark the most significant shifts in Tracy's recent work. Earlier in his work Tracy often seemed to espouse a hermeneutics of consent with all its presumptions concerning the innocence and adequacy of our traditions and their classics. More than ever before, Tracy is suggesting consent is inadequate; in the face of the inherent ambiguity of our classics and a history in which those have often been used to perpetuate great horrors, he now calls for strategies of suspicion and resistance. Moreover, he insists on giving priority to the voices of the oppressed stating, "among our contemporaries, their readings are those the rest of us most need to hear."[45] Thus in a significant way Tracy has aligned his position with that of liberationists for whom theological reflection seeks to serve those who have been history's victims.

In many ways Tracy and his revisionist companions can be said to have incorporated the strengths of postliberalism while avoiding its failures. Revisionist theology espouses the importance of tradition and the past, while increasingly maintaining a critical stance toward them. Revisionist theology also acknowledges the problematic character of modernity, jettisoning the ahistorical elements of that project and incorporating within its model the critical dimensions of historicism without abandoning the public sphere and the possibility of real encounter with the other. And finally, in its more postmodern turn, Tracy's version of revisionist theology has sought not unconcerned play but solidarity with those who suffer.

Despite these accomplishments, there remain questions concerning the depth and adequacy of historicism in Tracy's revisionist mode. Two central and connected issues come to the fore. The first is Tracy's continued emphasis upon the classics of a tradition. While he now sees these as fraught with ambiguity, classics nonetheless remain center stage in this revisionist approach. Hence, while we dialogue critically with the past we still do so with a fairly narrow, albeit changing, section of the historical heritage, one privileged by processes of power that left out much more than they included. This continued prioritizing of the classics suggests a lingering essentialism in Tracy's position that belies his historicism; it implies that there is a true core of the tradition and that the classics represent this core because they carry a freight—indeed perhaps an ontological freight—that separates them from the other events and processes of this particular history. A more full-fledged historicism would need not only to see the classics as ambiguous but would also need to deprioritize them and acknowledge their ontological equality with other historical events, texts, symbols, and persons. A fuller historicism would resist all essentialist interpretations of traditions and instead insist that the historical traditions with which contemporary theology must contend are thoroughly pluralistic and devoid of abiding essences that are stable over time. At times Tracy seems to be going in this direction himself as when he calls us to reflect upon "the ordinary ways practiced by most members of the religion" or when he declares "[i]f pluralists genuinely affirm plurality, they can hardly ignore, much less dismiss, the importance of ordinary and everyday examples of a living religion."[46] These claims are, from the perspective being argued for here, commendable. However Tracy's continued focus on classics undercuts and vitiates these moves, leaving them as empty gestures that have failed to alter his basic position.

A related issue is the fact that Tracy continues to view theology as primarily a hermeneutical enterprise in which the central task of the theologian is to correlate those classics of the past with present concerns and proposals. While a fully historicist perspective will readily agree with Tracy that the past contributes to the present and that we must therefore engage it, it is unclear that such encounter should be for the purpose of correlating the claims of the past with the contemporary situation. The more pertinent theological task would appear to be a constructive one that engages its particular historical tradition, along with those of other traditions, in order to create identities and visions of reality that are viable for today. When the past is shorn of its privileged status, then the hermeneutical moment is just one intermediate moment in the theological process, not its end and goal. Thus an historicist orientation suggests a move beyond the hermeneutics of revisionism toward a more constructive historicism.

Linked to the continuation of a primarily hermeneutical approach to theology is Tracy's ongoing emphasis on truth as a primordial manifestation. The motifs of concealment/disclosure and recognition on the part of interpreters still permeate Tracy's account of classics. But what truth as manifestation means has never been and is not now very clear in Tracy's work. It appears, at the least, to refer to the fact that whenever encounters of any type take place some interpretation of such interaction emerges. But Tracy seems to want to make more far-reaching claims than that. For he asserts that in genuine encounters or conversation the other is revealed in such a manner to make a claim to truth upon us. But what does this mean? Are all claims upon us to be assumed to be valid? Are all disclosures "true"? True to or about what? How does Tracy's growing recognition of the ambiguity of history play into his notions of manifestation? Philosopher Richard Bernstein has critically focused on this lack of clarity in Tracy's thought. As he states, "we must also always ask whether what is manifested is a true or false manifestation. The hard question that Tracy does not fully confront is what is the source of authority or legitimacy of truth as manifestation. Is the 'source' of this legitimacy to be found in the manifestation, in the disclosure/concealment, or in the communal critical practices of validating the claims to truth?"[47]

Accompanying this confusion about truth as manifestation is lack of clarity concerning Tracy's connected notion of the relative adequacy of interpretation. Tracy suggests that while classics manifest the truth in the dialogical moment interpreters, for their part, seek to give the best possible expression to that truth through their interpretations. Such interpretations cannot be seen to be absolute or timeless, Tracy avers, for as all things historical they are always limited, temporary, and fragile.[48] Hence all interpretation can ever aspire to is a relative adequacy that is always open to revision and challenge. On the one hand, Tracy's modesty here is commendable and certainly consistent with historicist insights. On the other hand, it does not help matters much. This is the case for several reasons. First, it is seemingly impossible to distinguish between the classic that is interpreted and our interpretation of it. As Tracy notes, we only have interpreted classics, not classics that are then subject to interpretation. Thus adequacy cannot be judged by comparing the "manifestation" and the interpretation of it. Moreover, as was noted above, when we are pushed back to the manifestation it is totally unclear what is to count as a true or false manifestation or on what bases such judgments should be rendered. Tracy's tendency to assume that we will know one when we see one simply will not do.

All this becomes even more problematic when the topic is religious classics. For these classics do not present some finite claim to validity but manifest the "whole of reality" through a particular finite reality. Not only does this seem to negate the particular significance of a finite historical reality by making it an occasion for ultimate reality to reveal itself, but it clouds the notions of truth as manifestation and relative adequacy even more. How does one assess as true or false a manifestation of the whole of reality through a finite moment? On what basis does one decide that this interpretation rather than another is more relatively adequate?

Now Tracy acknowledges that these are difficult questions and in part he tries to answer them by arguing that our various claims to adequacy of interpretation must be tested in the communal and public realms. That is, we must offer reasons. And Tracy has lately suggested, appealing to William James, that those reasons have to do with how our claims cohere with what "we otherwise know, practice and believe"[49] and with the consequences of such claims for life. These two norms, coherence and consequences, he links to William James's pragmatism. And as we will see, they do indeed resonate with the neopragmatism this work is espousing. But how these norms connect with the idea of manifestation and what content the pragmatic norm might have remain undeveloped. And while Tracy has recently referred to the need to develop interpretations of reality that foster resistance and hope, the reasons for moving in this direction rather than another also remain unarticulated.

In sum, this analysis suggests that Tracy has embraced a number of assumptions that are compatible with the position I am taking. There are many ways in which Tracy's instincts and explicit proposals will be seen to resonate with pragmatic historicism. But there are these other dimensions of his thought that lend confusion to his own position and clash strongly with the approach being developed here. His notion that "[t]ruth, in its primordial sense, is manifestation" smacks of an ongoing romanticism that presupposes that the really real, especially the ultimately real, resides behind finite reality waiting to be discovered and disclosed.[50] Such romantic presuppositions seem, moreover, to continue to tie Tracy to the classics of a tradition even though he has widened the category and now treats these artifacts of the past with a much more critical edge. And although Tracy now refers to pragmatic norms and criteria of coherence, the question of how they connect with assumptions about disclosure and manifestation remains much of a mystery. Thus, while Tracy has insisted, over against the postliberals' interpretation of revisionists, that hermeneutical theologians have been engaged in an internal critique fostered by growing historicist insights for several decades, key elements of that earlier tradition can be seen to remain in Tracy's own thought and to sit uneasily with the historicist directions his work seems now to be pursuing.

TOWARD PRAGMATIC HISTORICISM

The analysis offered thus far suggests that both postliberalism and revisionist theology reflect significant historicist insights that demand our attention and careful appraisal. They will continue to challenge the work of theologians who seek to rethink theology out of the recognition of our historicity. Nonetheless, our exploration has also led to the conclusion that many aspects of postliberalism and revisionism call into question the depth of their advocates' historicist commitments.

It will be the contention of this book that another theological approach is taking shape that carries out the implications of historicism more thoroughly. I have designated this theological option pragmatic historicism. It does not, as of yet, constitute a full-blown movement or a clearly defined school of thought. Rather, it is more of a trajectory, a direction toward which an increasing number of thinkers are moving. It is my purpose to give more definition to this movement, to define its parameters and its central contentions. It will also be my goal to push this trajectory along a little, to engage it, and by so doing, to contribute to its future shape and direction.

Pragmatic historicism will be seen to share much in common with the perspectives delineated above. But, at decisive junctures, it will also be clearly an alternative to the claims and assumptions espoused variously by postliberalism and revisionist theology. Thus, these other approaches will be conversation partners, perspectives to be criticized and critics themselves in the following discussion about the future fortunes of theology.

Before turning to the task of describing pragmatic historicism and presenting the arguments on its behalf, I want to refer once more to liberationist approaches to theology. Earlier I wrote that such perspectives, while continuing certain modern projects, also have been central expressions of and contributors to the sociopolitical assault on modernity. These approaches are still vital and compelling today. Yet I did not list them among my list of options for the present. I did not do so for several reasons. One is that it is difficult now, if it ever was possible, to refer to a singular liberation perspective. There are feminists, and African American and Asian and Latin American and African and Latino/a forms of theological thinking today that, while sharing much, also are distinctive in their own right and represent challenges to one another as well as to other forms of theology. Moreover, representatives of these orientations identify themselves not only as liberationist but increasingly carry out those commitments from within other theological perspectives. Thus, there are feminist postliberals, postmodernists, and revisionists, there are African Americans who have embraced the narrative perspective associated with postliberalism and others, as will be argued, who are pragmatic historicists. Liberationist orientations have therefore developed into multiple individual forms and have also found expression through various other schools of theology.

These are obvious reasons for not identifying liberationist approaches as one option among a series of clearly distinguishable alternatives. But my central reason for not adding this perspective as one more on a list is that I believe part of the challenge of liberationist theologians is the call to include liberationist concerns within any theological alternative being articulated today and to test its adequacy in terms of how well it incorporates and gives expression to those concerns. That is to say, no theology is valid today that is not in some form a liberation theology. This is not to deny that specific thinkers or groups are continuing to develop specific liberationist alternatives. It is to suggest the power of the liberationist critique has gained wide enough credence that it is, in this age, a central point for determining the validity of contemporary theological options, including the topic of this book: pragmatic historicism.

It is now time to turn to the specific rendering of pragmatic historicism. With the foregoing analysis in mind, aware of the other options available and cognizant of the ongoing challenges of liberationist thought, I will in the next chapter undertake the delineation of the overall historicist orientation that infuses this perspective and only then in subsequent chapters develop the theological approach that flows out of such a historicism and how this contrasts and resonates with other pragmatic approaches. Of particular importance in the last chapter will be the exploration of the pragmatic norms accompanying this form of historicism and how these emerge and function in a world of unequal and unjustly distributed power.

CHAPTER 3

Historicism and Human Worldviews

ASSUMPTIONS AND THEORIES

The purpose of this chapter is to begin to delineate an emergent theological alternative that I am designating pragmatic historicism, and that I believe carries out the dictates of the current historicism more fully than the options explored thus far. I want to commence such an analysis by exploring the guiding suppositions and underlying premises of this perspective and the larger theoretical picture that emerges when these assumptions are made explicit. While not all of the theologians designated pragmatic historicists in this study, or even all those to whom I will be making substantive reference in this chapter, would set forth their arguments in the manner proposed here, many of them, either self-consciously or implicitly appear to work out of a framework similar to the one depicted in this chapter.[1] Giving more precise expression to these underlying assumptions and theoretical frameworks allows us to explore the unique shape of pragmatic historicism while simultaneously probing several of the most tenacious issues raised by historicist sensibilities. In particular, I want to explore how a growing number of theologians are depicting what it means to be human, utilizing historicist categories, and what those categories assume or imply about the wider cosmos within which human life finds itself located. That is, I want to examine the anthropological and cosmological premises that undergird this incipient orientation.

To undertake such an exploration on my part, and certainly to attribute to others not only assumptions about the human and the cosmos but general theories concerning these, is an enterprise fraught with difficulty.[2] For today, as never before, theologians, as well as many other thinkers, are wary of any attempt to render explicit presuppositions and even more suspicious of articulating these premises in broad, encompassing theories purporting to speak of humanity, the universe, history, and so forth. These efforts seem, for many, to entail inevitably a covert return to universalism and new forms of essentialism. To refer to the human as such implies, it would seem, an isolatable human nature that constitutes all humans, no matter their temporal, spatial, and historical

51

location. It is precisely such grand theories about universal essences that contemporary historicism has repudiated so adamantly, as it has at the same time insisted upon the conditioned character of all our claims and their circumscription within particular localized traditions. Both theories about the human and the concrete humans to whom these theories refer are taken to be quite localized entities without universal reference or characteristics. Thus, postliberal theologians have been led to the discussion of human life within particular historical traditions and thinkers such as deconstructionists to a view of humans as unstable and variable individuals without any clearly definable common essence shared with all others.[3]

Therefore, for many thinkers today, any move to speak of humanity as such or to develop a general picture of the cosmos is highly questionable. Yet, if the recognition of radical historicity has led to the debunking of claims to absolute or unchanging truth and simultaneously to a sense of the futility of the search for ahistorical essences, such acknowledgment of historicity does not, in itself, lead to the conclusion that all general theories are useless or merely covert ways of smuggling in ahistorical assumptions about reality. For the flip side of asserting that there are no neutral or objective depictions of the world and humanity is the claim that *all* of our understandings of reality, even the most local and particular, are thoroughly conditioned and carry with them premises about the world, even if these remain implicit and unacknowledged. Indeed, the very appeal to categories such as historicity implies a theory of the human, that is, at least implicitly an anthropology. Stating that ahistorical or absolute claims cannot be sustained today does not automatically entail the further assertion that all general claims are de facto ahistorical and, therefore, cannot be made without betraying historicist commitments. Nor does it lead to the conclusion that it is unimportant or unhelpful in an historicist age to uncover and render explicit these assumptions.[4]

Not only does the current historicist sensibility entail consciousness that our positions are the bearers of operative assumptions about what it means to be human and to exist in a certain kind of world, but when examined, that sensibility also contains the recognition that these assumptions and the theories they become embodied within are value and interest laden and are held for a variety of purposes. As Frank Lentricchia has stated, "theory does its representing with a purpose."[5] Thus the implicit and explicit theories and premises that shape our views have not only descriptive intentions, contingent and tentative though they may be, but normative ones as well. They, therefore, have repercussions not only for how we view the world and our place within it, but also for what we interpret to be proper action and forms of relation with other humans and the broader world. To deny the possibility of general theories of the world and humanity is either to be naive about the working assumptions that in fact we hold as historical beings or to participate, wittingly or unwittingly, in the masking of interest-laden assumptions that have concrete and material effects on how we build our institutions, live our lives and relate to one another and nature.

A sense of radical historicity does not lead, therefore, to a naivety about a supposed absence of assumptions nor to the abandonment of the effort to give these systematic and coherent expression in more general theories of the human and the cosmos. Instead, it indicates the importance of rendering explicit the working anthropological and cosmological premises that pervade all of our thinking and doing, and of examining critically the concrete repercussions for individuals and society of living out of such presuppositions. Anything else is a form of self-deception and, perhaps more importantly, the deception of others.

A recognition of historicity is not the only reason why thinkers today, including theologians, need to set forth the founding claims upon which we build our positions. Several other reasons compel us to do so at this particular moment. First, when societies or cultures are fairly stable, the need to delineate and clarify guiding assumptions is not very strong. It is in times of crisis and transition, when firmly held presuppositions are challenged or faltering, that both the old and new premises and the contrast between them require greater examination and interpretation. As Alasdair MacIntyre states "generally only when traditions either fail and disintegrate or are challenged do their adherents become more aware of them as traditions and begin to theorize about them."[6] We find ourselves at just such a juncture in history, at the moment of transition from one era, modernity with its myriad assumptions, to a new period in history. Moreover, while I have spoken of a pervasive sense of historicity, it is not yet clear what this means or what repercussions it entails. New presuppositions may be forming but their broad-based and common appropriation is not yet in place and, hence, one of the tasks we face is articulating anew the assumptions we now hold and elaborating the status of these basic convictions about the world. It is at moments of historical metamorphosis that thinkers must seek to gain some measure of clarity about their most fundamental convictions, how they fit together and what they imply. Carrying out critical reflection on basic assumptions and setting them forth in relation to each other through theoretical elaboration will not, in a time imbued with a sense of contingency and fallibility, give us a new form of metaphysical comfort but it will provide us with a better sense of where we stand and why and how we differ or agree with one another.

Another reason for intellectuals and most especially theologians to make more explicit our guiding suppositions and their possible amplification in theory is a quite practical one: theologians have as one of our purposes the desire to respond to the conditions of our world and to offer theological positions that engage these in an effective and creative manner. What we consider effective responses and how we construe the terms of engagement differ from theological perspective to perspective as this book demonstrates. But in order to understand the responses theology has to offer the world today and to evaluate their differences from one another, it is imperative that we get a clearer picture of the assumptions that guide theologians as we develop our positions, the stances we hold toward other intellectual disciplines that are also reconceiving their central convictions, and what we consider effective or relevant interaction with the broader intellectual, religious, and cultural world.

This search for clarity is not only difficult for all thinkers given that our presuppositions are often inchoate, unsystematic, and at best implicit, and that our theoretical frameworks are often assumed but not articulated, but it is especially so for theologians. Theology has embodied over the ages diverse and conflict filled ways of relating to broader cultural and historical trends and beliefs; uncovering the basic convictions infusing a theological position, thus, entails becoming cognizant as well of its relation to these wider cultural contexts. Theological positions are, according to the historicist position taken in this work, not timeless expressions of truth, intelligible apart from their historical and cultural milieu but forms of cultural practice. To understand Augustine one must know about the late Roman Empire and Neoplatonism, Luther demands an awareness of the collapse of the medieval world and modern theology only makes sense in the context of the challenges of modern science, the rise of historical consciousness and the culture of critical reason. But it is not only a matter of what broader cultural and social realities and beliefs form the context within which theologians pursue their work but of how theologians *respond* to those beliefs, incorporating them into their theological perspective, or rejecting them for other convictions or social formations, or critically engaging them. What is certain is that some relation pertains between theology and its cultural context and to understand the former requires a sense of how it interprets and relates to the latter. Such a relation is often complicated and even conflicted; for example, theological postliberalism heartily endorses contemporary historicism but uses that endorsement to call for a return to the biblical worldview, even if that reversion entails the repudiation of other present-day assumptions linked to historicism.

Moreover, how the relation of theological convictions to other cultural beliefs and practices is interpreted also says something about how theological effectiveness is conceived and assessed. For postliberals, adopting, as they claim, a biblical perspective with its inevitable assumptions about reality, leads, in many instances, to a critical stance toward contemporary culture. In contrast the proponents of pragmatic historicism, while not discounting postliberalism's sometimes critical stance, reject the notion that theologians today can or should ignore the premises of one's own time. Instead the desire to develop effective responses to our current situation leads pragmatic historicists away from assuming a worldview from a bygone era, be it of the biblical world or otherwise, and toward a substantive engagement with our cultural context. This does not mean that theological and cultural assumptions are simply collapsed or that the only criterion for theology is how "contemporary" its underlying premises are. It does mean that, in Gordon Kaufman's words, theology must "establish effective contact with major presuppositions and perspectives of modern intellectual life."[7] To fail to do so is, finally, for Sallie McFague, as well as Kaufman, "blatantly wrongheaded" and entails an arbitrary adoption of another era's convictions, no less contingent and historical than ours, and leads at best to irrelevance and, at worst, to a dangerous intensification of our various crises.[8]

If it is the case that a historicist sensibility far from ruling out the legitimacy of underlying theories and convictions about reality indicates instead their inevitability, and therefore the necessity of continually making them more explicit and relating them to other assertions about reality, it is also the case that contemporary historicism renders such assumptions contingent, fallible, emergent in history, conditioned by temporal, historical, and spatial location and hence always open to modification. To refer to basic convictions of reality is not to discover self-evident or indubitable facts about the human self or world. It is instead to indicate operative assumptions that influence and ground our thinking and doing that are thoroughly historical, the product of specific historical processes. This contingent and fallibilist status applies not only to what was referred to earlier as implicit anthropologies and cosmologies but also to more self-conscious and fully developed theories about humanity and the rest of the cosmos, be they scientific, philosophical, or literary. Neither implicit convictions nor more comprehensive and systematic theoretical frameworks directly depict reality, human or otherwise; neither provides grounds for absolute certitude or claims to unassailable truth. Instead, as pragmatist Giles Gunn says quoting William James, theories are only, "hypotheses liable to modification in the course of future experience."[9] Recognizing the hypothetical, imaginative, and speculative character of our basic beliefs and most firmly held theories leads, according to Gunn, to a "more provisional relation to our convictions and a more quizzical attitude toward where they may carry us and what sorts of criticism they can sustain."[10] That is, it leads to an ongoing attitude of self-criticism that while continuing to hold strong assumptions nonetheless holds them a little less tightly, always acknowledging their fallible character.

CONVERSATION PARTNERS

The repercussions of letting go of earlier quests for certainty and indubitable foundations have, for theology, been varied. For postliberalism, the recognition of radical historicity has led to an affirmation of the centrality of traditions and to a view of theology as primarily concerned with the faithful rendering of the originating claims of particular traditions. While current historicist assertions play a pivotal role in this perspective, other contemporary claims about the world, be they scientific, those of other religious traditions, literary, or philosophical perspectives, receive only tangential roles in the substantive shaping of theological visions for today.

While postliberals have turned to a normative tradition, revisionists such as David Tracy have exhibited simultaneously an interest in the classical past and in broader contemporary conversation partners. Tracy's universalist tendencies, his more historicist notions of similarity-in-difference and his commitment to public discourse have all led him to an openness to nontheological perspectives and to conversations with proponents of other religious traditions. Tracy's commitment to a mode of correlational theology also propels him to utilization of nontheological sources. These perspectives provide insight into the contemporary condition and hence are indispensable for configuring the contemporary pole of theology. Finally, such extratheological sources have contributed significantly to the analysis of the classics of the past, helping make their relevance for today more available, and also shaping our present sense of their enormous ambiguity.

The current historicist mindset has even more significantly opened up new conversational avenues for proponents of pragmatic historicism. In particular, it has, for theologians like Gordon Kaufman, Sallie McFague, William Dean, and Delwin Brown, led to a renewal of theological interest in the sciences, both natural and social. This engagement with contemporary science marks a shift from the manner in which early modern theology and science were separated and it also gives an indication of the distinctive character of the historicist trajectory I am attempting to identify.

As suggested in chapter 1, science and theology have traveled separate paths for a significant part of the modern period. With the rise of the Enlightenment and its ideal of reason, science became the model for objective, universally valid, and empirically derived and tested truth. Religion, increasingly seeming to fail such criteria, was more and more relegated to spheres beyond the province of science, first to Kantian morality and, from the nineteenth century on, to the Schleiermachian realm of religious experience. And theology, banished from public discourse, engaged ever more in what Francis Schüssler Fiorenza has called a hermeneutics of human subjectivity, focusing on the depths of human experience interpreted as beyond the purview of empirical analysis or explanation.[11] Jeffrey Stout, referring to those theologians who followed in the line of Schleiermachian liberalism, contends that a truce was sought by them between science and religion, in which separate, inviolable spheres of influence were determined. Stout states:

> The truce was to be a pact of nonaggression—what Schleiermacher called an "eternal covenant"—which was to allot science and theology separate realms of human experience to govern and then to prohibit all trespassing across boundaries as the intellectual equivalent of imperialism. Science was to govern the realm of cognition; it alone would have the authority to tell us what we know. Theology was to reign in the realm of religious affectivity; it alone would have the authority to tell us what piety implies.[12]

There were certainly challenges to understanding religious faith and theology in such subjective terms including the Barthian repudiation both of science's claims to ultimacy and theology's anthropological focus, and, from the opposite perspective, the early Chicago School's conviction that science and theology might fruitfully engage and illuminate one another.[13] Moreover, it is also the case that modern theology, although situated within clearly demarcated boundaries, nonetheless has been confronted by the reality of the nonbeliever whose very existence has often challenged the supposedly protected realm of religious piety as no longer having any meaning or validity at all. Despite theological reservations concerning the separation of science and theology and notwithstanding the growing irrelevancy of theology and religion for many modern persons, for the most part the spheres have remained distinguished, and without substantive interaction.

The situation today, however, is significantly altered. As this chapter has been arguing, the profound consciousness of human historicity that has come to pervade life at the beginning of the twenty-first century has led to the repudiation of quests for certitude, the relativizing and fallibilizing of all our forms of inquiry and claims to knowledge and the historicizing of all our intellectual disciplines. One major result of these changes is that the privileged position of science has been increasingly undermined. While the sciences are still for many the model of truth and the purveyors of uncontestable "facts," for others, especially intellectuals, they have become, if not merely another language game, then less qualitatively distinguishable from humanistic endeavors such as literature. Moreover, such a reconstrual of science has been taking place within the scientific disciplines themselves, not only on the part of philosophers of science such as Thomas Kuhn and Paul Feyerabend who point to the historical and context specific character of scientific knowledge, but also by many contemporary physicists and cosmologists who readily acknowledge the imaginative and creative aspects of their speculations.[14] Now, as never before, scientific pictures of the world are, indeed, being viewed as James' "hypotheses liable to modification in the course of future experience."

If the sciences are being deprivilegized, if they are being displaced as the singular bearers and guardians of truth, why then should theologians turn again to these fields of inquiry? Indeed, as has been suggested, many theologians have turned elsewhere to poetry or literature or a normative past. But the proponents of pragmatic historicism have concluded differently and have set out a range of arguments contending for the importance of theology's engagement of both the natural and social sciences.

Generally stated, for many pragmatic historicists, the recognition of the historical and contingent character of inquiry should not lead to narrower conversations or isolation within restricted traditions or fields of inquiry, but should indeed have the opposite effect—it should open the places of conversation and debate, widening what counts as relevant. The reasons for science and theology not to talk no longer pertain. Ironically, postliberalism, though repudiating much of modernity, continues the separation of science and theology that was a hallmark of that heritage.

Why specifically should the sciences be listened to at this juncture of theological history? One reason is that if theology is to be able to respond to the crises that confront the contemporary world we can only hope to do so by taking account of the widest and best range of information that we can obtain in order to fashion a relevant and effective interpretation of our situation. Although the natural and physical sciences may no longer make claims to ultimate truth, they do continue to provide the parameters of at least tentative knowledge within which most contemporary westerners function. As James Gustafson, another thinker who has pursued such conversations, has argued, for theology to be "intelligible and persuasive," it must "engage the materials that inform both students and a wider public."[15] Likewise, Gordon Kaufman asserts that while there is no singular scientific viewpoint and, given the contingent and hypothetical character of scientific claims, there are no absolutely "coercive" reasons for adopting one scientific picture of the universe or of human beings rather than another, nonetheless, we must, in his words, "construct a conception of the world (and of God) appropriate to the knowledges we have available and to the problems with which we humans today must contend."[16]

It is not only a question of appearing intelligible to a public, including most certainly those within religious traditions who are deeply informed and shaped by the tenets of contemporary science, it is also that we, whether we acknowledge it or not, work out of sets of assumptions about the world and about humanity. Unless theologians are willing to live in either self-defeating ignorance or internal self-contradiction, it is imperative that we seek a critical congruence between our theological assumptions and our other beliefs and practices. We can neither pretend that we have no such assumptions nor adopt the assumptions of an earlier, long-departed time and worldview; rather we must analyze our theological presuppositions in light of what else we know and claim and set forth clearly their compatibility with or variance from these other components of our current worldview. And in our historical moment science is a central contributor to and ingredient in our worldviews.

Another reason for engaging the natural and social sciences according to pragmatic historicists has to do with what they see as having been left out of other forms of historicism. William Dean is most pointed in his criticism of many historicist orientations (including the pragmatism of such philosophers as Richard Rorty) when he notes that historicism has focused almost exclusively upon the human, depicted as a thoroughly linguistic being, situated solely within the confines of human history. The human as embodied creature existing in a physical universe is virtually ignored.[17] Sallie McFague likewise indicts the narrowness of contemporary historicism. Historicist insights have led to the acknowledgment of the context-bound character of all thought and action. But, McFague contends, "[t]he one context which has been neglected . . . is the broadest as well as the most basic, the context of the planet, a context which we all share and without which we cannot survive."[18] The result of this narrow historicism—what Dean labels humanistic historicism—is a truncated, often disembodied, notion of the human and a rampant anthropocentrism that not only fails to provide a perspective from which to respond to the current ecological and environmental crisis but, in fact, perpetuates and intensifies it. Ironically, the anthropocentrism and linguistic focus of postliberalism and poststructuralism are other ways in which they continue the very spirit of modernity they purport to critique and repudiate. For their part, pragmatic historicists claim the natural sciences—from microbiology to quantum physics to cosmological speculations—while not providing final truth or uncontestable solutions to our problems, do widen our view and locate us in the broadest possible context. By being situated in such an inclusive context, theological historicism is enriched and deepened and better able to contend with our perilous situation. Thus, these sciences claim our attention at this particular moment for very specific historical reasons. At other historical moments, different conversation partners might well take priority.

If contemporary historicism has had the unfortunate tendency to dematerialize humanity and to blind us to our natural and physical environment, it has also, in a quite strange manner, often left us ill-equipped to deal with the plurality and diversity of human communities and ways of being. It has, indeed, led us to recognize the plurality and particularity of human traditions and to the uniqueness that marks each individual. But that recognition has led in turn to contentions that human communities and their inhabitants are profoundly separated, fated to exist in insularity from one another with little hope of significant communication or understanding; it has led to what Richard Rorty terms, from his perspective positively, ethnocentrism.[19] Yet, despite these intellectual contentions, we find ourselves in a world where diversity is not half a planet away but in our midst and in which the interconnection of these diverse groups indicates that the survival of all depends on how we manage to relate to one another. A historicism that relegates us to isolated communities, to what anthropologist Clifford Geertz has referred to as "turned-in social totalities meeting haphazardly along the edges of their beliefs," provides little guidance in addressing this central character of our time.[20]

Pragmatic historicism contends that just as by attending exclusively to humanity and the human context our vision is too narrowly focused, so, too, by trafficking primarily with our own traditions and assuming the utter unlikeness of others much is dangerously left out. A historicism that effectively confronts diversity and difference must find a way both to affirm the historicity and therefore particularity of human existence while also seeking an "imaginative entry" into that which is alien, whether it is a world away or within our own society.[21]

The social sciences, as well certainly as the humanities, can aid in such a task. Anthropology, especially ethnography, and sociology provide not only in their theories but in the empirical data they set forth a means once more of widening our vision, of enriching and deepening our historicism. Cultural anthropologist Clifford Geertz again gives expression to the sentiments of many pragmatic historicists when he argues for just such a role for ethnography, stating that "it is the great enemy of ethnocentrism, of confining people to cultural planets where the only ideas they need to conjure with are 'those around here,' not because it assumes people are all alike, but because it knows how profoundly they are not and how unable yet to disregard one another. Whatever once was possible and whatever may now be longed for, the sovereignty of the familiar impoverishes everyone."[22]

Thus, for pragmatic historicists the recognition of historicity should lead theologians today to wider conversations, to the testing of our ideas about humanity against the claims and insights of other disciplines, especially those that can force us to contend with that which we seem to leave out of our accounts. Here, as with the natural sciences, exalted privilege is not being bestowed upon our fellow inquirers. It is, as it was in relation to the natural sciences, a case of being committed to an expansive historicism that can take account of and allow us to respond to the realities of our current situation.

And, finally, pragmatic historicists contend, the ability to respond to our present situation requires as well that we must recognize and take account of the dynamics of power that infuse how we conceive of both nature and of human communities and interaction. If historicism up to now has often been oblivious to its natural setting, it has just as frequently offered a view of the human social and cultural habitat that has not been adequately cognizant of the material and political character and conditions of culture. As developed in this work, an adequate historicism for today must not only give expression to the embodiedness of human historical existence but also to the material embeddedness of all cultural and social products, processes, and institutions. If we require a naturalized historicism and a historicized naturalism we also need a materialist notion of culture. Hence, those disciplines of political theory and social criticism that focus upon such dynamics are also conversation partners it is imperative to engage. A historicism that ignores these issues, that turns uncritically to a seemingly unambiguous history or to a playful, depoliticized self is, as Cornel West has argued, "thin."[23] In contrast, pragmatic historicism seeks a historicism that evidences an awareness of how ideas and beliefs both reflect and are conveyers of power, and how its own historicist assumptions also participate in such arrangements.

This chapter has set forth a line of argument that has contended that historicist insights lead neither to the denial of the presence of underlying premises about what it means to be human and about the nature of the cosmos that provides the context for human life nor to conclusions that more developed and self-conscious theories and interpretive frameworks are illegitimate attempts to express new unassailable foundations. Rather, it has been argued, a historicist sensibility should issue forth in the acknowledgment that such assumptions are always operative, that our ways of thinking, being, and doing are suffused with assumptions and often with theories that require not denial but elucidation and critical assessment; to make these explicit is not to engage in totalitarian adventurism but to open them up to scrutiny and criticism.

Thus, it can be seen, the theological perspective portrayed in these pages is proposing a distinctive orientation, one that is contending for a renewal of open and public conversation between theology and other intellectual fields of inquiry and that repudiates the isolation of theology within narrowly circumscribed traditions. By so doing, pragmatic historicism is not suggesting that any of these disciplines have access to ahistorical knowledge about reality nor that congruence with other contemporary cultural assumptions is the only concern confronting theology today. It is arguing that the empirical sciences, both natural and social, provide us with data and theoretical interpretations with which theology must contend if it is to offer viable visions for today. It is proposing that without such critical engagement, theology will have little persuasive power and few truly effective proposals for dealing with the world in which we live.

Pragmatic historicism offers, therefore, a variety of reasons for turning to a broad spectrum of conversation partners. It should also be noted, prospectively, that the picture of human existence that will take shape through these conversations supports and compels a view of theology open to and accountable in relation to multiple voices and perspectives. For the interpretation of human life and nature that will be laid before us in the next section will locate human historicity in the dense context of natural and social realities that are not divisible into small, unrelated enclaves without connection. This portrayal of human historicity will provide further impetus for wider conversations and suggests arguments for why theology must contend for its proposals beyond the boundaries of our local communities and traditions.

Before turning to this picture of human life and its wider setting that is emerging in pragmatic historicism, it is important to raise one more issue that seems to have been ignored in the orientation outlined above and that is the question of the traditioned character of life. While I have argued for the historicity of existence in terms of contingency and fallibility, and have used those to speak on behalf of opening new or renewed avenues of communication, far less attention has been paid to the equally important historicist insight that these contingent forms of knowledge always take shape in traditions; they never simply appear *de novo*, but emerge out of past interpretations, theories, assumptions, and practices. Indeed, postliberalism's rationale for its return to tradition is precisely its recognition of this dimension of historicity. Yet, thus far, my portrayal of pragmatic historicism seems more focused on the present and future than upon its past. Does this mean that the theological orientation labeled pragmatic historicism fails on this issue? There is no quick answer to this question; in part the argument of this book as a whole will need to stand as an articulation of how pragmatic historicism views the relation of present and past. And as we turn in the next chapter to more explicitly theological areas, the relation of contemporary theological claims to religious and theological traditions, especially "classics" or founding narratives will be focused upon much more explicitly and critically. But, at this juncture, it is important at least to note the general approach to these matters for which my version of pragmatic historicism will contend.

First, it is clear that for this perspective, ideas and beliefs certainly do not float free; they originate and take shape in particular temporal and physical locations and they bear all the marks of such specific locales. Moreover, they are passed down through traditions and gain their intelligibility and efficacy by virtue of their local nature even as those traditions extend through time and even when they offer the broadest pictures of reality. There may, indeed, be generalized beliefs but there are no unlocated and unattached beliefs—even scientific ones. Nor are there ideas or theories that do not depend in some real way on the history of which they are, at least in part, a product. Hence, pragmatic historicism as a theological movement must inquire not only how its assumptions cohere with the other claims being made today, but must also locate itself in relation to earlier theological and religious positions—something that several of the theologians I am now identifying as pragmatic historicists have often been accused of failing to do.

But to locate theological ideas in this manner does not, according to this perspective, require that the past be rendered normative. For that past is just as contingent and fallible as the present and merely by being past does not acquire some authoritativeness denied the present. Moreover, to recognize that humans are traditioned not only entails seeing that the present emerges from the past but also that in such a historical process the genuinely novel comes forth. To acknowledge our traditioned character is not to assume that historical lineages repeat unaltered some essence untouched by the contingencies of history, but that, in the process known as history, conservation, sometimes quite massive, and transformation, sometimes quite radical, both occur. Hence, for pragmatic historicists, the past cannot be ignored; it must be contended with, but this contention places no obligation of repetition or conformity upon the contemporary theologian. Moreover, as the above statement concerning the social sciences implies and as the next chapter will more fully argue, pragmatic historicism does not think traditions are insular or self-enclosed but rather porous, stitched together from many sources, internally multiple and open to the encounter with and influence of others. Thus, while it is imperative to struggle with history, that history is wider and, internally and externally, more diverse than we may have imagined.

With this prolegomenon as background, it is now time to turn to an examination of the anthropological and cosmological assumptions framing the theological trajectory of pragmatic historicism. The picture that is emerging here will be seen both to express central convictions but also to provide further reasons for conceiving of theology in the manner that will be set forth in the following chapters. Moreover, when set forth, they will elucidate the positions propounded thus far, further illuminating the bases of arguing as we have.

It is important to note that the picture that will emerge below is *generally* shared by the thinkers I am enlisting as pragmatic historicists. However, there are also significant points of divergence among these theologians that lead to both minor and, sometimes, substantial differences. Where differences are particularly acute will be indicated in the text.

COSMOLOGICAL AND
ANTHROPOLOGICAL PRESUPPOSITIONS

The form of historicism being developed in this volume has clearly entailed the rejection of claims of nonperspectival access to reality as well as notions that our theories and assertions about human selves and the world constitute indisputable depictions of such reality. Instead, we encounter ourselves, one another, and the wider world from particular locations shaped by language, history, and physical and temporal conditions. Hence, while we exist as participants in the midst of reality, that reality remains in a significant way a mystery to us, a context of ultimate unknowing with, as Gordon Kaufman has insisted, "no way to ever plumb the ultimate meaning of human life" and its cosmic setting.[24] Neither human life nor the cosmos is transparent to human knowers.

Present-day historicist insights have, thus, led us, more than ever before, to be cognizant of the speculative and imaginative quality of our theories and assumptions. Yet acknowledgment of the tentativeness, fallibility, and speculative character of all human claims does not lead to the conclusion that such claims can be merely jettisoned, nor that they are condemned to an arbitrariness in which each is equally valuable or valueless. Instead, it suggests that we fashion our pictures of reality in conversation with the broadest range of inquirers and out of engagement with the most defensible, albeit contestable, proposals of our time.

The proponents of pragmatic historicism contend that a general picture of reality is emerging from across the physical sciences that increasingly is being accepted as the "public portrayal of reality" for our times and that therefore demands our attention.[25] Moreover, this picture is one that historicizes the universe in the most fundamental way and thereby not only coheres with our assumptions about humanity but provides as well a broader interpretive framework in which humanity can be more integrally situated.

Sallie McFague has labelled this new view of reality emerging from such scientific locales as astrophysics, cosmology, and biology the "common creation story."[26] This interpretation, over against the dualistic assumptions of modernity, offers a conception of the universe as holistically interconnected and interdependent, as dynamic and ever changing, and as open and capable of genuine novelty. The founding assumption of this construal of reality is that all of the universe, past and present, has a common source, originating, it is speculated, in the cosmic explosion billions of years ago known as the Big Bang. From this singular event all reality, living and nonliving, has come forth.

Such claims of a singular, shared cosmic point of departure entail, according to McFague, a number of other assertions that are important both for how we conceive reality generally and for our view of humanity. Most significantly, the notion of a common creation leads to a sense of the wholeness, the oneness of the universe; "it has," McFague states, "a common history dating back fifteen billion years, gradually emerging through transformations of enormous complexity into billions of galaxies of the present, observable universe, including our own tiny planet, Earth."[27] To come from one source means that everything that is, is related to everything else. There is nothing that is totally alien, unconnected to other elements of the universe. For McFague, "From this beginning came all that followed, so that everything that is, is related, woven into a seamless web. . . . All things living and all things not living are the products of the same primal explosion and evolutionary history and hence are interrelated in an internal way right from the beginning. We are cousins to the stars, to the rocks and oceans and to all living creatures."[28]

This recognition of relatedness has the important repercussion of undercutting notions of the radical separation of humanity and the rest of reality that have been pervasive in western thought. While McFague and others I am designating pragmatic historicists will be seen to have a strong sense of humanity's distinctiveness, it is no longer possible, from this perspective, to interpret humanity as utterly unlike nonhuman, even nonliving, creatures. The universe of the common creation story is composed of entities whose ancient place of birth is a common explosion and whose history is one, infinitely complex process. Humanity is a product of this same cosmic process that brought forth all else.

In this interpretation of reality, not only is every element in the universe related but such relation means that the cosmos is a network of interdependent entities. Nothing exists in isolation from anything else in such a universe; to be at all involves dependence upon the larger context and upon its constituent elements. This is as much the case for humanity as for anything else; the modern portrayal of the human as an autonomous and uniquely independent being finds no support in this depiction of reality. Instead, human life, like all else, is contingent upon the cosmic web and both contributes and is subject to its variable conditions.

For Sallie McFague, the picture of reality taking shape in the sciences clearly leads to notions of interconnection and interdependence. But it also points to the distinctive, utterly unique character of all that exists in the universe. No star, no planet, no living earthly creature is the same as anything else. The cosmic process, with its singular beginnings, has brought forth infinite realities, unrepeatable both in themselves and in their configurations with one another. Hence, relatedness and dependency do not vitiate distinctiveness; on the contrary, they provide the bases out of which uniqueness emerges and upon which it depends. Distinctiveness and difference are not the corollary of autonomy and separation but of connectedness and the capacity for relation.[29]

This new world picture suggests, moreover, that while the interdependent and interrelated nature of reality means that everything is conditioned and shaped by everything else, at least remotely, nonetheless the universe is not a closed, deterministic system. Instead, the cosmos is, in this view, an open creative process in which everything is conditioned *and* self-constituting and in which the really new emerges. In McFague's words, "This is an unfinished universe, a dynamic universe, still in process."[30]

Thus, out of the scientific interpretations of the origins of the universe, a general construal of reality is emerging that depicts the cosmos as a relational web of interconnected realities extending over vast stretches of space and time. It is an emergent universe in which interdependence issues forth both in the conditioned character of all reality and in the possibility of novelty. It is a universe that is quite thoroughly historical in which the past, immediate and distant, is literally the raw material out of which a new and unique present continually comes forth. As such, this view embodies on a grander scale similar historicist insights as have been proposed about human existence throughout these chapters. Both the status of this world picture—interpreted as tentative, partial, liable to challenge and change—and the categories that structure its claims correspond to and will be seen to reinforce the other historicist assumptions that have funded the arguments set forth thus far.

William Dean's historicist assumptions and his appropriation of contemporary scientific theory lead him, like McFague, to argue for a holistic interpretation of reality in which the bifurcation of history and nature is overcome.[31] Dean concurs with other historicists that there is nothing that is not historical, neither extrahistorical realities nor ahistorical truths. However, he asserts, many contemporary historicists, including theologians, fail to carry through the implications of such claims for the wider cosmic sphere and instead limit their historicist assertions to the confines of human history. This limitation, in part due to the historicist tendency to avoid grand theories and leave unexamined underlying presuppositions, has the unfortunate effect of keeping intact outmoded construals of reality and of humanity's relation to the rest of the universe.

The overcoming of these deficiencies is an important goal of Dean's work. A major way he seeks to contribute to this overcoming is through the extension of historicist categories to nature, including categories that have heretofore been almost exclusively applied to conscious human behavior. This stretching of categories helps Dean simultaneously to historicize nature and to locate humanity in a newly conceived natural context but does so through the controversial process of anthropomorphizing nature in a way that other pragmatic historicists, such as Gordon Kaufman, will be seen to resist. Dean, for his part, contends that the portrayal of reality emerging from the sciences lends credence to such a move and provides the theoretical means to talk of the human and nonhuman spheres utilizing one coherent conceptual framework. In particular, Dean finds the work of physicist John Wheeler supportive in reconfiguring nature as historical. Wheeler, building on the uncertainty principle that claims that the very act of observation alters the results of observing, moves toward notions of a historicized natural world and the historical character of natural laws. Reality, far from being static or ahistorical, is a dynamic, emergent process whereby new reality issues forth from the interaction of observer and observed. Wheeler, in Dean's account, argues that "reality should be treated as nothing but the interaction, the evolving relatedness, between the observer and the observed."[32] In this view, the cosmos becomes a "participatory universe" in which "every observer's interpretive reaction contributes to present reality's new definition."[33]

The repercussions of rendering reality in such "participatory" terms are, in Dean's perspective, far-reaching. First, Dean suggests that construing reality as an ongoing interpretive process, where interpretive refers not to the conscious elucidation of meaning but to creative and transformative engagement whether conscious or not, leads to a historicist understanding of nonhuman reality, for it is not just conscious human beings who alter reality by virtue of interpreting it. Rather, all of reality interprets itself; nature and the universe as a whole are constituted by the interaction of the past and present whereby new realities emerge. Thus, the radical distinction between human historical processes and natural ones can no longer be maintained in this view. Nature, too, is historical.[34]

Second, the bifurcation of history and nature has had as a concomitant assumption the notion that the human self was separable from its world. In this participatory universe, in which the effects of interaction reverberate throughout the universe, this separation is no longer conceivable. In a cosmos where reality is constituted by the interplay of its elements, there is nothing that exists apart from its relations with its world, including with the natural and biological world.[35]

Third, as with McFague, to view the universe as a network of relations is not, for Dean, to interpret it in mechanistic or crass materialistic terms, nor is it to view the cosmos as "the creature of a solipsistic or nihilistic relativism."[36] On the one hand, a participatory universe is an open one; new, unpredictable realities do emerge through the temporal engagement of past and present. While there may be trajectories within the universe, directions of development, there is no evidence that either the past—earlier sedimented history—determines rigidly the present or that some teleological lure pulls reality irresistibly toward a predetermined end. On the other hand, the past does exist, in Dean's terms, as "a causal mandate" that sets boundaries within and in relation to which the cosmic interpretive process takes place. In his words, "the universe's history is not just whatever we subjectively make it. The observed past contributes also to the interpretation and the observer has no control over the content of that contribution."[37]

Fourth, Dean's construal of reality as participatory, as a web of interconnectedness through which novelty emerges, highlights the centrality of relations. Building on the claims of earlier American thinkers such as William James, Dean argues for a form of radical empiricism. Giles Gunn, speaking of James, states that "[r]adical empiricism conceives of life as an interwoven, interdependent structure that can only be grasped in its fullness by being grasped in its relations, its transitions, its tendencies, its fluidities."[38] For Dean, such a recognition entails a number of important factors. It suggests that it is through the experiencing of relations, both humanly and nonhumanly, that reality is constituted. But such experiencing of relations is not, according to both the early radical empiricists and their latter-day proponents, confined to conscious, linguistically structured awareness on the part of humans. For

Dean, clearly all of reality participates in such "grasping" of relations—indeed comes into being by virtue of it. Moreover, humans experience our world, according to Dean, more broadly or deeply than most linguistically oriented historicists allow. While humans relate to the world in a linguistically shaped manner, we are also aware of and connected to our world in a largely prelinguistic or nonlinguistic and mostly unconscious manner. Human beings not only perceive their world through the five senses and conceptualize and shape such perception linguistically, but also engage our world in another, more fundamental mode of relationship by which we literally feel the world physically and causally impinge upon us. We perceive the world through what might be termed an affectional sensibility and thereby grasp the world in its relations. Thus, for Dean, humans engage our environment on this fundamental level in a manner similar to how the nonhuman world relates to its world, hence strengthening our sense of being part of and at one with that world, not separate from it.[39]

And finally, for Dean, radical empiricism not only broadens our conceptions of how humans interact, it also indicates the valuational character of not only our linguistic experience but also this primal experience of relations. On the one hand, the experience itself is not empty but is laden with value and significance; on the other hand, that which is experienced comes as valuable and quality filled, it is not neutral itself. Reality, in this view, does not only have value imposed upon it, but value is ingredient in it as well. For Dean, as will be seen in subsequent discussions, this affirmation of value will be extremely significant in the attempt to give pragmatic historicism a normative direction that avoids subjectivism and relativism.[40]

Dean, thus, calls for a "naturalistic-humanistic historicism." He contends that the testimonies of science provide "an indispensable voice" that must be attended to if our historicist constructions of reality are to be persuasive in our age. Such testimonies broaden the case of contemporary historicism, locating humanity within a historicized natural world and providing infinitely increased data in relation to which historicist construals of humanity and the world might be tested. For Dean, therefore, "Unlike a humanistic historicism, [a naturalistic-humanistic historicism] would effectively require historicist theology to justify itself not only before the bar of an interpreted human history but also before the bar of an interpreted natural history."[41] By so doing, this form of historicism would not gain indubitable truth but would, according to Dean, avoid the pitfalls of an exclusively self-referential humanistic historicism while remaining within the confines of a now enriched and expanded history.

Dean is not alone among those who I am labeling pragmatic historicists in undertaking the renewal of radical empiricism. Delwin Brown is also a proponent of a variation of radical empiricism that while it resonates with Dean's position is, as the next chapter will indicate, utilized for different purposes and steadfastly rejects the criteriological thrust of Dean's approach and the anthropomorphic sound of Dean's language of interpretation. Brown's major concerns in articulating a form of radical empiricism relate to his desire to account theoretically for the role our bodies seem to play as a central means by which we engage the world, to acknowledge theoretically the apparent fact that human behaviors fall along a continuum, and to emphasize his conviction that the largely nonlinguistic and preconscious dimensions of human experience require greater attention than they have been given, even by historicists, if we are to understand, or significantly affect, the dynamics of religious or cultural traditions.[42]

Brown sets forth his version of radical empiricism through the articulation of four points. The first is "the proposal that our primary connectedness with things is at the level of largely nonconscious feeling. It is an activity of the body, or at least of the self as an embodied organism, rooted in and interacting with the rest of nature."[43] Brown contends that while consciousness, structured and conditioned by linguistic and symbolic inheritance and resources, is certainly significant to human experience in fact we traffick with reality primarily as bodies, encountering the world physically. Such interaction takes place through the senses but for Brown, along with other radical empiricists, it also occurs on a more basic level of feeling from which sensory experience is derived.

A second component of radical empiricism, à la Brown, is that not only do we come to the world from our own perspectives but that the world we encounter and engage through this bodily commerce comes to us "weighted, patterned, or directional."[44] According to Brown, we inherit a world rich with value, "not innocent, indifferent buzzes" but "values that incline us, influence us, move us."[45] Not only do we bring value to the world, assessing, imposing, and constructing it, but the world in which we are always already immersed is also heavy with the tendencies and character of its infinite components.

A third point, already implied by the above, ingredient in radical empiricism is the assumption that the relation pertaining between humans and their environments is an interactive one in which self and world mutually constitute each other rather than a one-directional movement whereby either the self receives a world or in some idealist fashion creates it.[46] We are not, on a nonconscious level any more than on a conscious level, blank receptors who receive or mirror a world that is simply given nor do we wholly construct a world out of our own bodily or imaginative activity. Instead we interact and in the interaction both we and the world come into being.

And fourth, Brown proposes that radical empiricism, or at least his version of it, is not espousing some sort of "pure experience." In humans, "the more primitive level of experience is intertwined with sensation and reflection" with influence going both ways.[47] Moreover, even on the most basic level of feeling all experience is perspectival, the feeling of this body in relation to this particular environment.[48] As such Brown's version of radical empiricism does not deny the dictates of a historicism that emphasizes the local and particular character of experience but reinscribes them in relation to fundamental bodily experience. If historicism cannot disregard our bodily commerce with the world, neither can a turn to bodily experience ignore the conditioned and located character of this dimension of human life. Radical empiricism, for Brown, is not a path back to discounted notions of immediate, nonconditioned experience.

In sum, Brown sees radical empiricism as a speculative hypothesis, one that makes sense of the judgment that "we are bodies more than we are minds."[49] Such a hypothesis should not be interpreted to claim that humans have some sort of ahistorical, unmediated experience that can be called upon to prove other claims or, against the sometimes present tendencies of Dean, to provide some sort of criteria or direction for determining which conscious proposals are best or most valid. Instead, it allows us to develop a view of humanity and the world that can more adequately account for the role of the body in experience and knowledge and that links our experience to other, nonlinguistically developed creatures. In this latter sense, radical empiricism for Brown, as for Dean, naturalizes our historicism and historicizes all forms of our experience including our bodily experience.

For Gordon Kaufman, as with Dean, Brown, and McFague, there are no uninterpreted descriptions of reality but only value-laden theories that then have repercussions for what we see as appropriate ways of being in a particular kind of world. Nor can these ideas be totally separated from one another or neatly derived one from another. Instead, our ideas of the world and the human self and especially the divine exist in dialectical relation informing and shaping each other. Thus, where one commences an analysis of these topics is somewhat arbitrary and always refers back to other ideas and assumptions. Much of Kaufman's work has focused upon the idea of God, how it functions and the ways in which it, for him, needs to be reconstructed. Anthropological assumptions about the nature of language and the role of symbol systems within cultures often framed these more distinctly theological discussions. But, in his most recent work, Kaufman, while certainly not forsaking his interest in analyzing and reconstructing the God-symbol, has offered, in his most extensive effort yet, a full anthropology that both grounds his conception of theology and provides a normative direction for his constructive theological proposals.[50] Hence, for Kaufman, it is from an anthropological vantage point that both cosmology and theology are engaged. With him, we turn to a fuller examination of the anthropological assumptions that inform at least the Kaufmanian expression of pragmatic historicism.

Kaufman, no less than McFague, Dean, and Brown, locates humanity in the broader natural and cosmic context developing what he terms a biohistorical interpretation of the human. It is, according to him, "not possible to understand human existence apart from its wider situatedness in the ecology of life on this planet; and, of course, planet Earth can be understood only within the context of the solar system and the wider universe. So our anthropological work leads ineluctably into cosmology."[51] All cosmological renderings of the universe are, Kaufman acknowledges, imaginative and highly theoretical world-pictures whose adequacy and accuracy can never be fully empirically determined. Yet our visions of reality, if they are to function for us, cannot be merely arbitrary but must give the fullest account of the universe possible predicated on our best current knowledge. And, for Kaufman, as for the other thinkers invoked in this chapter, the picture of the universe depicted by contemporary science as an historical evolutionary process provides the most comprehensive interpretation and best foundation for interpreting human life today.

Stated succinctly, Kaufman adopts a now familiar interpretation of reality as an organic, dynamic, open-ended movement that continues to generate varied and new forms of existence. The universe is, for him as for the other persons examined in this chapter, an interconnected and interdependent web, evolving over time, a cosmic eco-system in which all forms of existence are both related to each other and dependent upon the entire network for their maintenance and development. Moreover, in this view, while the universe gives little or no evidence of a deterministic teleology, the evolving cosmic process has produced increasingly complex forms of existence, including eventually the emergence of conscious human life.

For Kaufman, this last fact that human life and history have arisen from the evolutionary movement is most significant for our anthropological construals and eventually will be, for him, important for how we might today reconceive specifically theological ideas, including God. First, it clearly situates human life as part of and inseparable from the wider fabric of existence. For Kaufman, "humankind is emergent from other forms of life, and it continues to be sustained by the web of life as

a whole. . . . Humanity, thus cannot be thought of as a distinct and independent reality, separable from the world; it must be thought of as
essentially in the world, part of the eco-system within which it
emerged."[52] Locating humanity "in the world" implies, secondly, that
not only has humanity emerged within a physical and biological universe, evolving out of earlier biological forms, but also that human
beings remain corporal creatures whose biological needs must be met in
order for human life to survive and flourish. Human life has its matrix
in a physical universe upon which it is utterly dependent. Thus to understand what it means to be human at all entails the fundamental acknowl-
edgement of our biological nature and the further recognition that it is
only the maintenance and development of the cosmic web of existence
that insures the continuation of human life.[53]

For Gordon Kaufman, therefore, interpreting humankind as a product of a vast, complex evolutionary process signifies our bodily and
physiological nature. But it also implies much more, both about the cosmos and humanity. For the dynamic process that brought forth human
biological life has also resulted in the emergence of consciousness and
the development of a distinctively human sociocultural form of existence. The universe, no matter how else we interpret it, must be seen as
a creative process capable of developing and sustaining not only life but
conscious existence. And, human existence, while clearly biological,
must also be conceived in terms of its unique capacities for language and
culture.

Kaufman's argument concerning these matters, while not differing
substantially from the other theologians examined in this chapter, does
have a different tone from the ones offered by McFague, Brown, and
especially Dean. They have recently focused upon the problematic separation of nature and history, of humanity and the rest of the universe, of
culture and the body. They, therefore, emphasize the cosmic and natural location of human life and have stressed the continuities between
human existence and other forms of existence. McFague, thus, contends
for a more "earthly" interpretation of human life.[54] And Dean not only
historicizes nature, but he and Brown, with their articulation of radical
empiricism, challenge the singular focus upon conscious experience and
its linguistic and cultural construction, thereby contending that humans,
like all other experiencing subjects, significantly traffick with reality in
physical and nonconscious ways. For Kaufman, too, human life clearly
emerged out of and continues to depend upon matrices of interconnected biological life that evolved over the eons. However, from early
on, human life has also existed within and been dependent upon the cultural and social webs that developed as humans acquired language and
symbol-creating capacities. Hence, human life is not only biological but

also, in a manner more strictly tied to distinctively human capacities, is sociocultural or, in a narrowly human sense of the term, historical.

To be sociocultural beings entails a good deal for Kaufman. It means that in all our ways of being and doing, humans are "qualified and transformed by the cultural patterns which we have learned through interaction with other human beings from infancy onward."[55] Human life, from the moment of birth, and likely before, is colored by its cultural and social context. For Kaufman, this means, in particular, that language plays a pivotal role in shaping distinctively human experience. It is through the acquisition and use of specific historical languages that humans name their world, develop interpretable patterns and gain the orientation that permits self-conscious behavior. It is, in this schema, the attainment and deployment of language that renders to humankind its distinctive form of existence; indeed without language and culture, human beings could not exist at all. Moreover, culture conveys through its language, as well as through other nonlinguistic means, roles and practices, values and ideals. What specific ways of being human are possibilities for us and how they are valued all depend upon the particular culture within which we find ourselves and how that culture has evolved over time.

For Kaufman, then, culture and language are ingredient in all human forms of being and modes of activity. The possible ways humans enact our humanity, the roles we can take, the forms of activities open to us, and our interaction with both our fellow humans and the broader world are all made possible through and are dependent upon the linguistic, symbolic, and cultural forms that human communities create. These assertions of the sociocultural status of humans carry widespread implications in Kaufman's schema. In general, they entail the acknowledgment of humanity's fundamental and inescapable situatedness within particular historical locales. This means, first, that language and culture are always specific; there is no such thing as a universal culture or a general, nonhistorically specific language. Instead, these originate, develop, and change through particular historical processes, uniquely conditioned by time and location. What is possible in one historical period or cultural milieu is inconceivable in another. This specificity further indicates that human cultural and linguistic development has issued forth in multiple, distinct, noninterchangeable but not *necessarily incommensurable*, human communities and traditions; that is, human diversity is the unavoidable by-product of our being sociocultural creatures.

A second implication of an historicist reading of the sociocultural nature of humankind is the admission of our dual status as conditioned, traditioned beings and as creatures capable of change and self-transcendence. On the one hand, it is clear that, for Kaufman, to interpret humanity in historicist terms, especially when these are explicated in relation to language and culture, entails the recognition that humans are products of particular historical lineages upon which we are fundamentally dependent. In Kaufman's words, "everything about us, including all our ideas and values, our standards and norms, our ways of living and our patterns of action, have been shaped by and in the culture within which we have emerged; that is, by tradition. Without such historicocultural shaping we would have no form at all; we would not even be."[56] But, such dependence does not, on the other hand, deny the dynamic, changing and self-transcendent quality of societies, cultures, and traditions. For language and cultural forms are not fixed, exhibiting some ahistorical essence unchanging through time. Instead, they are the product of the creative interaction of humans and their past and present environments whereby new possibilities continually emerge. For Kaufman, "humans have a power of creativity, a power to transform their inherited conditions of existence, which is unique among all living beings of which we know."[57] While Kaufman might concur with Dean that the cosmic evolutionary process embodies this transformative creativity as well, he asserts that with the emergence of consciousness and language that creativity has taken on new dimensions; in particular, it has become self-directing and thereby responsible for the content and directions of its own development. This last point is of great importance for Kaufman, for it indicates that humans, with their particular human form of historicity, have evolved into creatures with the capacity for relatively free and self-conscious actions, who not only inherit language, culture, values, and so on, but also are responsible for their conservation or transformation. Thus, for Kaufman, to be historical beings existing in the twin matrices of culture and the natural world means finally that humans are moral creatures, participants in the creation of both their natural and cultural environments and, in part at least, accountable for their condition and future development.

The fact that self-conscious historicity has emerged in the universe says something as well, for Kaufman, about the cosmic evolutionary process itself. That process has now brought forth and continues to sustain conscious and self-directing life. Thus, whatever else we say about the universe, we must say it is a sort of reality that is capable of creating conscious, purposeful, and moral existence. Moreover, in the very process of so doing, the cosmic process itself has become self-conscious, capable of deciding, in part, its own future direction. The emergence of distinctly self-conscious modes of organization and activity mean, according to Kaufman, that "the irrevocable cosmic movement into the future is no longer one that is completely blind and purposeless; it has become deliberate in certain respects, intentional, permeated with meaning."[58] Thus, human beings as self-conscious historical creatures bear not only the necessity and responsibility of creatively engaging their particular histories, but also by so doing, of contributing to the future direction not only of humanity and its earthly context but literally of the cosmic process itself.

For Kaufman, theological engagement with the sciences, natural and social, can be seen to yield a persuasive picture of the universe that indicates both humanity's enmeshment in a broader natural order and its distinctive characteristics as a uniquely linguistic and cultural species. There is no doubt that, according to him, the biological and cultural-historical dimensions of human life each need to be accounted for in any theological interpretation. It is also clear that in Kaufman's work the fact that conscious, purposeful, and moral existence has emerged within the evolutionary process signals a creative advance whose appearance, maintenance, and further development should be central theological concerns. In particular, how the nature of theology is to be construed, the location and content of its norms and its substantive proposals will all be seen to be related, for Kaufman, to the portrayal of humanity in social and cultural terms. Hence, both cosmological and uniquely anthropological assumptions will be seen to have direct theological import. For it is, finally, as historical creatures acting for historical purposes that we carry out the theological task.

I stated above that the group of thinkers I have been introducing as pragmatic historicists while not contradicting each other do offer different emphases, with Kaufman continuing his long-held attention upon the importance of language and uniquely human history and McFague, Dean, and Brown pushing for the importance of our natural context and bodily experience. Kaufman tends to separate material views of the cosmos and humanity from historicist ones. I and the other pragmatic historicists, while not neglecting the distinctive human capacity for creativity, are more likely to bring materialist and historicist views together by emphasizing the ongoing creative process that is the cosmos. And though Brown, McFague, and I are somewhat wary of Dean's anthropomorphizing tendencies, we share his concern to keep humanity's locatedness in nature central to our theological considerations.

On one level these differences have to do with a matter of style and decisions about what elements it is most important to give theoretical prominence today; Kaufman, thus, does not deny we are bodies and the others are clearly cognizant of the significance of language and symbols. But on another level these differences will, as this book continues to unfold, shape how individual pragmatic historicists determine what is adequate, what field of experience should be the testing ground for theological inquiry, their understanding of the importance of the past, and how they construe the relation of inheritance and historical agency. Thus while my purpose in this chapter has been to offer a general picture that I think is emerging that sets off this trajectory from other options, it is also important to keep in mind the plurality and indeed tensions that characterize what I am calling pragmatic historicism and to recognize that there are not only options between this perspective and other historicist positions but also within pragmatic historicism as well.

And finally, before turning to my concluding remarks for this chapter, I want to ask what has been left out of or is underdeveloped in the positions that I have been detailing and how must they be altered if they are to be adequate. The kind of historicism that I have been describing here is bold in its insistence that its presuppositions and theoretical frameworks should be made clear. Moreover, in its desire to be expansive and to avoid a disembodied form of historicism, its proponents, to varying degrees, have turned to nature, the broader cosmos, and the body. However, I noted earlier in the chapter that pragmatic historicism needed not only to be naturalized but also politicized. On this point I think many of my fellow theological pragmatic historicists do not follow through their historicist insights thoroughly enough. While all the thinkers designated pragmatic historicists acknowledge the importance of culture and indeed in the case of someone like Gordon Kaufman focus intently upon culture as the distinctive expression of human historicity, frequently the interpretation of culture, language, and symbols that emerges appears abstracted and isolated from social relations and from the operations of power. What, I think, pragmatic historicism requires is not only a theory that accounts for the bodily based character of experience but one that offers a more material view of culture.

Materialist views of culture have come to characterize a number of perspectives including neo-Marxism, some forms of poststructuralism, certain feminist and liberationist orientations, anthropology, especially ethnography, and perhaps most prominently, cultural studies. Certainly these perspectives offer distinctive theories of culture that deserve more focused analysis. But for our purposes I want to highlight several points that I believe it is imperative for pragmatic historicism to take into account. First and foremost is the insistence that culture, taken as a way of life, cannot be separated from an inclusive web of social relations. Too often even pragmatic historicists, such as Kaufman, while nodding in that direction still focus on culture primarily as a system of meaning and upon symbols as the embodiment of meaning; the task then becomes to relate meanings to other meanings and a major concern becomes the internal coherence of an intellectual system or its agreement or disagreement with other so-called systems. A materialist view of culture, while not denying the significance of meaning systems nor the importance of how ideas and assumptions cohere with other ideas and premises, nonetheless asserts that these cannot be abstracted from the social and political forces, institutions, and material conditions within which they are located and in relation to which they function. If such abstraction is ruled out, it will not do only to ask what theoretical assumptions underpin our positions and how our theological ideas relate to other ideas abroad on the contemporary scene—important as these questions are. We must also ask how they relate to political, economic, and other social orders and forces. If pragmatic historicism is truly to be both pragmatic and historicist, it must not only turn to culture but recognize that culture is social and material through and through.

Such a recognition entails, in an interesting parallel to radical empiricism, the insight that "meaning" is not only constructed and produced linguistically and discursively but also that it is created through nonlinguistic and nonideational means. For pragmatic historicism to give a more materialist account of culture, including especially its religious manifestations, means that it will need to turn not only to systems of thought but to other sites of meaning and value, including such things as rituals, institutions, and other nondiscursive formations. Furthermore, this suggests that, as the next chapter will explicitly argue, for pragmatic historicism to be efficacious it must not only transform ideas but engage the full range of human practice and feeling.

Another element suggested by a more material construal of culture is the all-important assertion that the intersecting forces from which culture emerges and in relation to which it functions are also deeply connected to power, its distribution and circulation. Not only can we not separate cultural formations, including religion and theology, from their social matrix but we must recognize that these forces are not neutral, equally benefiting everyone and equally contributed to and controlled by all. If a materialist view of culture turns us to a complex network of social relations and to practices, institutions, and formations not easily reducible to ideas, it also pushes us to interpret this matrix as infused with power and as often conflictual in nature.

Earlier materialist theories of culture attended to these dynamics of power but often embodied a tendency toward deterministic and mechanistic views in which all power was located in one site or in which one sector, say economics, controlled and dominated all other human realms. Such one-sided views have diminished among theorists of culture to be replaced by interpretations of culture as dynamic, interactional, and creative, as processes of negotiation, invention, and struggle in which power is never purely repressive nor the sole possession of one group or sector of society.[59] Thus while no dimension of culture can be understood apart from social relations and the operations of power that inhere in them, neither can cultural formations be reduced to simple mirrors of some hidden but all-determinative power dynamic of class, race, gender, religion, sexual orientation, or any other of the categories by which we are tempted simplistically to analyze the causes of evil and good. As with the claims concerning bodily based experience (which as the radical empiricists insisted cannot be simply divorced from cultural and social processes) both constraints and creativity characterize all the dimensions of human historical existence.

If pragmatic historicism, especially in its theological expression, is to avoid becoming a truncated linguisticism and an apolitical abstraction, it must attend, in theory and practice, both to the bodily basis of our experience and to its embeddedness in social relations. Doing so will result neither in a new determinism nor in reconstituted notions of unconditioned experience but in a richly nuanced understanding of historical existence. And such an expansive historicism will chart, as we will see, new directions for theology in the pragmatic mode.

Finally, this recognition that human historicity is embedded in and part of complex social relations also suggests that there are other, more functional kinds of coherence that characterize human individual and communal identity and organization. While this chapter has focused upon the task of theologians to integrate and make sense of a variety of cognitive and conceptual claims that shape our contemporary condition, it is also the case that in the concrete specificity of lived existence, persons and groups bring the myriad factors that influence them, including social ones, together in complex ways. Moreover, as the next chapter emphasizes, human identity emerges out of the intermingling of plural strands of interpretation, not singular ones. These claims combine to remind us both that new conceptual configurations take shape from myriad influences and that, individually and communally, humans continually create functional ways of life that transgress boundaries and utilize varied resources that may appear to external analysis to be incompatible.

CONCLUDING COMMENTS

The theologians and positions discussed above do not agree on everything. Yet, taken together, they are suggestive of a new orientation in theology. While historicist insights have turned some thinkers inward to their narrow religious group or cultural experience, these theologians have concluded very much the opposite. The recognition of the historical character of all our ideas, interpretive complexes, and underlying convictions and values opens up the possibility of public, broad-based conversations in which multiple disciplines, none of them privileged, contribute to one another. In this view, public does not mean some neutral arena in which all participate out of a common set of assumptions in search of universal and uncontestable claims to truth. Instead, the public sphere is the diverse and messy arena in which various contending visions converse with one another. And, for pragmatic historicists, such conversations take place not so we can find new unassailable foundations for our claims, but in order that we can more adequately be about the construction of contemporary visions of reality and human life, knowing full well that they are contingent and fallible and will, in the future, be superseded.

This chapter has defended open boundaries between disciplines out of the conviction that each age reconfigures its understandings of reality in the face of new knowledge, altered social relations, and changing challenges. It further examined the results of such attention to other fields of inquiry by setting forth portrayals of the cosmos and humanity that certain theologians are developing out of conversations with the sciences and other disciplines. These portrayals, it was contended, do not contradict our historicist assumptions, but instead locate human historicity within a much larger historical setting. The broadening and deepening of historicist assumptions were seen to have far-reaching implications, including the connecting of all humans to one another and all else that exists, the decentering of humanity as it is interpreted to be a small part of a much larger and ancient process, the simultaneous recognition of humanity's unique position of responsibility in relation to its own future and that of the cosmic process itself, and the refusal to abstract such human historicity from either social or physical reality. Thus, for pragmatic historicists to espouse historicist assumptions leads, when examined, to much more extensive claims about humanity and the cosmos as a whole. The question now becomes what such cosmological and anthropological construals imply for the theological task. If humans are historical creatures, enmeshed in webs of natural and cultural reality, both products of and contributors to the historical process, what does this say about what theologians are doing when we reflect theologically, about the status of our claims and purposes for which we make them, and about the norms by which theological proposals should be evaluated? What, in short, can theology consist of within a historicist interpretation of reality? It is to these questions that we now turn.

CHAPTER 4

Theology in a Historicist Perspective

PRELIMINARY COMMENTS

All humans, as argued in chapter 3, live out of basic assumptions about reality. Often these premises are implicit and unsystematic; other times they flow from more fully developed and comprehensive theories about the nature of life and human existence. But recognized or not, they are there and they are operative in the way we understand ourselves and deal with the world. The pragmatic historicism being formulated here, moreover, contends not only that all humans in fact make assumptions about reality but that it is imperative for intellectuals and, in this context, particularly theologians to be as clear as possible about these central premises and to explore openly the differences they make for how we construe and respond to the wide range of dilemmas facing human life today. But while calling for theoretical candor, this perspective at the same time eschews all pretensions of grand theories and instead invokes a theoretical modesty fully cognizant of the speculative, imaginative, and tentative character of its claims. And finally this sense of the provisional quality of assumptions and theories leads pragmatic historicism to an openness to a broad variety of views in the quest to develop a picture of reality adequate for our current situation.

The individuals I have designated pragmatic historicists have begun, through engagement with the natural and social sciences, to articulate a general picture of reality and human existence for our times. That depiction stresses the dynamic, evolutionary nature of an interconnected cosmos in which human beings are embedded in the matrices of material and physical existence. It is out of these matrices and in dependence upon them that human existence has developed. Hence humans are quite thoroughly a part of the natural world. But the human creature that has emerged over many millions of years is not only a biological being but also a cultural one shaped within and dependent upon the distinctively human resources and tools of language, cultural and social practice, and human institutional organization. Thus humans are not only biological beings but also cultural entities existing within the context of humanly created worlds of meaning, value, and practice.

The question before us now is what implications does this kind of general depiction of human life hold for theologians as we seek to think out theology's nature and role in the present context. There certainly is no one understanding of the nature and function of theological reflection that by necessity flows from these general assertions about reality and humanity; a variety of construals of theology, including revisionist and postliberal theologies, might claim such a portrait as their own. Nonetheless, pragmatic historicists have self-consciously and with unusual rigor explored these claims to see what they imply about human reflection in general and theology in particular and further they have attempted to develop a contemporary interpretation of theology that is consistent with this broad picture of human existence.

HISTORICIST THEOLOGY AS
IMAGINATIVE CONSTRUCTION

Among pragmatic historicists it has been Gordon Kaufman who has attended to these issues most thoroughly and who has set forth the fullest argument about the nature of theological discourse.[1] Elaborating upon the broad picture sketched above, Kaufman has detailed a conception of human life that accounts for the emergence of what we have come to call religious traditions and their secular counterparts and for the peculiar kinds of reflection termed theology. Moreover, for Kaufman, this account is suggestive about the status that should be accorded these traditions and the theological reflection that accompanies them as well as the critical norms that should be invoked to evaluate them.

The general picture of human life we have been unfolding emphasized that human beings, while physical animals, have, over the millennia, evolved into culture-creating and symbol-using beings. According to Kaufman, this evolution of humans from an animal state to that of complex cultural and linguistic—albeit still biological and embedded in material realities—beings has been fraught with profound implications for human life. For as cultural and linguistic beings, humans do not, at least on a conscious level, experience reality in a nonperspectival or unmediated fashion but always encounter it within the interpretive context their culture has provided. Thus language and culture provide a major access through which humans experience their world.

Now all languages, symbols, and practices are cultural artifacts that allow humans to survive and function. But, Kaufman argues, another development has occurred in the history of human evolution that is of particular importance; humans have not only created language and symbols, they have also, over vast stretches of human history, utilized these tools to elaborate comprehensive interpretations of reality, visions about the nature of reality and of humanity's place within the cosmic scheme. Humans not only interpret reality locally, so to speak, but those interpretations are always situated within these broader, encompassing renderings of reality that name the cosmos and humanity's position within it. Thus Kaufman's explication of humanity's cultural nature leads him to the claim that humans are also world creators, imaginers of overarching interpretations of reality within which all their more localized interpretations gain credence and intelligibility. Not only do humans, as linguistic and symbolic creatures, require cultural artifacts to survive but, according to Kaufman, we seem to require them on this grander scale if we are to negotiate our way through existence.

It is precisely these comprehensive interpretations or worldviews that we have come to label religious traditions.[2] For Kaufman, religious traditions, along with their secular analogues, are best understood precisely as general frameworks of meaning providing, through symbol, belief, ritual, and practice, descriptive and normative construals of reality and thereby orientation in and meaning for life. In his words, "if we ask what human societies are doing when they create religious traditions, and what individuals are doing when they participate in them, we can answer that they are seeking to gain orientation in life and some measure of understanding of the human place in the world."[3] As such human religious and secular worldviews express humanity's basic convictions about reality and locate human values and commitments in a cosmic context.

What, then, does it mean that humans engage in such world construction and, in particular, what does it signify about what we call religion? It means, to begin with, that our historically derived imaginative renderings of reality, including our world pictures, are not options that can be foregone but contribute centrally to the functioning of human life.[4] The very fact that we exist in a context whose character we can never fathom with certainty entails that we live out of the resources made possible by our own historically developed imaginative capacities.

Kaufman also argues that if world construal is ever prevalent, it has a particular character. First, as has been repeatedly indicated in this analysis, such worldviews are human constructions built up out of the materials of human life. The raw materials for world construction are none other than the bits and pieces of localized human life.

Second, as human constructions they are also historical products; they have not materialized spontaneously or without reference to earlier human imaginative efforts. Rather, over time, stories about the universe and human life have emerged, developed, and been transformed as the conditions of life have changed and the challenges human communities have faced have been altered; each age has inherited, borrowed from, and rearranged the visions its forebears have bequeathed it.

Third, because those conditions and challenges have varied according to geographical locales, time periods, and cultural settings, differing visions of reality have taken shape, offering distinctive interpretations of existence and ways of being human, not simply culturally diverse expressions of common human assumptions about or experiences of reality.[5] Thus, according to Kaufman, humans exist in a pluralistic world of contending conceptions of reality and ways of being human. And it is always from the perspective of some particular vision that humans encounter the world. There is, for humans, no cosmic point of view, unfettered by historical particularity.

Fourth, for Kaufman, while worldviews or comprehensive interpretive perspectives are clearly human constructions, assembled from human resources, they, nonetheless, seek to portray reality as it is; they intend the real. They embody a community's or culture's or civilization's fundamental sense about the way things are. In times of crisis, as noted earlier, the constructed character of our visions becomes clearer. But for the most part, their adherents assume the validity of their worldviews. Even when that confidence is shaken, the choice is not, Kaufman contends, between holding a worldview and existing without one, for the latter is impossible. Instead, the choice is clinging to an outmoded vision or being about the construction of a seemingly more adequate interpretation.[6]

Fifth, if our comprehensive interpretations of reality intend the real, they also present to those who live within their purview a normative vision of how life is to be lived, of the values to be sought and the commitments to be lived out. They tell a tale not only of how life is but how it should be and the role humans have to play in the cosmic process.

And finally, this normative tale is deeply affected and infused with the interests of those who weave it, including the interests of class, culture, race, and gender. Human interpretive traditions are not neutral or necessarily benign; they embody both life-giving and life-denying possibilities and are ever the conveyors of social and political power. Precisely because they are so conditioned, we may not claim, according to Kaufman, an absolute status for any human construction. "None," he asserts, "of our values, norms, or insights (including those of our religion) can, therefore, claim absoluteness; however important they may be to us, they are always relative to our needs, our language, our social problems and structures, our race and gender and class, our cultural setting."[7]

Kaufman makes another claim in relation to his analysis of traditions of meaning and practice. He suggests that these interpretive schemas are organized and focused by central symbols or ideas that unify and give order to the overarching vision. These centering ideas do not exist apart from the broader framework and are intelligible only within those complexes of meaning. Moreover, they exhibit the same characteristics that have been detailed in relation to the encompassing pictures; they, too, are the products of human history, carrying convictions about reality and replete with normative import for human life. What is most significant about them is that they provide centering points for organizing the worldviews, for focusing their visions and conveying their commitments and values. When traditions of interpretation are challenged or undergo substantive reconstruction, it is often at these nerve points that change occurs.[8]

Gordon Kaufman, thus, elaborates a view of humans as such, not just the so-called religious among us, as world makers, creators of cosmic visions and interpretations of the human. Such visions are human constructions, historical products, plural in number and diverse in content, descriptive in intent and normative in purpose. To be human is both to live out of these interpretations and to participate in their creation and continual reconstruction in response to the contingencies of life.

Out of these assumptions Kaufman has fashioned an interpretation of theology as imaginative construction whose primary task is the "analysis, criticism, and reconstruction" of comprehensive interpretations of reality, in particular, their centering symbols so that these might better serve their function of ordering and giving direction to human life.[9] Now, traditions, as historical processes, continually undergo criticism and change; lived religion is never static or merely repetitive of what has been inherited. Hence, participants in traditions hold and are shaped by visions of reality and are also ongoing agents in their renewal and transfiguration. But there has also emerged in some traditions the particular practice of self-conscious critical reflection upon those traditions. It is this practice that is, for Kaufman, theology.

Theology, from this perspective, has a very particular character. As the analysis thus far has suggested, for him, theology is ultimately carried out in order to contribute to the construction of worldviews, systems of meaning and interpretation for today. It is, therefore, a fundamentally practical undertaking whose goal is the shaping of habitats of meaning, value, and practice so that contemporary persons might function in a universe construed to have significance and direction.

On one level, for Kaufman, every contemporary discipline and every historical tradition can be seen legitimately to offer insights for this constructive effort. As chapter 3 suggested, historicist assumptions need not lead to closed and narrow conversations within traditions but to open borders in which many perspectives and claims, historical and contemporary, might be investigated. Indeed, if we are to develop interpretations of reality adequate for today we must not reject out of hand any tool or resource but must be as open as possible to the broad expanses of human reflection and conviction.

Still, on another level, Kaufman recognizes that such openness has its limits; while in principle no line of thought or tradition of interpretation can be ruled out as a conceivable resource, it is impossible for humans, as historical beings, to entertain all possibilities at once. Moreover, traditions of value and meaning present alternative construals of reality; while they may overlap, they also challenge the claims of other traditions and may not be reconcilable with these. Thus, although all interpretive visions have the same, so to speak, ontological status and while, in principle, there can be communication between frameworks, nonetheless theologians always, according to Kaufman, "conduct their explorations and reflections in terms of some particular meaning-and-value-complexes, some framework of interpretation which commands their respect and commitment."[10] That is to say, theologians are always located within a tradition. But what does such location mean? To begin with, just as one cannot entertain all claims to knowledge at once, neither can one attend to every part of a tradition simultaneously; thus, theologians situated within a particular complex of meaning and value inevitably focus their attention upon certain dimensions or elements of that particular tradition as they undertake the task of forging a viable interpretation of reality for today. Predicating his argument on the claim that "the basic structure and character of a world picture are determined largely by a few fundamental categories which give it shape and order," Kaufman asserts it is to these, what he terms a tradition's categorial scheme, that theology should first and significantly turn.[11] And for theologians working within the Christian tradition the central categories to which they must attend are humanity, the world, Christ, and, most especially, God.

But is this interpretation of theology not similar to the ones Kaufman has repudiated? Once Kaufman has admitted that "only in and through appropriation (and/or study) of Christian history and Christian traditions (including the Bible) can the God of Christian faith come into view for us,"[12] is he not led to relate to the Christian tradition in either the authoritarian form of postliberalism or the hermeneutical mode of the revisionists? And does not his categorial scheme look very much like Lindbeck's grammar of faith or Tracy's classics of the Christian tradition?

While there are, indeed, similarities among these positions, Kaufman contends that his construal of the Christian categorial scheme and theology's task in relation to it represent significant alternatives to other current options. First, Kaufman asserts that he is not attempting to identify an unchanging essence of Christianity. For him, there is no content-filled, permanent core, only an abstract, categorial one. While his categorial scheme of Christ and God, humanity and the world have been developed within Christianity (and its antecedent traditions) no single content has been present throughout that history, no final or definitive way of construing these notions has taken shape.[13] Hence, for Kaufman, to say that theology should attend to the basic categories of the Christian tradition does not suggest that theology should narrowly focus upon some particular interpretation of these, some "classic" portrayal, and certainly not some exclusive body of texts. Instead, theologians must be open to the wide, diverse, and even contradictory renderings of these symbols or complexes of ideas that have developed across Christian history. And while theologians will certainly need to offer definitions of what these categories refer to (e.g., the symbol God might refer to the ultimate point of reference for human life or the source of all reality, meaning, and value) such definitions should not privilege at the outset one historical version of these ideas nor one elevated source for their interpretation, such as the Bible. Instead these fairly abstract definitions provide the heuristic impetus for exploring the complexities of the tradition.[14]

Thus Kaufman shares with postliberals and revisionists the conviction that theological reflection has its starting point in tradition. But that starting point is neither an unchanging grammar given in the originating narratives of the tradition nor the classical texts of the tradition but rather the central symbols of the tradition through which access is thereby gained to the broadest reaches of Christian history. For Kaufman, a tradition is not something that receives its definitive content in its inaugural moments or textual expressions; it is, instead, a dynamic process in which real change occurs and diversity is ever present. Hence, to turn to a tradition can never mean to focus narrowly on one aspect nor to assume some singular normative construal of that tradition.

Kaufman's view of tradition also leads him, in the second place, to argue for a different relation to the past than is suggested by postliberalism or revisionist theology. If a tradition is a dynamic historical process without a content-filled core that is unchanging, then the theological task is not to recapitulate that past or correlate contemporary issues with the classic answers of the tradition. Nor is it to appropriate or translate, however creatively, its visions into contemporary idiom. It is rather to start with the varied options that have historically developed within the tradition and to evaluate and assess—but not assume—their potentiality for contributing to the construction of viable contemporary visions.[15]

And finally, for Kaufman, though the development of an adequate interpretation of reality begins in a tradition, in the explorations of historical possibilities, it must also move away from what he has termed a single tradition focus. To construct viable notions of God, the world, humanity and even Christ requires broader conversations than even engagement with the widest expanses Christian history can provide. It requires openness to and input from other historical traditions and contemporary forms of knowledge. These, too, are the raw material out of which theology forges its interpretations.[16]

Kaufman calls, therefore, for a holistic, multidimensional form of theology that takes into account historical construals but also draws upon what we now know about our world and human life. This mode of theology attempts to hold together engagement of a particular past and openness to other histories and to the contemporary world so that, in the critical intermingling of these, new ways of understanding and being might emerge. The interpretations that come forth from this process will be human products, fallible and fragile attempts to name reality, what is most ultimate within it, and how humans should live life today in the face of the final mystery and unknowing that pervades all historical existence. As such they are imaginative constructions for which each generation must claim its own responsibility and therefore must be open continually to critical analysis and revision in light of new circumstances and challenges.

This interpretation of theology clearly is a powerful rendering of the historicist perspective being articulated in this book. But it is also possible to discern problems with Kaufman's position not only from theological locales that differ from the general approach of this work but from the very perspective of pragmatic historicism. In particular questions emerge concerning what might be termed Kaufman's disproportional stress upon the agential character of human historicity and the resulting anemic and uncreative view of tradition that is a feature of his view of theology.

While Kaufman acknowledges the traditioned nature of human existence, he interprets the distinctiveness of human historicity primarily in terms of freedom and the power of creativity, the power to transform all inherited traditions and to shape future history, in both its human and natural forms. While agency is clearly a central dimension of historicity, Kaufman's almost singular focus upon it has unfortunate effects. From the perspective being articulated here, this overemphasis on human agency leads in particular to an inadequate understanding of the role of inheritance and traditions in the constitution of individual and communal identity. As will be argued momentarily, agency and influence by others—including our pasts—are not antithetical but require one another.

Moreover, this failure to theorize the relation of past and present more adequately results in a far too abstract and contentless relation between the present and our inheritance when Kaufman does refer to these. Kaufman's relation to the Christian past is, methodologically at least, an almost solely formal and abstract relation. What we are concerned with as theologians are the *categories* of God, Christ, humanity, and the world, *not* the concrete specificities of a living tradition. Even when Kaufman makes reference to the Christian past, it has the quality of an illustration, not substantive engagement. Thus Kaufman evidences some surprise when, in his recent work, his doctrine of God takes a trinitarian turn.[17] Such developments are felicitous, but not necessary. In sum, while theology begins in a tradition, it need not concern itself overly much with its concrete historical manifestation. There is, in this view, little real sense that historicity entails being concretely funded by the past and that existence so funded can also be creative in character.

There is also another crucial way in which Kaufman's version of historicity will be seen to be at odds with the form of pragmatic historicism taking shape here. That has to do not only with the fact that Kaufman offers a thin view of tradition, but that his position is characterized by a lingering essentialism and an abstractionism that run counter to his own historicist insights. The charge of essentialism may seem strange since Kaufman has denied that the Christian, or any other tradition, has a material essence that gives it identity. But while he repudiates any material essence to Christianity, he replaces that kind of substantive core with an abstract one—that is, the categorial scheme of God, Christ, human, and world. His maintenance of this particular set of categories, however empty and versatile, as representing the peculiar structure of Christianity is very dubious from the standpoint of pragmatic historicism. As Kaufman acknowledges, Christianity is diverse but much of that diversity is formed precisely by giving prominence to other categories than these four. While many versions of Christianity may have favored these, from a historicist perspective one cannot thereby bestow upon them the essentialist reading that Kaufman does; in some settings other categories may have greater valence, and what categories will emerge in the future to shape Christianity are as yet unknown. Moreover the concretely diverse ways these particular categories have historically been rendered is vacated by their ahistorical appropriation in Kaufman's scheme. Stated succinctly, for the kind of historicism taking shape in this book, if Christianity has no intrinsically privileged material construal—whether found in its "grammar" or its "classics"—then neither does it have this complex of categories, however, abstract, as its privileged essence. Religious traditions are not reducible to either material or abstract essences but are conglomerations of all that developed throughout their history.

Going along with these claims is also a tendency to view the past in a simplistically negative way. When the concrete past does emerge, for Kaufman, it is most often interpreted as a restriction to be transcended or a set of problems to be overcome. If other pragmatic historicists such as Sallie McFague and, as we will see, Delwin Brown offer views that lead to over-estimating the potential resources of our inherited traditions, Gordon Kaufman tends to offer insufficient recognition of the past as a source of creativity and, potentially at least, of resources for today.

Finally, Kaufman's discounting of the past issues forth in a failure to recognize the power of the past. The past seems to be there passively, awaiting our attention if necessary. But in fact, the past, those inheritances, continually impinge upon us for good and ill. A truly pragmatic historicism needs to account for the power of the past and what that power implies for a constructive historicism.

In sum, when Kaufman focuses on this categorial essence, it leads to a most abstract relation with the Christian tradition. "Real Christianity" in all of its concrete messiness falls by the wayside, replaced by categories emptied of any substantive content. Such a position acknowledges, analytically, the diverse concrete history of a tradition, but it does so in a manner that then justifies its nonengagement. An adequate historicism must point us back not to some arbitrarily elevated element of the past, be it a grammar of faith or a set of classic texts or abstract categories with variable content, but to the full range of concrete historical existence that has shaped us and that funds the historical process.

Thus, for all the strengths of the Kaufmanian position and its contribution to pragmatic historicism, it must be acknowledged that Kaufman's view of theology is too one-sided. While it clearly and strikingly embodies historicist consciousness in its recognition of relativity, partiality, and plurality and in the responsibility it conveys upon the theologian, nonetheless, this interpretation of theology offers too shallow an understanding of how people are, in fact, shaped by their histories, materially and substantially, and not just by a somewhat abstract categorial scheme. Without a more tangible connection with the material tradition, in its concrete manifestations, Kaufman's proposals run the risk of being coherent and consistent interpretations of reality that lack precisely the efficacy whose pursuit guides his entire theological project.

HISTORICIST THEOLOGY AS METAPHORICAL ELABORATION

Sallie McFague was characterized in chapter 3 of this work as a pragmatic historicist. She was portrayed as espousing a naturalized historicism, focused upon humanity's place within a dynamic and evolving universe. But McFague is also important because she has developed a historicist interpretation of the theological task that clearly acknowledges the human character of theological discourse and insists on the necessity of ongoing critical revision of religious traditions influenced by contemporary sensibilities. Her work, in this context, is particularly significant because while she shares these and other convictions with other pragmatic historicists, she offers a somewhat different understanding of how theology should be construed especially as it relates to its past. Hence her portrayal of theology and its task both supports and offers a distinctive version of the theological approach taking shape in this work.

McFague has most fully developed her views of theology in two interrelated works: *Metaphorical Theology* and *Models of God*.[18] In both works she emphasizes the uniqueness of the contemporary context within which theology carries on its task. It is a context imbued, in a manner not known before in history, with a sense of profound historical relativity, pluralism, and the diversity of human thought and ways of being. This sense of the contingent quality of experience and thought is magnified by the fact that human existence and indeed the existence of the entire earth are now threatened by the twin dangers of ecological deterioration and potential nuclear annihilation.

Given this context, McFague has asked what kind of theology is possible and appropriate. McFague, has, in the past, answered these questions by espousing a form of revisionist theology that has had much in common with the work of David Tracy. However, her particular version of that form of theology and her recent constructive work have moved her more in a direction akin to pragmatic historicism, making her a viable candidate for inclusion in this context.

McFague has for a long time insisted on the importance of language for human existence. While humans are embodied creatures, located fully in the matrix of material existence, they always experience themselves and their worlds from particular perspectives; all experience, even on a subatomic level, is perspectival. Humans, however, as conscious beings, experience in a manner shaped not only by physical location and bodily state but also by the interpretive lenses provided by culture and tradition. Humans are, she tells us, "the preeminent creatures of language."[19]

But language, for McFague, has a particular quality; it is tensive, both attempting to grasp and name reality but always doing so in a way that is never directly referential but is always interpretive, shaped by human needs and values. Hence, there is in all language what McFague terms an "is" and "is not" quality. McFague's way of stating this is to suggest that language is highly metaphorical, indirect, seeking to name its object but always characterized by a dissimilarity between it and that object.

Now McFague thinks that all language is to some degree metaphorical, that "metaphorical thinking constitutes the basis of human thought and language."[20] This is as true for science as for poetry, as humans extend their knowledge by gaining insight into the unknown through elaboration of the familiar. One way this occurs is that individual metaphors are singled out as primary, as what she labels root-metaphors, and these are then amplified into more comprehensive interpretive models and schemes. But such models are, according to McFague, also indirect ways of understanding reality, bearing the marks of human imaginative interpretation. Thus from individual metaphors to elaborate and detailed conceptual systems, humans through language seek to name, gain orientation within, and give significance to reality, but that naming is always characterized by a tensive "is" and "is not" quality that leaves every metaphor and every interpretive schema open to challenge and reconfiguration.

There are several elements in McFague's understanding of language that contribute in particular to her construal of theology. By focusing upon the metaphorical quality of language, McFague hopes to hold together both the discontinuities that pervade language, the gaps that can never be overcome, and the relative "is" quality of language. This latter point is very important for McFague because according to her we do not simply live in an idealist world of our own making or a world in which all constructions are equally valid. Language does not wholly construct its world but also, to lesser or greater degrees of adequacy, names or intends to name it accurately and, therefore, is in some manner accountable to that world. Hence, McFague has called herself a critical realist.[21] Her desire to maintain both the is and is not quality of language will be seen to affect what she thinks is required of theological language today.

These presuppositions of the historically and linguistically conditioned character of human existence and of the relative, incomplete, and indirect nature of language have led McFague to fashion an understanding of theology, in at least one of its modes, as metaphorical theology. Theology, in this form, sees as its task the elaboration of imaginative pictures of the world and especially of the divine-human relationship through which humans might encounter reality and interpret their existence. Such a theology would, in her words, be about the "remythologizing" of the world in order to provide better interpretive frameworks for contemporary persons.[22]

This task of remythologizing is imperative for McFague. She contends that, from our contemporary viewpoint, theologians increasingly recognize that humans have always lived out of interpretive pictures of reality. On a theoretical level, this has led to relativizing religious and theological claims, acknowledging the partial and incomplete character of interpretive frames of reference, and so on. But McFague argues on another, more basic, level that little change has occurred; in terms of foundational metaphors, models, and images, where lives are grasped and transformed and basic commitments find embodiment, theologians and believers alike continue to live out of outmoded and ever more dangerous images of reality. Contemporary persons are living, she claims, "in our imaginations and our feelings in a bygone world."[23] Thus if theology is to have a role to play today it is important that it tend to this imagistic level of interpretation as well as more elaborate conceptual schemas.

McFague, therefore, proposes metaphorical theology as a mode of theology whose particular task would be the elaboration of material and concrete metaphors. It would identify, analyze, and explore the repercussions of various root-metaphors in order to assess their viability for focusing human life today. In this sense it would turn theology toward the imagistic and away from an all-pervasive fixation on the abstract and conceptual. It was precisely this rehabilitation of the concrete that McFague undertook in her work *Models of God* and that she has now continued in *The Body of God*.[24] But the exploration of and elaboration of root-metaphors also requires attention to the presuppositions that are embedded within them and the wide interpretive framework that endows them with content and meaning. Thus, metaphorical theology not only is about the development of individual images and metaphors but also, as her most recent work illustrates, their location in wider systems of thought and models of reality.

Theology in this mode acknowledges its fictive and constructive character. It eschews any claims of being directly referential or of offering literal descriptions of reality or God. Instead it sees itself to be about the heuristic task of building up complex imaginative pictures of reality through which humans might express their basic convictions about reality and the foundational values that animate their action and which, in turn, will lead to new ways of existing in the world.[25] It is, thus, thoroughly historicist, experimental in orientation, self-critical in posture, pluralistic in form, and openly interested. As such it resonates strongly with Gordon Kaufman's position and with the other approaches that this chapter will examine. But does it provide a more adequate view of the past? Does it offer us a historicist interpretation of tradition?

In order to evaluate whether McFague offers pragmatic historicism a helpful way to proceed on this issue we must examine more closely how she conceives of the Christian tradition and what role it plays for her in theological reflection. In much of her work, McFague has proposed a form of correlational or revisionist theology though one that is clearly distinguishable from Tracy's version.[26] She has suggested there are two poles or constants that set the parameters of theological work and that provide, albeit in a tentative manner, the norms for evaluating the adequacy of metaphors and models. The first pole is what McFague has termed the contemporary sensibility, that is, the basic interpretation of reality that has gained widespread consent in our era and that informs all knowing and doing in the present situation. McFague has argued strenuously that theology does not engage in the articulation of timeless truth but must embody the ethos and respond to the needs of its particular context. To fail to do this means that theology will present outmoded, irresponsible, and ultimately unpersuasive pictures of reality that do not serve those who live within them.[27] We must, therefore, do theology for our time and that means that in an important sense the criteria for evaluating theological proposals lie in the present.

The other pole or constant that McFague has often invoked is that of the tradition or what she has termed the Christian paradigm. The question now is what does this pole consist of and what role does it play in theological reflection? Is it a version of Lindbeck's grammar, Tracy's classics, or Kaufman's categorial scheme? First, for McFague, to exist within the purview of a tradition requires a continual return to its historical expressions. The Christian theologian, as well as theologians of other traditions, is, thus, according to McFague, "constrained by the constant of the tradition, however interpreted, in attempting to deal with the other constant, that of the contemporary situation."[28] In this sense, McFague shares with revisionists such as David Tracy and postliberals like Lindbeck a stronger sense of the traditioned character of life and theology than was evidenced by Kaufman's approach.

Having invoked the constant of the tradition, however, McFague proceeds to construe that tradition in such a manner as seemingly to avoid any authoritarian readings of it. She, therefore, stresses, in the second place, the human character of the tradition. The past and the present are on, so to speak, an equal ontological footing. The new and the old, in her words, "are in the same situation and no authority—not scriptural status, liturgical longevity, nor ecclesiastical fiat—can decree that some types of language or some images, refer literally to God while others do not. None do."[29]

Moreover, in the third place, there are varied interpretations of the Christian paradigm, not one decisive one. The tradition is multivalent, rich in meaning, full of ambiguity. And each era must name, through engagement with the past, what it takes to be the Christian paradigm. Such decisions are always partial, incomplete, and deeply influenced by contemporary needs and sensibilities. Hence no construal of the Christian paradigm can be taken as self-evident, completely objective or final but must always be open to refutation, challenge, and revision.

McFague, therefore, concludes that what the past provides is not a stable, unchanging Christian interpretation of reality to which contemporary theology should submit as if to a uniquely authoritative norm. Rather than providing norms for later theology, the Christian past, including its "classic" biblical texts and various interpretations of Jesus, offers examples of theology, prototypes for us to emulate of the process of imaginative interpretation of the world and God.[30] Thus, the scriptures should be seen as a model "of how theology should be done, rather than as the authority dictating the terms in which it is done."[31]

What of McFague's notion that contemporary theology, including her metaphorical type, must express "demonstrable continuities" with its historical Christian pole? On a formal level, this means that contemporary theologians and religious persons should be about what their ancient forebears were, that is, thinking through what it means to live and act out of an interpretation of reality centered in belief in God as that is shaped by the paradigm of Jesus. Therefore, for McFague, "[t]he formal criterion for theology, then, is that it reflect, in tough-minded, concrete ways and in the language and thought forms of one's own time, about what salvation could, would, mean now, to us."[32]

But McFague has also argued that Christian theology has a material criterion of continuity with the past. In relation to this norm, McFague takes great pains to avoid either an essentialist or authoritarian reading of the past. She does suggest that, in the most general way, Christian faith can be construed to entail the claim that "the universe is neither indifferent nor malevolent but that there is a power (and a personal power at that) which is on the side of life and its fulfillment."[33] This is, however, an extremely broad assertion, perhaps even characteristic of most other religions. Now, for Christians, this claim gains some specificity and material content through Jesus of Nazareth, who is, McFague claims, understood as the paradigmatic embodiment of this faith. But the turn to Jesus does not provide a clear-cut, independent, or fully adequate norm for determining the validity of theological assertions. First, the story of Jesus plays a pivotal but not all-determining role in providing contemporary persons clues and hints for expressing the conviction of reality's gracious character. It furnishes, therefore, some of the insights needed for theology but clearly not all that are required.[34] Second, as the argument above claimed about the Christian tradition as a whole, there is not a singular self-evident and indisputable interpretation of Jesus that constitutes the material norm to judge all subsequent theological claims. There are diverse, competing construals of Jesus and the designation of one of those interpretations as paradigmatic is a matter not just of what contemporary historical studies tell us about Jesus but also what particular individuals or communities choose to highlight and make normative. How present-day thinkers specify what distinguishes Christian faith is deeply influenced by the contemporary pole of theology and its commitments and convictions; there is no construal of the past that exists independently of the interests and claims of the current interpretive context. Hence, the Christian pole, far from providing an indisputable given against which to test contemporary claims, offers up a partial, limited model that is only one, though a very important, resource among several for theological construction. "Continuity," in this view of theology, can never consist of conformity to the past or repetition but a kind of resonance with what is being set forth as the Christian paradigm; it is, in part, therefore, the theologian's task to state clearly how particular contemporary models are "appropriate and persuasive expressions of Christian faith for our time."[35]

McFague has in much of her work, thus, proposed an approach to theology that affirms both contemporary and historical sources and norms. In relation to each pole, McFague emphasizes the tentative, thoroughly human character of these resources and criteria of evaluation and the necessity that any particular model or metaphor demands balancing from other models and images and none, whether ancient or present-day, can claim an absolute status. Humans require imaginative interpretations to live by but they are always human creations, there are always alternative ones, and they are ever vulnerable to changing circumstances and to what they inevitably fail to render meaningful or intelligible.

On the surface, McFague's appeal to the two poles of theology—the contemporary situation and the Christian tradition—appear to hold the past and present in creative tension in a manner that can move pragmatic historicism toward a more adequate understanding of how historical creatures are constituted not only by present relations and circumstances but by the past out of which they emerge. But does her position really do so? Positively viewed, McFague's position indicates that we are located in traditions and that those traditions are concrete, not abstract. Moreover, it keeps alive the recognition that in fact there are competing construals of the tradition, not definitive or uncontested ones. However, invoking the "Christian pole" in the manner McFague does continues, for all of its qualifications, to carry a tone of narrow essentialism, especially when this pole is labeled as the paradigmatic rendering of Christian faith or of the "heart" of Christianity. There are several reasons that this way of speaking appears problematic from a historicist perspective.

First, despite all McFague's talk of plurality and diversity in the tradition, references to the Christian pole reduce what are really multiple traditions to a single paradigmatic rendering of Christianity. By so doing it leaves out much of the vast richness of our historical lineage, focusing our attention prematurely on a narrowly, if only vaguely, portrayed paradigm. It does not open up the past in a true historicist way but continues to lead us along the essentialist path, arguing that we have isolated and identified the true meaning of our tradition even if we immediately admit that what we have identified is our construal of this meaning.

For the form of historicism taking shape in this volume it is finally not adequate to admit that we historically construct our versions of the heart of a tradition and that there are competing ones. For this view, traditions have no essences, they are plural, diverse, and contentious to the core. While we may assert that particular elements of the past make more of a claim upon us today than do others, the reasons for doing so relate to their continued viability and usefulness, not to an assumption that they represent the true center of a tradition or are its paradigmatic rendition. Language about the Christian paradigm or Christian pole retains an essence-like quality that has more in common with postliberalism or revisionism than the nonessentialist pluralism of pragmatic historicism.

A second, related way this essentialist inclination is expressed resides in McFague's tendency to have her Christian vision trump, without clear argumentation, competing claims. This move is clearest when McFague confronts conflicts between the evolutionary model she espouses and her version of a Christian model of inclusive love and preferential alignment with the weakest and most vulnerable. McFague has taken pains to note that the common creation story that so fully shapes contemporary sensibility in many ways resonates with her articulation of a Christian vision, especially as it pushes us to consider nature as an arena compelling religious and theological concern. But she also argues that these two perspectives clash, the one pointing to a ruthless and chance-ridden process in which the powerful prey on the weak and some forms of life are eclipsed in favor of the emergence of the new, while the other calls for commitment to the vulnerable and powerless. When this clash occurs, McFague strenuously argues that it is the Christian vision that is normative.[36] The question is why.[37]

One answer might be that since hers is a theological interpretation of reality, priority is given to the religious tradition. That is, despite all the talk of contemporary norms finally the historical pole carries a greater normative weight. But is this in fact what is going on? First, the story of Jesus or the Christian paradigm to which she appeals is, according to all McFague has argued and what this analysis has revealed, not a historical deposit definitively given in the past. It is one construction of that story, not a description. But second, McFague's vision is not just an imaginative rendering of Jesus' story; it is a self-conscious extension of the "hints and clues" she finds in her version of that story.[38] That is, McFague argues that now, in a way quite inconceivable in Jesus' time, nature must be included in a vision of radical love and solidarity with the oppressed and that, hence, the Jesus story is significantly altered. Moreover, this extension of inclusive love and solidarity with the outcast to include nature is as much dependent upon contemporary interpretations of reality as thoroughly interdependent as it is upon the hints to be found in the Jesus story; it is the contemporary, scientific story that makes this revision of the Christian story possible and intelligible.

What we have here, then, is not a case of a historical story versus a contemporary story or the pole of the Christian tradition versus the pole of contemporary sensibilities but two competing contemporary interpretations of reality each of which is the result of engagement with historical traditions, with one another and other traditions and stories. Nor does it appear that the basis for choosing between them is that one embodies the "heart of Christian faith," for what we have is not what Christian faith has always been, in essence, or even what it once clearly was but a very contemporary interpretation of what this living tradition should be for this moment.

This all suggests that McFague's sense that history cannot be neglected and that the Christian tradition must be materially and concretely engaged in an extensive manner remain helpful reminders of certain dimensions of our historicity. However, when she advocates for the normativity of the Christian vision by seemingly sole appeal to its status as paradigmatic, then there remains the suspicion that she is continuing not only essentialist tendencies but assumptions that these claims carry a different character than do competing historical visions. When this is the case, then her turn to the Christian tradition is not a way of tracing historicity but of surreptiously and, from the perspective of pragmatic historicism, illegitimately bolstering what is inevitably our own contemporary judgment by implied appeal to more than historical grounds.

It is the contention of this work that a full theological historicism must not only admit there are no essences to religious traditions but also that what makes a theology Christian or anything else is not that it demonstrates continuity with a paradigmatic tradition; what locates a theology in a tradition is that it emerges out of, in conversation with, criticism of this history and not another. And finally and most importantly, the historicism articulated here maintains that whether a vision deserves our allegiance is not a matter of continuity with any tradition but a question of how it will function today.

The point of the criticisms offered here is not to dismiss the importance of the positions developed by McFague and Kaufman; both methodologically and especially substantively they have made among the most significant contributions to the trajectory that this work is seeking to delineate. My own approach affirms both the general direction of their work and many of their explicit claims. Still, the analysis worked out here suggests that on the issue of how theology should conceive of its relation to the past—a most central issue for any historicist perspective—neither Kaufman nor McFague offer an adequate view to support the form of historicist theology being proposed here. The question now is whether there are views of theology that concur with McFague's instincts about the importance of history without the confusions attending it and embody Kaufman's strenuous defense of constructivism without his jettisoning of material history. That is, are there forms of historicist theology that can more adequately attend to both the agential and patient dimensions of human historicity without falling victim to all the dangers apparent in postliberalism and revisionism?

TOWARD A MORE CONSISTENT HISTORICISM

Three other theologians I am locating within the trajectory of pragmatic historicism are making both general contributions to this approach to theology and are specifically helpful in working through these ever so thorny issues of how to understand the nature of traditions and the relation of past and present. I will turn first to William Dean and Linell Cady, who, while not developing the extensive arguments offered by McFague and Kaufman, offer specific valuable contributions to the discussion. After dealing briefly with Dean and Cady, I will examine the fully articulated theory of tradition proposed by Delwin Brown.

William Dean has explicitly called for what he terms a new historicist theology. Such a theology will be marked by a number of specifically historicist characteristics. Theologians in this mode would not be searchers for or articulators of a timeless truth but rather those who traffick only in the "web of natural and human history."[39] Thus Dean's historicist theologians are thoroughly situated thinkers, located within specific traditions. He suggests that such theologians might see themselves as "interpreting historians"[40] or as thinkers who apply our interpretive imagination to particular religious histories.[41]

To envision theology in this manner acknowledges, for Dean, "the present's dependence on the power of the past."[42] Moreover, it recognizes that the tradition within which one is located is always concrete, never abstract and to be a successful interpreter of a tradition requires both the content and the form of theology to be concrete as well. In keeping with the argument set forth in the last chapter that all of reality consists in the ongoing historical interpretation of what has gone before, Dean suggests that the past that constitutes us is really a set of diverse and multiple interpretations whose ongoing reinterpretation constitutes every new present.[43]

Dean draws several other conclusions from this view that distinguish his position from many other thinkers who also espouse the power of the past. The past, as the body of earlier interpretations, carries the same ontological weight as the present; it, too, never escapes the web of natural and human history. Second, the past includes not only ideas and symbols, linguistic constructions and conventions but also, *pace* his radical empiricism, all that has gone before, including physical and natural reality. Third, when the past is seen in this way there is no inherent reason, though there may be specific historical reasons, to focus upon only a narrowly defined segment of the past or tradition. Indeed Dean suggests that one mark of a true historicist theology is its explicit attempt to include within its purview the widest, most diverse range of material possible. Rather than limiting oneself to the grammar of faith, the classics of a tradition or to its supposed central categories or paradigmatic expression Dean opts for a radical inclusiveness, what theologian Bernard Loomer termed "size." Dean states that "[t]he interpretation with the greatest size is the interpretation which includes historical experiences so diverse, appreciations of history so wide-ranging, that it stops just short of being so inclusive, so filled with the ambiguities of natural and human behavior, that it would destroy the integrity, the unity, the sanity of the interpreting individual or community."[44] The historicist theologian, thus, stretches the boundaries, opening him or herself to the wide ranges of a radically diverse and tension-filled history.

Dean argues for this way of proceeding not only because historicism removes the mandate for prematurely focusing or narrowing by category our relation with historical traditions but also because theologians engage in our interpretive work for the practical purpose of responding to current needs. Ongoing interpretation, both consciously and nonconsciously, is the way human reality is constituted and constitutes itself. Theologians engage in their work not in order to conform to a normative past but so that they might, using any and every resource available to them, contribute to the fashioning of a more adequate present.

Such reinterpretation is not, finally, for Dean a matter of reiterating something from one's tradition in contemporary idiom. It is neither translation of some given nor a new embodiment of a paradigm. Instead, out of the ongoing engagement of the present with a widely diverse past, new and novel realities emerge, new and distinctive forms of a historical tradition. In Dean's words the effect of applying the interpretive imagination to Christianity (or any other tradition) "is not merely to alter the form of the Christian message, as though leaving some eternal substance intact, but to work apart from such finally dualistic distinctions and to acknowledge the continual creation of fundamentally new Christianities."[45]

William Dean, thus, stresses the concrete character of traditions and their continual development in new forms while eschewing the abstractionism of Kaufman and the essentialism of McFague. He pushes us, thereby, to take seriously the radical pluralism that internally constitutes the past. In all of this I think Dean's work moves us closer to a more adequate rendering of historicist theology. There is, however, one particular issue that I wish to highlight that will also emerge again in relation to Brown's work. Gordon Kaufman was seen to argue that while we are located thinkers and hence always begin somewhere, not everywhere, nonetheless, if we are to respond to the needs of our day we cannot turn only to the resources of our own tradition, plural though they are. Instead we must in a sense widen our histories to explore the possibilities of other traditions. Dean locates himself in a more narrowly circumscribed tradition than Kaufman calls for. Thus Dean states that "an interpreting historian is, above all, loyal to a specific communal past."[46] The desire to avoid a false universalism makes such a statement understandable. However, a position that stresses that we traffick with reality not just discursively, that traditions cannot be captured in some enduring essence, and that we carry out our theological task for the sake of the present suggests that our identities are not necessarily or always tied so closely to single traditions and that our theological mandate requires just the sort of commitment to size that Dean has articulated, including openness to other traditions. These assumptions lead to the question, which I will explicitly explore momentarily, of whether we are not only traditioned but are or should be multitraditioned.

In *Religion, Theology, and American Public Life*, Linell Cady, another theologian closely aligned with the perspective being developed in this book, also offers an approach that contributes to this discussion in suggestive ways.[47] She posits, in a vein similar to other thinkers portrayed as pragmatic historicists, that "[t]he theologian . . . is primarily involved in investigating the meaning, truth, and power of the religious worldview(s) that shape human experience."[48] Cady's work is motivated by a desire to interpret theological investigation as being a public inquiry while simultaneously acknowledging that humans are deeply traditioned beings and that all theology is embedded in historical traditions of thought and practice. In the final chapter we will examine Cady's historicist revisioning of the public realm but in this context it is important to explore how she explicates the traditioned character of theology, and ways in which the past informs and constrains the present.

Cady is particularly concerned to avoid two extremes that she thinks fail to embody historicist insights fully. The first extreme is found in modes of authoritarian and confessional theology that elevate isolated elements of the past and assert that the task of contemporary reflection is to conform to these givens. The other consists in those "instrumentalist" forms of theology, including some forms of pragmatism, that neglect or are indifferent to the past, either assuming that it should be escaped or has nothing to offer the present. Both miss, for Cady, the real but dynamic power of tradition.

Over against these Cady espouses what she terms an extentionalist form of theology. She develops this view by borrowing from philosopher of law Ronald Dworkin's distinctions between conventionalist, naturalist (renamed by Cady extentionalist), and instrumentalist modes of legal reasoning. Dworkin opts for an interpretation of juridical reasoning as that which seeks to extend a legal tradition by forming and testing its judgments against a sense of the legal tradition taken as a whole and considered "charitably" in its most positive form.[49]

Cady, suggesting that theological reflection can be seen as akin to legal reasoning, argues that its task, too, should be the extension of a living tradition so that its inhabitants might continue to develop and flourish. If for Dean theologians contribute to the creative renewal of their traditions by striving for a form of radical inclusiveness, Cady suggests that such extension is achieved another way. For her, like Dworkin, theologians expand their traditions by construing it as "a whole" and in its best possible light. Hence, theologians focus on the ongoing reconstruction of what the tradition is thought to be generally about. This approach can, with conventionalist modes of theology such as postliberalism, affirm the importance of continuity with a tradition. "However," Cady asserts "the continuity it seeks is not a narrow consistency with isolated elements of the tradition, but with the principles of that tradition interpreted as a whole."[50]

This approach offers an interesting but, I think, somewhat problematic view of the theological task. It positively argues that to be traditioned and contextual does not mean being confessional and fideistic but creative, critical, and constructive. For what is taken as a tradition interpreted as a whole or as its "fundamental principles and insights" is always a function of present reflection and decision making and how those are then utilized is also a matter for contemporary critical discernment.[51] Moreover, the resources for deciding these matters are not tied to narrow components of the past be they classics or scriptures or some authoritative set of doctrines but can be garnered from the full tradition.

However, Cady replaces what she takes to be, from a historicist perspective, the illegitimate elevation of "isolated elements," with a notion of the whole abstracted from a concrete and lived tradition, and then claims for it, to use McFague's term, a paradigmatic significance. I want to contend, however, that from a full historicist perspective, there is no "whole" of a tradition in this sense, no "general thrust" as she phrases it.[52] There is only the vast stream of historical developments that embody not one thrust or set of principles but multiple, contending ones. While theologians in a historicist perspective must acknowledge the "whole" of a tradition in Dean's sense of the encompassing sweep of our historical lineage they must avoid the abstractionism that attends Cady's portrayal. Cady herself attempts to mitigate these problems by distinguishing between historical description of the multiplicity inherent in any tradition and normative claims of the theologian who "seeks to distill the most compelling trajectory in order to extend the tradition."[53] I am suggesting that as constructive historicists we can, indeed, turn to particular developments within our tradition, claiming them as particularly relevant for today or perhaps as the best or most challenging the tradition has to offer. Our arguments for so doing should be predicated, however, on their viability for today, not on the suggestion that they somehow are the embodiment of either the "fundamental principles" of a tradition or of its general character. Language of "general thrusts" or "general principles" or the "tradition taken as 'a whole,'" both deflect us from the contentious multiplicity of traditions and subtly lead us to misconstrue the location and process of validating our claims.

Much else that Cady argues for in this work might well point her and us in another direction than does talk of general principles, central thrusts, and "wholes." For at other points, Cady stresses in a powerful manner that traditions are "extraordinarily pluralistic" and that religion is always "enacted" in localized and diverse contexts.[54] Moreover, she proposes toward the end of her book that it is precisely to these particular concrete sites of lived belief and practice that historicist theology must attend and, therefore, it should move away from the focus upon texts and originating narratives that has captured theology's attention for centuries. According to Cady, recent inquiries into the nature of culture, myths, and symbols compellingly indicate that "the interpretation and evaluation of religious narratives and symbols cannot be prosecuted in abstraction from their instantiation in specific contexts. Far from having static, essential meanings that can be retrieved from a text, they are cultural strategies that cannot be deciphered except through their embodiment in local settings."[55] Hence, Cady urges that theologians converse less with textual exegetes or philosophers and more with historians, social scientists, and political theorists in order that they might better contend with the profligate "morass of lived religion."[56] Insofar as

Cady follows these historicist insights, I think her position will move away from generalizations about any tradition, be they descriptive or normative, and closer to a critical examination of contending concrete configurations, theoretical options, and symbolic expressions. Theology will, indeed, involve, as Cady asserts, extension of religious traditions. But it will more clearly emphasize the critical and constructive tasks and open theologians to the multiplicity of traditions and countertraditions of our religious inheritances. Delwin Brown's interpretation of tradition offers a fuller theoretical justification for just those moves to the morass of lived religion that Cady espouses and the kind of extensionist theology she envisions. It is to that theory that we now turn.

In a recent essay Brown concurs with many other contemporary thinkers that we are now in an age that is shaped by a profound sense of historicity.[57] Brown suggests that this historicism has three characteristics or, as he terms them, principles. The first is the principle of historical particularity. All humans live within particular cultural processes that determine both the limitations and potentialities of specific historicized existence. There are no humans in general, only humans located in particular contexts and traditions of inheritance.

The second and third principles of contemporary historicism point to, as Brown states it, the paradoxical character of human particularity. On the one hand historicists acknowledge the given, inherited, traditioned, and conditioned nature of human existence. We are, according to this second principle—the principle of givenness—created and constituted by what we inherit and the current network of relations within which we reside. But on the other hand, historicists also assume another principle—the principle of agency. We are not only created but also historical agents who impact, transform, and bring into being new forms of human and natural existence. We are, thus, both constituted and creative, made by the past and our environments and constructive agents of the present and the future.[58]

In his book, *Boundaries of Our Habitations: Tradition and Theological Construction*, Delwin Brown explicates the relationship of particularity, givenness, and agency by articulating a theory of tradition and of tradition's proper relation to contemporary theological construction.[59] This theory takes shape through the elaboration of three central notions: culture, tradition, and canon. Building upon the work of Hans Georg Gadamer and especially of contemporary post-Geertzian cultural theorists such as James Clifford, Marshall Sahlins, Roy Wagner, and Raymond Williams, Brown defines culture not as an arena of stable symbols and meanings but literally as the "struggle to create, maintain, and recreate individual and collective identities."[60] It is, Brown tells us, "the negotiation of identity amid chaos and order."[61]

Tradition, in Brown's theory, is a specification of such cultural negotiation. It is "a continuously reformed and formative milieu, a dynamic stream of forces in which we live (or die), move (or stagnate), gain (or lose) our being."[62] Traditions are historically constructed and passed-on complexes of being and meaning within which communal and individual identities are formed. Moreover, the specific identities that take shape within traditions are always characterized by both continuity with those historical lineages and departure from them. And finally, and perhaps most importantly, such continuity and creative novelty are not oppositional dynamics but are both continually and simultaneously at work in the formation of historical identity.

Brown makes the case for this claim by further specifying his analysis of tradition in terms of what he labels canons. Traditions are given their particular shape by canons, by "complexes of myths, stories, rituals, doctrines, texts, or institutions" that ground and give shape to historical lineages.[63] But such canons, and therefore the traditions they ground, are very complicated phenomena that cannot be related to in any singular or simple fashion. Most importantly, for Brown, canons are not just textual or even cognitive. They encompass "the continuum of human functioning and responsiveness" including certainly symbols, stories, institutions, but also moral practices, rituals, and even feelings.[64] To capture the complexity of any canonical inheritance Brown suggests that canons have six characteristics:

1. They are bounded, having some, though very loose, parameters that need to be contended with or against in any interpretive process.

2. They are curatorial, collections of multiple, diverse, and conflictual meanings, values, and commitments. They are never singular or univocal and can, therefore, never be reduced to one core or authoritative meaning.

3. They are normative, alleging, as diverse and complex aggregates, to provide adequate forms of human identity for those who reside within their boundaries.

4. They are contestable with both their content and their boundaries and the evaluation of these open to debate and ever matters of contention. They are, thus, never finished matters and in this sense a tradition's canon is never definitively closed but is always open to renegotiation.

5. They are contemporaneous, meaning that canonical commitments are to be tested in the arenas of contemporary evaluative discourse.

6. They are existential; it is through negotiation with our canonical inheritance that we humans become the specific individuals we are within our unique historical communities.[65]

Together these elements suggest a picture of traditions and their canons that is quite different from many found in theological reflection today but that resonates well with the findings of extratheological disciplines. Canons are clearly not tied to a small body of classical texts that have been given definitive shape in the past. Nor are canons reduced to singular, unchanging depth grammars that we need to be faithful to in each new historical moment. Nor are canons limited categorial schemes, providing abstract but not material continuity throughout a tradition's history. And finally, canons are not paradigmatic construals of what the tradition is at heart or as a whole. Instead canons are the fluid, porous, and exceedingly diverse complexes of meaning and value that have accumulated throughout the history of a tradition and indeed continue to emerge as that tradition unfolds. Hence, to attend to a tradition and its canon is not to look solely to some ancient source or a particular defining symbol but to the whole inheritance in all its messiness, diversity, and internal contradictions.

But how should contemporary theologians relate to such complexes and what role should this widely diverse accumulated inheritance play in contemporary theology? First, it is clear that for Brown, jettisoning or ignoring the past is both impossible and, even if conceivable, not very advisable. Humans as historical are, by necessity, shaped by that which has gone before them, both their ancient and more recent history. The present is funded by the past; the past provides the raw material out of which the present and any future emerges. To use language, to have feelings, to engage in meaningful action all require the resources wrought by our forebears. Moreover, Brown argues continually in his work, precisely because humans are historical and traditioned, those who seek to be efficacious contributors to present human life and organization must effectively engage, negotiate with, and, as he says, play with and be played by that inheritance of meaning, feeling, and value. In particular, theologians who engage in the preeminently practical task of constructing worldviews must do so through the reconstruction of their tradition's conceptual and material pasts.[66] In this sense, for Brown, the past is always constitutive of the present.

But, in the second place, if the past constitutes the present, if human life is always receptive in nature, molded by its history, it is never merely responsive or only repetitious of some settled past. This is the case because of the nature of the past; as Brown has argued, the past is diverse and full of contending values and meanings. A tradition's canon has no unitary center or self-defining core that contemporary persons could faithfully replicate even if they wished to do so. It is full of multiple possibilities that could never be appropriated simultaneously. It is, moreover, continually contested, setting boundaries that are temporary and shifting. As Brown states, "Canons have no intrinsically privileged construal or adequate summation. Indeed, canonical diversity and fluidity is such that, while offering a particular construal for a particular circumstance is inescapable, in the nature of the case no single rendering, however complex, can finally get a fix on canon."[67] Hence, it is in the nature of a canonical inheritance that no replication of that past, certainly as a whole, is possible.

But it is also the nature of human interpretation and appropriation that renders mere repetition impossible. Humans engage the canons, the broad inheritance of their tradition, from particular locales for particular purposes and these shape what is engaged, highlighted, criticized, and even discerned as being present in the tradition at all. All appropriation of a tradition entails, therefore, its creative transformation into something new that then becomes a part of that inheritance. As there is no construction of worldviews *de novo*, neither is there any simple repetition or perfect translation of them into a new idiom that somehow retains their essential meanings or, as for postliberals, adheres to "the same directives" that were involved in the creation of a tradition's founding narratives.[68] Engagement with a tradition always results in the new, in a novel contribution to the ongoing development of historical life. Thus, for Brown, there can be no construction of contemporary interpretations of reality without the constitutive contribution of the past and there can be no appropriation of history without its reconstruction. Humans, as historical, are shaped and shaping beings but these are not two distinct activities; it is as inheritors that we are agents and it is only as constructors of new realities that we can appropriate our pasts.

Thus Brown offers an articulation of the historicist principles of givenness and agency in a manner that does not set these against one another but argues for their intimate interconnection. He does so by simultaneously emptying historical inheritance of any essentialist content and debunking any notions of free-floating and unattached agency. Finally, in his more recent work, Brown pushes the multifaceted and multidimensional character of tradition and canon even further by insisting that historicism also should be characterized by another principle, the principle of materiality. This principle points to the fact that our historical inheritance cannot be reduced to the textual and the cognitive dimensions of a tradition but also includes noncognitive and nonlinguistic elements as well. This principle is in many ways the most innovative of Brown's proposals, for it pushes historicism beyond its fixation on the linguistic and conceptual and toward the nondiscursive, the physical, and the natural. In *Boundaries of Our Habitations* Brown's commitment to materiality takes, as was indicated in the last chapter, the form of a reappropriation of radical empiricism, stressing that we traffick with reality more with our bodies than our minds. This means for Brown that not only are our inheritances much richer than streams of disembodied ideas but that if we are to creatively engage such inheritances we must do so not only on the level of intellectual debate and construction but also through ritual, bodily enactment, and feelings. Traditions live or die not only because of their intellectual content but also because of the richness of their nondiscursive practices and sensibilities. If theologians seek to be effective, they must attend not just to ideas but these as well.[69]

Brown, in his most recent work, articulates the principle of materiality not only in terms of the insight that we are bodies as well as minds but also in terms of the contemporary claims that ideas are intimately connected to social practices and to the circulation of power. Not only do ideas not stand apart from nondiscursive practices and feelings but these are both the product of and response to social and historical realities not reducible to linguistic formulations.[70]

The arguments set forth by Delwin Brown are compelling in many ways and especially helpful in moving pragmatic historicism—or, as he terms it, constructive historicism—toward a more adequate understanding of tradition and theology. His dual insistence that our traditions have no enduring essences that can or should be conformed to and that it is only through engagement with concrete, diverse, and dynamic traditions that historical existence emerges at all pushes contemporary theologians to return to their traditions but to do so shorn of any pretensions that those traditions are uniform, settled, or adequate. Instead theological reflection is unavoidably and unapologetically constructive, forging out of the diverse elements of the past new possibilities for the present. And finally, Brown's move beyond narrow linguisticism to materiality moves theology into new arenas and provides a theological contribution to the growing concern within religious studies and cognate disciplines to de-throne texts as the primary vehicle of religious meaning, or as Harvard historian of religion Lawrence Sullivan states it, "to bring an end to an overly literary approach to the religious condition."[71] Brown, thus, challenges historicist theology to become not only naturalized but also politicized and fully cognizant of its sociality.

Despite these strengths I have, as I have had with my other pragmatic compatriots, several issues with Brown's position. For my present purposes I want to indicate three such concerns. All three have to do with what might be termed Brown's "monotraditionalism." This monotraditionalism is found on many levels of Brown's argument. The first level has to do with his very conception of traditions and how they emerge and develop. While he admirably acknowledges that traditions do not have stable essences, that their contents are diverse and inherently conflictual and their boundaries are porous and changing, nonetheless, Brown neglects to appreciate fully what might be termed the hybrid or composite or even syncretistic character of many traditions. Brown focuses upon how traditions develop once having emerged in history. But new traditions also come into being and we must also inquire how that takes place. Traditions are not just created by the recovery of their diverse elements or by "alien" elements being absorbed into a dominant tradition. Instead traditions also emerge as the novel syncretistic combining of varied strands of historical existence. Traditions do not just react to external forces as Brown notes; sometimes they are the combination of multiple forces in new ways, composite in origin and syncretic in development. Examples of this might be ancient Manichaeism, or modern Santeria, or numerous forms of popular religion that cannot easily be reduced to a variant of Christianity or Islam, or perhaps even the combination of Greek philosophy and the Hebrew tradition that resulted in Christianity. Moreover, even when we focus upon the development within traditions and not the emergence of new ones, it is not at all clear that the way that occurs is primarily through the recovery of past elements or the sublation of foreign elements into dominant traditions. While both of these certainly take place, many studies of culture today indicate far more complex processes of the intermingling of historical materials, including both conscious and unconscious intermingling—bricolage—through which takes place the "formation of new cultural forms from bits and pieces of cultural practice of diverse origins" and the interaction or combination of elements from different traditions in syncretistic processes.[72] Moreover such intermingling takes place for many reasons including advancing a new tradition, preserving other traditions and practices, and, not unimportantly, as a form of resistance and subversion. The point here is that Brown's model of tradition for all of its flexibility still focuses too singularly on the internal dynamics of individual traditions and less adequately accounts for the radical interpenetration of historical movements and the broader cultural, social, and political mechanisms that in fact characterize and create concrete religious traditions.

Accompanying this form of monotraditionalism is a tendency on Brown's part to see personal and communal identity taking shape within dominant traditions instead of at the crossroads or out of the interaction of varied traditions. Even when Brown admits that humans may reside in more than one tradition at once, he tends to assume that identity is wrought through bringing those various traditions under a dominant tradition. I want to suggest that while sometimes this may be the case, it is in fact not the way many persons' identities are formed.[73] It is not enough to acknowledge that traditions develop and accumulate new content as they go along and that therefore they and the identities they nourish are pluralistic. Nor is it sufficient to admit that traditions interact along their boundaries and are altered. All this still makes it sound as if most humans reside within clear, if ever changing perimeters, receiving orientation in life predominantly from individual traditions. In contrast to this view I would argue that humans are rather shaped by many conversations, by plural traditions that not only affect each other but are commingled in historically specific ways. I am not denying that humans are traditioned but suggesting that we, especially today, are multitraditioned. James Clifford, one of Brown's favorite advocates for internal creativity and inventiveness *within* traditions, also argues for recognition of our multitraditioned status, putting it eloquently when he refers to contemporary life as "existence among fragments."[74] Clifford states that "[t]wentieth-century identities no longer presuppose continuous cultures or traditions. Everywhere individuals and groups improvise local performances from (re)collected pasts, drawing on foreign media, symbols and languages."[75] At any moment, an interpretive framework or an identity emerges not just out of the backward-looking engagement with one historical tradition, however pluralistic and porous; instead, identity and interpretive frameworks are, as Clifford argues, conjunctural, the product of the constructive intermingling of varied influences, historical and contemporary, from different strands of interpretation.[76]

Finally, Brown's monotraditionalism is evident, though in a more muted fashion, in the fact that his position easily lends itself to the further claim that adequate visions for today can be constructed through the recovery of elements internal to particular traditions. While Brown acknowledges that traditions not only give life but kill and not only provide resources but also sometimes fail to and therefore die, his other assumptions about traditions tend to encourage an excessive confidence in our inherited traditions and to discourage an interest in other traditions. This confidence follows from the conviction that traditions most effectively develop through the utilization of indigenous materials and that human subjectivity takes shape within dominant traditions. It is, further, bolstered by Brown's assertion of the extreme inner plurality of traditions and his conclusion that because of this plurality, traditions exhibit remarkable adaptability. From the perspective of this work's version of pragmatic historicism, Brown's position lends, at least tacitly, support to a too easy leap from the plurality of resources to the adequacy of such resources. While the past may contain potentialities for today, that recognition should not lead to the much more sweeping claim that they do so or that those resources are adequate to the task before us. Increasingly some theologians, including myself, assuming more syncretistic views of traditions and of human subjectivity, are arguing that we must intentionally cross the boundaries of our inheritances in order that we might create interpretations, symbols systems, and practices through the self-conscious intermingling of our manifold pasts.

This is all to suggest that Brown's historicist interpretation of traditions is a great improvement on much of the competition. However, while it embraces pluralism it still seems to long for pure, if plural, traditions. If theology is to embody thoroughly historicist mandates, it must acknowledge not only the plurality within traditions but must also be open to new identities and traditions wrought at the crossroads.

This chapter has engaged in a conversation with a number of theologians I have termed pragmatic historicists. The portrayal that has emerged is not of a unified or homogenous point of view. Instead, by placing these thinkers in juxtaposition to each other and emphasizing particular features of each, a suggestive direction for theology appears that is distinctive from the other forms of historicism on the current scene. Moreover, I have sought through my critical analysis of each thinker to add my own voice to this conversation and to push this historicist trajectory in those directions that I deem most fruitful. As a way of closing this part of our analysis I want to draw together the insights that have emerged and for which I especially want to advocate. The version of a historicist view of theology summarized here is a product of conversation with all of the theologians studied above but, in good historicist fashion, does not exactly replicate any of them (indeed it points in directions that certainly some of them would not care to follow), but seeks to push their insights and my own to, from my perspective, their appropriate historicist conclusions.

A PRAGMATIC HISTORICISM

The perspective taking shape herein clearly and emphatically grounds itself in the assumption that human beings, as biological and cultural creatures, reside within complex fabrics of interwoven realities that mutually depend upon each other and the fabric as a whole to exist, survive, and flourish. We are creatures of our natural and specifically human history, and our human future and the future at least of our planet depend upon our capacity to contribute to the unfolding of such historical processes in life-sustaining and life-enhancing ways.

While sharing with all other entities participation in and contribution to the physical matrices of life, humanity's historicity has also taken specifically cultural forms. Thus we are entities whose lives are shaped significantly through the cultural organization and practices that have emerged in human evolutionary history. Such cultural forms, embodied in language, institutions, ritual actions, feelings, and so on, cannot be divorced from their physical setting and in turn have enormous impact on that context. Nonetheless, they give human historical existence its particular character, distinctively shaping its evolutionary development.

A central repercussion of the cultural character of human existence is the fact that humans always exist within and receive direction from humanly devised interpretations of life, meaning, value, and practice. As Gordon Kaufman so strongly emphasizes, humans cannot survive outside the historically developed traditions of interpretation that have emerged over the vast span of human history.

These streams of interpretation and practice have emerged and continue to take shape in different places and out of unique circumstances. Traditions of meaning, value, and practice are, thus, always specific and concrete, developing in localized, not general or abstract ways, intertwined with other social and cultural factors. They are, therefore, internally pluralistic. Every tradition is in reality many traditions, conglomerations of distinctive and even heterogeneous interpretations, sets of meanings and practices that cannot be assimilated to or reduced to any universally present factor. Even when certain symbols or beliefs or rituals recur they always do so in concrete forms that render them distinctive and make them unique construals of reality, not variations on a common theme. If human cultural, including religious, traditions do not express some transtraditioned common understanding of life, neither do their subtraditions embody common cores, centers, or essences.

What makes these minitraditions, so to speak, part of one particular tradition instead of another, then, has to do with the fact that they emerge out of a particular historical lineage, in its complexity, not that they exhibit some continually present essence or some internal consistency. While certainly continuities are present or family resemblances can be discerned when a tradition such as Christianity is examined over time or in different historical locales, these continuities or resemblances are not always the same in all places and times and their presence cannot be determined in abstraction but only through historical analysis. This historicist perspective wants to maintain, therefore, that, broadly speaking, different traditions have emerged that can be generally distinguished from each other as different historical configurations or strands of development, but that internal to each strand are various, often heterogenous, voices that resist reduction to one another and whose plural character should not be obscured through the art of abstraction.

Moreover, this historicist approach maintains that while historical configurations of meaning and practice are always particular, they do not thereby exist in isolation from one another or in some sort of splendid self-enclosed purity or incommensurability. Traditions continually interact with one another and are reshaped by those encounters. Traditions, while distinctive, are also porous, as Delwin Brown argues, having boundaries but moveable, negotiable ones that are never set or final. Distinctions between them are hence real, at least for some purposes, but relative and ever changing.

These notions clearly indicate that traditions are complex historical configurations of interpretation and practice. They are held together, loosely as is becoming evident, by the fact that they emerge out of a particular historical movement, by the fact that each new form is historically contiguous with some other expression of the tradition, though not to all other expressions. They do not all exhibit a common vision of reality or utilize a common symbol system or continue a common paradigmatic story. The surreptitious return of much contemporary theology to some form of commonality, albeit presented in historicist guise, represents a lingering essentialism that continually runs the risk of treating concrete particularities as disembodied abstractions. In the view present here, what makes a tradition a particular tradition is not that something specific is retained or can be identified in each new moment (be it Lindbeck's grammar, McFague's paradigmatic story, or Kaufman's categorial scheme) but that something is contended with and that out of that contention new, even widely deviant, portrayals of reality and of human life take form. Therefore, in James Clifford's words, "There is no going back, no essence to redeem."[77]

But something else follows from these insights as well, something that has great import for how theology is to be conceived. It is not only that traditions are internally pluralistic or that they take in elements from one another. It is that communal and individual identities are often composite, hybrids, sometimes fragmented and hyphenated, whose unity is frequently temporary, wrought out of multiple resources and constraints. Whether in the great urban centers of the world or isolated rural settings, humans' communal and individual identities emerge at the intersection of plural traditions and historical developments. Humans listen and contribute to numerous conversations simultaneously, we both advocate and resist, consciously and unconsciously varied political, social, economic, cultural, and natural developments and who we are as individuals and communities result from the combination of these factors. Or to use another metaphor, we do not just stand on one side of our tradition's fence talking to others in another tradition's field, but we both continually wander across boundaries and frontiers or find ourselves refugees far from home residing, if momentarily, at ever new crossroads. This is, as I stated above, not to deny that humans are traditioned; it is rather to contend that many humans are multitraditioned.

Pragmatic historicism's version of the multitraditioned and contextualized character of human existence is further specified by the recognition that interpretive traditions and their symbol systems are not disconnected from the material practices of those traditions, and that neither can be understood apart from wider cultural and societal institutions, discourses, and networks of power. To imagine that the human is reducible to the linguistic, or our diverse human worlds to human languages, or that language can be understood internally and apart from its interaction with the nonlinguistic dimensions of human reality is to commit the fallacy of linguisticism. A full-bodied historicism must recognize that symbol systems and beliefs are not just abstract linguistic configurations to be interpreted primarily in relation to other linguistic expressions. They are thoroughly embedded within, reflective of, and have impact upon the material processes of life including biological, political, economic, and psychological processes. Only by such recognition do we avoid an anemic form of historicism that is no more than an abstract and truncated linguisticism.

What has emerged here is a picture of humans as multitraditioned beings residing at the crossroads of dynamic, plural, incremental, and porous traditions that are continually interacting and creating in new historical moments novel understandings of reality and human practices that are connected to what has gone before but cannot be reduced to it. It also suggests that what we call particular traditions are really heuristic fictions that we should utilize but hold to lightly lest we mistake our abstractions for concrete reality and in the process empty history of its material content. This portrayal also pushes in the direction of a very particular way of understanding theology in a historicist mode.

The task of theology, in this mode, is the identification, examination, assessment, and reconstruction of historical traditions of interpretation and practice so that humans might more fruitfully and responsibly live within our complex and interdependent universe. This view of theology affirms that for theologians to carry out this task we can only do so through the full recognition of the historical character of human life and, hence, through the engagement of the historical traditions that provide the raw materials for the construction of the present and the future. Pragmatic historicism will not turn its back on the past.

However, the view of theology espoused here rejects the reduction of such historical inheritance to an essence capturable in a singular moment, claim, or person; we are, as historicists, continually returned to tradition but never to The Tradition, for there is none. Moreover, pragmatic historicism refuses as well to narrow our consideration of the past only to texts, doctrinal formulations, or symbol systems. Rather, to engage historical traditions is to respond to their multiple concrete particularities, the full range of history.

To broaden the raw material of a tradition beyond a focus on a supposed essence is certainly an important mark of distinction for this view of theology. But the claim that theology must engage not only texts, symbols, and doctrines also has great import. While language remains an important focus of theological reflection, it now takes on a new cast. Pragmatic historicists will certainly continue to be interested in belief and symbol systems; theology might even be termed, to use a phrase of Delwin Brown's, an "ethnography of belief."[78] But such belief systems cannot be separated from their material locations and conditions and an adequate theology will need to trace the connections between these and other institutions, discursive formations, and nondiscursive practices.

If pragmatic historicism seeks a modified, more materialist view of language, it also suggests that our views of culture require revision along the same lines. As this book has posited, historicists generally have emphasized, along with the importance of language, the significance of culture as the arena within which human meaning is constructed and conveyed. Pragmatic historicism clearly maintains the centrality of culture but insists that it must not be interpreted as a separate sphere of symbols and ideas linked primarily to one another. It, like language, is part and parcel of other processes.

Moreover, pragmatic historicism suggests that while language should be viewed as part of culture, culture is not just linguistic in nature. This point is significant because often, in the contemporary context, language and especially texts have been invoked as the models for interpreting all other human practices. When this is the case, exegesis and textual hermeneutics become the preferred method for approaching not only beliefs and symbols but nondiscursive practices as well. This model has yielded much, especially in contexts of the so-called "book" traditions and cultures. But this approach has also limited our investigations. As Lawrence Sullivan has stated, such a fixation on textual metaphors and methods misses the reality that "the religious conditions of humanity lie largely beyond the sacrality of scripture."[79] Pragmatic historicism pushes theology to take these insights seriously as we engage historical traditions for the purposes of creating visions and practices for today.

Thus, the view of theology espoused here avers that a truly historicist orientation must resist all tendencies toward essentialism and the desire for purity of traditions. Traditions are simply what they have historically come to be; they are not the bearers of abiding meanings or values but multiple, historically produced ones. Hence, to engage a tradition is always to respond to its concrete particularities, to contend with this particular history. It is not limited to replication of, or even resonance with some elevated dimension of that tradition (though it may in part entail all of these). "Demonstrable continuities" between the present and the past do not entail material or conceptual recapitulation but the fact that this new present has come out of engagement with this particular past.

Moreover, the drift of the present argument has been to suggest that it is no longer adequate for theologians to understand themselves as engaging one, predominant tradition and from within clearly defined boundaries conversing with (or as in the case of some current theology announcing that one cannot converse with) those outside in other traditions, be they Buddhists or cosmologists. Instead, theologians must trace our own locations as multitraditioned; we must learn to decipher and bring to clarity the multiple and contending assumptions and values that shape us and the concrete settings in which we reside. This suggests that theologians both need to contend with vastly more concrete material, not only the Christian traditions in their multiplicity but also the other traditions of nation, ideology, gender, race, class, and other systems of belief and practice, increasingly including other religions and cultures.

This call for the relinquishment of essentialism, the desire for purity, and an exclusive focus on the linguistic results in what might finally be termed the democratization of tradition and culture. In this view it is no longer adequate to focus only on the formalized doctrines of a singular tradition, its prevailing symbols, its regnant classics, or even its dominant rituals and practices. Instead our theological reach must extend to consideration of and engagement with the worldviews, beliefs, symbols, and practices of ordinary persons who far from being passive recipients of the construction of value and meaning by those more powerful, are significant contributors to and conveyors of the traditions within which they reside. But if pragmatic historicism argues for the rehabilitation of the ordinary, resisting the long-standing theological tendency to attend to and valorize the views and practices of the powerful, it also urges that we avoid the temptation to romanticize popular culture and religion as inherently more liberatory or valuable. In this view no belief or practice has an inherent or automatic value but can only be judged in concrete contexts; all are on the same ontological playing field. It is what they do that matters.

All this suggests that if the historicist version of theology contended for here is to be carried out, then the traditional conversation partners of at least Christian theology—classical philosophy, especially metaphysics, and biblical studies—are no longer sufficient on their own. Neither gives us material access to or conceptual tools for assessing the vast mosaic of the Christian traditions and neither prepares us to trace the intricacies of other traditions that shape us or the complex contemporary contexts within which we reside. The mode of theology taking shape in this book increasingly appears as a form of cultural analysis, critique, and reconstruction and as such it seeks conversation with those disciplines and methodologies that will better equip theologians to enter the world of lived beliefs and practice. To that end, pragmatic historicists advocate that theologians attend to the developments in social and cultural theory, the shifting theories of the physical sciences, and the developments in the study of religions as we forego the quest for timeless truth or an assumed to be adequate past but rather immerse ourselves in the concrete specificities of historical existence.

But if pragmatic historicism urges theological openness to the natural and social sciences, it also indicates the importance of the study of religion, including theological reflection upon networks of belief and practice, for these disciplines. Not only has the study of religion generally been marginalized in much of the academy today but theology especially has been ignored or reduced to forms of confessionalism that do not merit a place in contemporary intellectual conversation. The position developed in this work contends that theology contributes to the vital extension and reconstruction of traditions of belief and practice and that it also provides valuable insight into and information about these traditions to other intellectual disciplines that seek to understand human historicity. If theologians must listen to others, we also have significant contributions to make to the current intellectual debates.

Undergirding all of this is the assumption that traditions of thought and practice are the products of humanity's thoroughly practical need to survive as cultural beings. Insofar as they seek to contribute to the enhancement of historical communities and identities, the formation of theological claims is pragmatic. Hence, pragmatic historicists do not seek eternal truth or even the most "authentic" version of Christianity. We have more localized purposes; our theologies are not only for particular times but also, for both good and ill, for particular places and circumstances. In this historicist view, theologies always have been thus and will, despite our pretensions, continue to be so.

And finally, the conviction that the formation of theological ideas is practical entails the judgment that in the last analysis the validation of theological positions is pragmatic. It is ultimately pragmatic norms developed in every present, localized setting that determine the viability and adequacy of theological construals of reality. There can be no appeal to some ahistorical source of truth, for there is none, nor can there be an appeal to a historical artifact arbitrarily elevated. Neither can a clear norm be discerned in the welter of our historical inheritance but only a multiplicity of options awaiting our critical evaluation. This form of theology, therefore, pushes us to the present as the site of our normative decisions as we construct visions and practices for today. But it also raises the specter of balkanized communities, groups, and individuals, each asserting the validity of their particular claims with no way to adjudicate among those claims except the rule of power. Thus, the historicist perspective being espoused here raises the question whether it is all, as pragmatist Richard Rorty states, a matter finally of weapons and luck or whether historicist theology can offer some other understanding that maintains its historicist commitments while avoiding the descent into continual warfare.[80]

We will turn to these questions of truth, normative criteria, and historical contingency in the last chapter. But before we examine how theological pragmatists are answering these concerns it will be helpful to take one final side trip in our exploration of the historicist landscape and examine how nontheological pragmatists have understood these issues. Therefore, we will turn to the work of pragmatists whose work has most closely paralleled that of theologians and will focus upon Richard Rorty, Jeffrey Stout, and Cornel West.

CHAPTER 5

Philosophical Fellow Travelers: Rorty, Stout, and West

PHILOSOPHICAL PRAGMATISM

Chapter 4 set forth a statement of pragmatic historicism as a form of theology emerging on the present scene. It contended that it offers a distinctive alternative to other theological historicisms and that it indicates a particular pragmatic trajectory for theology to pursue. In conclusion it argued that theology in this mode not only understands theological claims to be formed for the practical purposes of negotiating with and through reality but that finally we evaluate such positions according to pragmatic norms of how well our interpretations of reality, symbolic traditions, and communal practices fulfill these purposes.

Theologians are not the only thinkers grappling with these issues. Historicism, as this book has argued, is now widespread in our era. And a number of thinkers across the intellectual disciplines have also linked historicism to pragmatism. Prominently among these are representatives of a resurgent pragmatism in philosophy that seeks to distinguish itself from classical philosophy in a parallel manner to theological pragmatism's turn from classical theology. But, while often concentrating on many of the same concerns as theological pragmatism, central pragmatic philosophers explicitly reject any theological agendas, interpreting theologians as captive of their classical or traditional inheritances. Thus, before turning again to our theological task, it is helpful to inquire into this other trajectory of pragmatism to see how it supports or questions the project underway here. While it is impossible to refer to all the thinkers who might be termed philosophical pragmatists or even to examine in detail those thinkers with whom we will deal, nonetheless even sharply delineated exploration will contribute to honing the issues before us. With that heuristic purpose in mind, we will turn first to Richard Rorty, then Jeffrey Stout, and finally, as a bridge to theological pragmatism, Cornel West.

RICHARD RORTY

Richard Rorty has been among the most significant voices on the contemporary intellectual scene proclaiming the demise of central Enlightenment assumptions and their attendant philosophical pursuits.[1] He has done so by articulating positions that resonate strongly with many of the historicist insights espoused in this volume, though there are a number of places where theological pragmatists and Rorty will part company. In particular, Rorty has proposed a view of philosophy that no longer seeks absolute truth or certain knowledge but is now one voice, one set of social practices among others in our historicized world.

Rorty's work is defined by a clear bias against realist ontologies that assume that the world or reality not only exists independently of humans but that it has a definite nature or essence that can be identified and known by humans.[2] While Rorty has little doubt that the world is "out there," that is, "that most things in space and time are the effect of causes which do not include human mental states," he nonetheless rejects all claims that we have access to that world in a direct or neutral manner that provides us with a means of assessing our ideas and their correspondence to the way things really are.[3]

Linked to this antirealist orientation is Rorty's rejection of all forms of epistemological foundationalism. Foundationalist views of knowing argue that there is some way to stop the infinite regress in the knowing process by an appeal to some point or source that is self-evident and self-authenticating and that thereby serves to validate claims that build upon it. There is, for Rorty, no such "ultimate source of evidence" that stands outside of or beyond the historical context within which contingent and fallible claims to knowledge are proffered. All the likely candidates for such transhistorical and transcultural status, be they clear and distinct ideas, sense experience, pre-linguistic awareness, intuition, or God's self-revelation, turn out, on inspection, to be thoroughly caught in the web of historical existence, tied inevitably to the linguistic and social practices of particular communities. Together Rorty's antifoundationalism and antirealism lead him to eschew notions of true knowledge as that which corresponds to or represents or expresses reality grounded in and validated by an ahistorical point of reference. There is simply no way to move outside of the humanly created languages, cultures, institutions, and practices within which humans reside, know, and act.

In all of this, language plays an enormous role for Rorty, as it was seen to play for a number of other historicists dealt with in this work. As David Hall states, Rorty has substituted language for experience and has, moreover, focused on the contingent and historical character of all linguistic systems.[4] There is, according to Rorty, no standpoint outside "the particular historically conditioned and temporary vocabulary we are presently using."[5] This assertion implies several other claims as well. It articulates Rorty's antiessentialist orientation toward not only the world but also human nature. There is no universal human nature hiding behind or lurking in the depths of the human defining what it really means to be human. There is no "core self" shared by all humans that gives inviolable content to that which is naturally human and defines for all time what is inhuman. The human self is rather a web or tissue of contingent linguistic and social practices that is relative to its time and place, created by "its use of a vocabulary rather than being adequately or inadequately expressed" in one.[6] There is no given or common knowledge of reality or the good nor what it means to be human. Finally, for Rorty, there is only "the sense that there is nothing deep down inside us except what we have put there ourselves, no criterion that we have not created in the course of creating a practice, no standard of rationality that is not an appeal to such a criterion, no rigorous argumentation that is not obedience to our own conventions."[7]

Language, in this view, takes on a particular, nonrepresentational, character. It is not a "medium that is gradually taking on the true shape of the true world or the true self."[8] It, like its human progenitors, is historical, contingent, and arbitrary, emerging in history, developing out of earlier linguistic practices and continually being rewoven in response to particular situations. It is, thus, most helpful to interpret languages as tools, made rather than found, functioning for various purposes in distinctive contexts.[9] Neither the physicist nor the poet are closer to reality; each develops and deploys different vocabularies to accomplish different aims.

Rorty's linguistic focus raises the question of how change occurs in human history. First, Rorty acknowledges that languages and vocabularies are rarely created out of whole cloth but take shape as humans continually reweave their various inheritances. Thus, humans depend upon the vocabularies, languages, and cultural practices that their forebears have created, living out of other's pockets.[10] Despite this acknowledgment of the "parasitical" nature of human life, Rorty's central interest is on the creative act of redescription by which novel vocabularies and narratives come into being. It is by the creation of new, abnormal discourses that cultural change is driven. Thus Rorty advocates both the proliferation of discourses and vocabularies and the protection and tolerance of cultural spaces within which new linguistic forms can be freely created. Such creative practice, ascribed most often to what Rorty terms the strong poet, continually opens up new avenues for human becoming while concomitantly resisting tendencies to assume that any one vocabulary has it right or is the correct description of the way things are.[11]

This all leads Rorty to eschew philosophy understood as metaphysics or the construction of overarching and encompassing theories that explain or describe reality and as epistemology, interpreted as the quest for certainty and foundations beyond those offered by contingent history. These construals of philosophy reflect what Rorty terms the "platonic urge to escape from the finitude of one's time and place."[12] Instead philosophy becomes therapeutic and edifying, an interpretive practice in which humans trace various language games and contribute to the construction of ever new stories and narratives about human life and the rest of reality. As such it enjoys no special status; it becomes one voice among many and thereby foregoes its historical self-designation as the final arbitrator of conflicting claims to truth and value.[13]

Rorty's historicist turn and his insistence upon the contingent, indeed arbitrary character of human existence has raised questions about whether he is an advocate of a form of nihilism in which anything goes and every claim is as good as another. What does truth mean in Rorty's vision or is it a notion that no longer has any function to play? In some ways Rorty sounds as though he considers the idea so infected with ahistorical elements that we should just let it go; truth is that which we should no longer talk about.[14] And certainly Rorty is clear, as were many of the other thinkers examined in this volume, that classical notions of truth as correspondence to reality or as that which is "capable of being made evident to anyone, regardless of background" cannot be maintained in a historicist perspective.[15]

However, when Rorty is not suggesting we simply change the subject when the topic of truth is brought up, he articulates more precise distinctions that clarify his position, distinguishing him from nihilists and even very strong relativists, and that stake out his position as a pragmatist. First, Rorty repeatedly argues that truth is a concept that is only relevant within particular language games or modes of inquiry, not a relation that pertains between an idea or claim and an independent object. Truth is a property of sentences and how they relate to one another and is therefore specific to the particular language system within which various sentences function and to the criteria that govern how they are to be used. For Rorty, truth is not "out there": "The world is out there, but descriptions of the world are not. Only descriptions of the world can be true or false. The world on its own—unaided by the describing activities of human beings—cannot."[16] Since, for Rorty truth is a property of sentences and sentences are part of particular human languages and human languages are contingent human creations, to ask, therefore, the question of truth is to ask how a claim functions in a particular linguistic configuration and how it coheres with other elements of that configuration; it is not to inquire into its nonhuman grounds for justification. Truth is finally a human creation or fabrication; it is made, not found in or disclosed by the depths of reality.[17]

When truth is defined as a relation pertaining to the internal dynamics and criteria of particular language games, one of the central tasks that appears is the tracing of the various ways claims are used and justified within particular language systems and how these claims relate to one another. Here Rorty's affinity with postliberal theologians is evident; one can never get outside of his or her linguistic framework to compare it with reality so in a central way the question of truth is an intrasystematic one. But Rorty abjures another postliberal move, that is, the further assertion that languages and cultures are at their most fundamental level self-enclosed and impenetrable and that therefore critical assessment can only take place within a framework, not across differing systems. In contrast, Rorty argues that we can and need to be about the critical evaluation of various languages and narratives even though that evaluation cannot consist in testing these against reality or the true nature of what it means to be human. Rorty, rejecting the postliberal-like notion that differing vocabularies and cultures consist of irreconcilable "axiomatic structures" and therefore cannot be analyzed in relation to one another, urges us to compare and contrast these human constructions, "playing vocabularies and cultures off against each other."[18] Among the reasons for needing to undertake such comparison is the fact that humans do not live in only one community and through one vocabulary but in and out of loyalty to a number of sometimes compatible but often conflicting ones. Indeed, for Rorty, "[m]ost moral dilemmas are thus reflections of the fact that most of us identify with a number of different communities and are equally reluctant to marginalize ourselves in relation to any of them."[19]

Comparison is, thus, a major means by which we evaluate competing claims and seek to render judgment. Comparison and evaluation, in this view, entail the recognition that languages and vocabularies are tools that allow us to get around in life, making certain things possible and inhibiting others. Hence, a central dimension of this form of analysis is the pragmatic one of assessing the fruitfulness of certain ways of construing reality for varied purposes. In Rorty's pragmatism there is no one purpose that all language seeks to fulfill, such as accurately depicting or predicting reality or creating a moral universe; the languages of science, poetry, and morality play different roles in human life and we should neither reduce them to one another nor cavalierly elevate one over all the others. In this view the line between the hard and soft sciences, and science and the humanities is transgressed and their hierarchical ranking is challenged. Each is to be judged not by how far or near to reality it is but in terms of how well it works when compared to alternatives, both present and imagined.

Now Rorty readily admits that all such comparisons, both within and between cultures and languages, are not impartial nor are they carried out from ahistorical standpoints. They are situated, presupposing the norms and values of their location. Hence they can only make their case in the historical arena, seeking to justify themselves according to the local canons of their context. The task is to convince as many of your fellows as possible of the merits of your version of things. Here, as Rorty states, "the desire for objectivity is not the desire to escape the limitations of one's community, but simply the desire for as much intersubjective agreement as possible, the desire to extend the reference of 'us' as far as we can."[20]

Rorty's historicist narrative thus points us away from large theoretical justifications for our positions and instead suggests that critical evaluation takes place in more localized contexts through appeal to our temporal and indeed temporary norms of social practice and is carried out through the imaginative exploration of how they advance our varied purposes. He has thereby linked his rendering of historicism not with the potential nihilism of much postmodernism but with a resurgent pragmatism that retains its critical capacities while letting go of modernity's pretensions of absolute truth and objectivity. But if Rorty has rejected the justificatory maneuvers of Enlightenment modernity he has not forsaken all of its values and dreams. In particular he has emerged as a staunch defender of Enlightenment-inspired democratic liberalism as the best form of societal organization that we have on the current historical scene. Here, as with his pragmatism, Rorty has separated himself both from communitarians, those thinkers who offer a critical interpretation of the dangers of pluralism and espouse a return to localized communal traditions, and from those postmodernists that disdain liberal democracy. In particular he refuses to participate in what he, following Jonathan Yardley, calls the "America Sucks Sweepstakes."[21]

Rorty ties his defense of democratic liberalism to a number of different factors. First is his contention that the source of an idea is not defining of its eventual value. Both critics of liberalism and its supporters have contended that when the Enlightenment philosophical presuppositions that funded its emergence have been dismantled then liberalism and its values cannot long survive.[22] Rorty, in contrast, does not believe we need metaphysical or cosmological support to recognize the value of tolerance, freedom, and the rights of the individual. All we need is to recognize that these beliefs contribute significantly to a better way of life than alternative beliefs. And we can come to this recognition through, Rorty believes, comparison with the alternatives.[23]

But it is not just a general defense of liberalism that elicits Rorty's support. What he espouses as particularly valuable is the separation between public and private that has come to characterize contemporary democracies and especially North American society. The distinction between the public sphere and the private arena runs throughout

Rorty's work though how the two terrains relate has undergone considerable revision in his thought.[24] The public is the sphere of shared obligation and responsibility to one another; it is where we need to contend with others' claims upon us and in which we are required to justify our actions and beliefs to those affected by them. It is the space of politics and morality and often, though not exclusively, of communal relations. The private is the province of the voluntary though not thereby solitary; it is the context in which obligation to our fellows is not primary and wherein our actions and beliefs require no public justification. It is the arena of self-creation and the quest for self-perfection where novel and abnormal discourses emerge and new narratives and redescriptions come forth. The private is to the public what love and creativity are to politics and morality.

Rorty has candidly acknowledged that he has struggled both personally and theoretically to make sense of the relation of the public and private or what he has self-referentially referred to as the problem of how to hold together "Trotsky and wild orchids" in one coherent vision.[25] Nancy Fraser has interpreted Rorty's preoccupation with these two spheres, and his ongoing struggle to conceptualize their relation, as a contest between his pragmatism and an equally powerful romanticism while David Hall has traced Rorty's commitments to the aesthetic side of American philosophical thought.[26] Whatever the lineage of these interests, Rorty has concluded that it is not possible to hold, quoting Yeats, "reality and justice in a single vision," to see solidarity and private perfection as necessarily, rather than incidentally, mutually enhancing.[27] Hence, the separation of the public and private expresses for Rorty the abjuring of single visions and the quest for "purity of heart" in which all our motivations, beliefs, and practices are disciplined by one set of commitments, values, or beliefs. Contemporary liberal democracies protect an arena in which humans are responsible to one another, where all voices are included, and public debate reigns, while at the same time providing space for that which we do not share with others, where our "idiosyncratic loves" prevail. Liberal democracies, thus, not only fare well by comparison to, say, totalitarian states, but also are uniquely suited to an age that has accepted its finitude and foregone its Platonic urges.

Where, if at all, do religion and theology fit in Rorty's narrative? Succinctly put, theology has no place for him. Rorty tends to equate theology with metaphysics, that desire to hold all things together, and to see both as manifestations of "the temptation to look for an escape from time and change."[28] While apparently philosophers can change their self-understanding, theologians remain prisoners of their longings for ahistorical meaning and truth. The kind of theology proposed in this volume seems not to have ever been entertained as a possibility by Rorty.

Though Rorty rather cavalierly dismisses theology, he has found a way to speak of religion in his historicist narrative. Religious discourse and practice, like all other human creations, are shorn of their ahistorical pretenses and with them, any claims to absolute validity. They become simply another narratival expression. But what is most interesting in Rorty's rehabilitation, thin though it be, of religion is that he locates religion utterly in the private sphere, where it becomes one more manifestation of our search for private perfection. As such it has more to do with, taking Whitehead out of context, "what we do with our solitude" than with what we do "together in churches" and takes on a primarily aesthetic tone rather than a moral one.[29] It becomes what Rorty terms a form of "romance," promoting only "private projects."[30] And while Rorty admits that religious beliefs, just like so-called secular ones, will influence how we comport ourselves in the public arena and how we assess social and political options, nonetheless these private beliefs should not count as evidence for or against our public positions; the private sources of our visions are not important, only their affect. On the other side, the public sphere should not care about our private quests for perfection except insofar as those quests "frustrate the needs of other human beings."[31] Thus Rorty combines a historicizing and aestheticizing of religion with support for the modern privatizing of religion and the separation of the public and private sphere. While such moves diminish religion's role in our world just as the historicizing and relativizing of philosophy chastened its function, nonetheless this is a small price to pay to secure both religious liberty and public tolerance.

Richard Rorty can, thus, be seen to have articulated a position that eschews the philosophical supports for modernity but not the political and cultural liberalism that flowed from them, and to have replaced the narratives of modern philosophy with a historicist narrative that links itself profoundly to contemporary forms of pragmatism. Both his historicism and pragmatism show obvious resonance with many of the positions espoused in this work. However, there are clear places where the theological pragmatism advocated here finds Rorty's position inadequate and develops in significantly different directions. It is impossible to cover all of the criticisms that have been leveled at Rorty's extensive work. For our purposes, what is important to do is to suggest the ways in which the theological form of pragmatic historicism significantly differs from the historicism and pragmatism articulated by Rorty as well as noting the challenges his position presents to the vision unfolding here.

The first issue to be enjoined relates to Rorty's reluctance to engage in any general reflection about the nature of reality or the cosmos or human nature. According to Rorty, all such reflection smacks of the

very metaphysics he wants to leave behind. The broad-based cosmological and anthropological proposals espoused by Kaufman or McFague
find little support in Rorty's versions of historicism and pragmatism.
However, the analysis ventured in chapter 3, while concurring with
Rorty's rejection of traditional metaphysics, argued strongly that generalizations, theoretical frameworks, and encompassing visions do not in
and of themselves harbor Rorty's feared "platonic urges"; they do not
of necessity embody absolutist and ahistorical intentions, nor do they
depend upon theories of correspondence or representation. Instead, such
encompassing theories seek to bring to light the assumptions that frame
positions and to clarify the possible repercussions that follow from our
fallible beliefs and values. Rorty commentator David Hall voices a similar concern when he states that Rorty moves too quickly from banish-
ing traditional metaphysics and its pretensions to also dismissing generalizations that "attempt to advertise the implications of one's admittedly
contingent commitments."[32] Without such examination many elements
of a philosophical or theological position simply go unexamined and
thereby unchallenged. As Linell Cady states in a criticism of Rorty's
metaphysical shyness, without such wide-angled analysis "we are too
apt to limit our conversation and debate to choices that do not challenge
the fundamental assumptions and values of the dominant paradigm."[33]
And indeed, Rorty's refusal to uncover presuppositions in the name of
abjuring metaphysical, cosmological, or anthropological comfort leaves
unanalyzed such things as the public/private disjunction, the separation
of language and the material realm, the alliance between democratic liberalism and capitalism and their relation to poverty and oppression elsewhere, the individualistic presuppositions of an aestheticized religion,
and so forth. The form of pragmatic historicism ventured here urges
such further exploration, arguing that such critical reflection plays a significant role in assessing the relative strengths and weaknesses of our
positions.

In particular, this book is developing an encompassing interpretive
framework that differs significantly from Rorty's present but unacknowledged assumptions. For example, it proposes a biological, historical, and social portrait of human existence that raises serious doubt
about whether such stringent distinctions can be drawn between public
and private, between the moral and the aesthetic, and between the realm
of private perfection and public morality. Instead, while agreeing that
not all our beliefs and practices entail the same amount of obligation to
our fellow humans, it suggests that in a social and interdependent world
there are no purely private projects whose implications need not be
examined or justified. Moreover, it refutes Rorty's tendency to draw the
boundaries of local contexts in such a manner that how one locale

affects another is simply left out of the analysis.[34] The expansive pragmatic historicism advocated for here insists that while all contexts are
particular their borders are permeable and their reach is extensive and
that both these factors must be considered when we ask what is relevant
evidence and whose voices need to be heard in our critical assessments
of our normative proposals for human life and society. Or again, the
theological position being set forth here stresses a materialist interpretation of culture and a view of language as material practice in a manner
that mandates a much more thoroughgoing political and cultural analysis. In this view, Rorty's assumption that social change is driven by
strong poets creating new languages appears elitist or doomed to support, albeit inadvertently, the status quo in a way that is antithetical to
many of Rorty's own commitments to justice and solidarity. Thus pragmatic historicism, in its theological mode, pushes us not only to explore
more cosmological assumptions than Rorty is willing but also, out of its
anthropology, to widen its analysis beyond the linguistic to the cultural
and political and to trace the interconnection among these spheres of
human existence.

Of all the differences between Rorty and theological pragmatists
perhaps the most obvious are the differing assessments of theology and
religion offered by each. In relation to religion, Rorty's tendency to
reject communal religion—"what we do in churches"—as at odds with
contemporary intellectual historicism and to replace it with a thoroughly aestheticized religion suitable only as a personal quest for perfection limited to the private realm seems premature at best. Rorty's
admonitions that the moral is not the only value in human life, that religion need not be reduced to it and that what is idiosyncratic to an individual may carry as much worth as what is shared among people are
important insights that can, if tended to, creatively temper pragmatic
historicism's overtly moral and political orientation. But pragmatic historicism also suggests that the historicizing of religious beliefs and communities need not result in their privatization but in a renewal of their
communal and, indeed, public role. It is, as Henry Levinson has noted
in relation to reconstructed Judaism, possible to acknowledge the contingent and historical character of our beliefs while simultaneously
affirming our historical heritage in communal practice and life.[35] The
fact that many religious persons do not yet accept this is no more telling
against this understanding of religious traditions as contingent interpretations of human existence and reality than is the fact that many
philosophers do not yet espouse Rorty-like historicism is compelling evidence against his position. Convincing our fellows of the viability of our
positions remains a task before us all.

The question of religion's public role is a more vexing one. Theological advocates of pragmatic historicism tend to agree with Rorty that the fact that a proposal's or belief's source has been designated religious should not count as evidence on behalf of its viability any more than if its source is Enlightenment modernity or contemporary postmodernism. Moreover, as Gordon Kaufman has noted about interreligious conversation, trying to adjudicate between competing overarching frameworks in terms of which is closer to reality is simply, as Rorty rightly asserts, a fruitless task.[36] But despite these agreements between Rorty's position and that of pragmatic historicists, we theologians are much more convinced of the positive role religion can play in the public realm. Though not voices that can claim special stature, adherents of various religious and secular traditions can openly set forth their interpretations of human existence, history, and practice and can critically engage and be engaged by others in terms of the practical and concrete repercussions for human life and organization that flow from such convictions and commitments. Religious communities can, as Linell Cady will presently be seen to argue, contribute to debate on our common life without denying the contingency and historicity of our religious visions.[37]

And finally, the whole import of this book is to suggest that Rorty's dismissal of theology as hopelessly ahistorical is unwarranted. Theology, like philosophy, can accept the contingent and fallible character of all human claims and can thereby reconfigure itself in a historicist mode. By so doing it may indeed give up the pretension of articulating absolute truth but in its place it can engage in the identification, analysis, and critical construction of forms of human belief and practice more adequate for today. At least that is the case that pragmatic historicism seeks to make for itself.

JEFFREY STOUT

Jeffrey Stout is another thinker associated with pragmatism whose work both supports and challenges theological modes of pragmatic thought. Stout, a moral philosopher, has emerged as a sensitive chronicler of the demise of the premodern worldview and the rise of a modern world increasingly fraught with pluralistic and diverse moral languages in which questions of justification and truth are contentiously debated.[38] For our purposes, Stout's 1988 book, *Ethics after Babel: The Languages of Morals and Their Discontents*, provides a helpful access to the issues that confront historicist thinkers of the type examined in this volume.[39]

Ethics after Babel is a sustained discussion of the plurality of moral languages that characterizes late-twentieth-century liberal societies and of the seemingly intractable moral debates that appear to accompany that pluralism. Contemporary liberal societies, such as the United States, are comprised of a wide variety of communities and traditions, whose members often live out of diverse and not easily reconciled worldviews, beliefs systems, and moral interpretations of what human life is and should be like. There is little consensus about important moral issues and endless debate about both private life and public institutions and policies. Many thinkers, perhaps most prominently philosopher Alasdair MacIntyre and his communitarian cohorts, regret the demise of more unified traditions of values and practices and see in the pluralism of today great dangers. For them, this situation of radical pluralism is the outcome of the Enlightenment and its subsequent failures, and signals not the Rortian "best of all the options we have discovered up until now" but the emergence of a new dark ages in which the moral life is deeply imperiled. "What matters at this stage," MacIntyre tells us, "is the construction of local forms of community within which civility and intellectual and moral life can be sustained."[40] For MacIntyre, we must, therefore, return to communal traditions of value and practice lest we succumb to the barbarians who are not at the gates but already in our midst. Stout's work, while taking these concerns with utmost seriousness, seeks to interpret the current situation in another, less negative, manner and to propose a "modest pragmatism" in which pluralism and moral judgement and truth are not antithetical.

Stout assumes, as do the communitarians he engages in his book and the historicists dealt with in this volume, the traditioned character of human life. Humans always find themselves in contexts and those contexts always have histories. All human reflection, including moral reflection, and all social practice bear the marks of such historical situatedness. Stout, thus states:

> None of us starts from scratch in moral reasoning. Nor can we ever start over again, accepting only beliefs that have been deduced from certitudes or demonstrable facts. We begin already immersed in the assumptions and precedents of a tradition, whether religious or secular, and we revise these assumptions and set new precedents as we learn more about ourselves and our world. Our starting point is not so much arbitrary as inescapable. We are who we are, the heirs of this tradition as opposed to that one, born into one epoch rather than another, our intuitions shaped by the grammar of our native tongue.[41]

Stout explicates this assumption of the historicity of human existence in a number of ways that concur with the position being developed in this work. He is neither surprised nor alarmed at the multiple languages and traditions that have developed in human history. While there may have been periods of less intense plurality than our own, Stout suspects human history has long been marked by a plurality of traditions and a creative diversity within particular traditions, even those traditions MacIntyre so enthusiastically elevates for our admiration. Thus the characterization of contemporary life as having "lost a prior moral and linguistic unity" seems questionable to Stout.[42]

But even if the pluralism and diversity of our current situation bears some resemblance to that of other times and places, nonetheless questions remain about whether both their fact and present intensity do not undermine our capacity for rational and especially moral decision making and adjudication. Is it possible for differing traditions and cultures to understand or criticize one another? Are they self-enclosed and self-referential? What happens in a culture such as ours "when we seem to have too many moral languages for coherent public discourse"?[43] Once we have admitted the historicity of our human beliefs and convictions and have let go of dreams of ahistorical foundations, have we also lost any basis for claims to truth or justification other than arbitrary appeal to current social practice?

Stout suggests that neither the fact that there are no ahistorical grounds for judgment nor the widespread plurality characteristic of our own society lead to these rather dire conclusions. He argues that, in part, such conclusions are predicated on problematic understandings of traditions and languages as self-enclosed and static. First, according to Stout, languages and cultures are not hermetically sealed off from one another, untranslatable, and, by virtue of being untranslatable, incommensurable. Stout, borrowing heavily from Donald Davidson's arguments about translatability, stresses that while languages and cultures or traditions within cultures may be very different from one another, they can still be seen to share a good deal in common that makes communication possible. Without such commonality we would not be able to recognize another language as a language or be able to delineate other beliefs as different from ours. Thus, translation is not, Stout argues, impossible in principle.[44]

But there is another, connected reason beyond the assumption that languages can be seen to share enough to make understanding possible that Stout proposes as a basis for communication. Languages and the traditions they embody are not fixed, decided for all time at some distant place of origin. Instead they are dynamic and changing, capable of hermeneutical innovation and enrichment as they encounter that which is other than themselves or face new situations with which to deal. According to Stout, "Natural languages actually in use are not static systems. That is why cultures are not, simply by virtue of conceptual diversity, hermeneutically sealed. Nothing in the nature of conceptual diversity itself prevents one culture from developing the means for expressing an alien culture's moral propositions or grasping their truth."⁴⁵ The process of understanding and translation may be long and difficult but the difficulties associated with it are contingent and historical and thus capable of being overcome through innovation and the imaginative enlargement of our world.

If conceptual diversity does not rule out understanding or translation neither does it imply that, underneath, all languages and conceptual systems are saying the same thing or espousing the same moral visions. Traditions and languages do indeed, to varying degrees, propose different candidates for truth and falsehood.⁴⁶ Moreover, being able to understand what is different from us does not entail agreeing with what we understand; we can understand others and recognize that others' values and beliefs are in fact irreconcilable with our own and through that understanding we can render negative judgments concerning those belief or value systems. Or conversely, we can experience their judgment of our positions. Thus to be historical and traditioned does not mean that humans are prisoners of their own contexts or histories; languages, traditions, and cultures are all, for Stout, dynamic realities that are open to ongoing change through a process of hermeneutical responsiveness to what we encounter both within and beyond our boundaries, a responsiveness that involves not only understanding but also critical judgment.

Being within a tradition also does not imply for Stout that while we can make judgments about other traditions from our own perspective (and they, us), we nonetheless uncritically live out of our own locations, simply appropriating what we have inherited from those who have preceded us. Historical situatedness does not mean an incapacity for critical reflection about our own locales; tradition and critical reflection are not antithetical. For Stout, "We may have no power to transcend our traditional inheritance completely—for we are finite, historically situated beings—but we do not have to rise above history to call assumptions in question."⁴⁷ We can call our own assumptions into question, if not all of them at the same moment, not only because of the capacity for hermeneutical enrichment occasioned by encounter with the other and by the challenge of novel situations. But we can do so because, as Delwin Brown also argued, traditions are internally plural providing challenges to any particular rendering of a tradition as well as resources for critical adjustment and change. Historical traditions, by virtue of their inherently dynamic and internally pluralistic character, have the capacity for immanent criticism through which we make decisions about what is valuable in our inheritance, what needs to be challenged, and what possibilities deserve our loyalty and commitment.⁴⁸ Stout thus states:

To find oneself in a cultural tradition is the beginning, not the end, of critical thought. There is no simple opposition between tradition and critical reason or between conservatism and reform. Our task is not simply to bring as many possibilities into view as we can but also to judge what is worth preserving, what requires reformulation, and what must be left behind. And we have nothing to go on but the critical resources of the tradition itself, extending its horizons with the help of history, anthropology, and creative art.[49]

Thus Jeffrey Stout presents a view of traditions that both supports and invites critical reflection, forms of immanent criticism responsive to alien traditions and new situations and capable of harnessing their diverse internal resources in new and creative ways. Such a process Stout calls, borrowing a phrase from Claude Lévi-Strauss, bricolage. Bricolage is a process of critical retrieval, judgment, and reconfiguration of a tradition's inheritances and the resources of other traditions that the hermeneutical encounter makes available. It pragmatically brings together bits and pieces of traditions, utilizing whatever is at hand to fashion more adequate responses to present situations and challenges. It is less worried about the purity of origins or lineages and more concerned with the ways in which resources can be harnessed for contemporary use. It simultaneously preserves and transforms and is both creative and critical. The moral bricoleur is, thus, for Stout, a reflexive ethnographer, offering a thick description of the moral heritage, and a creative pragmatist, eclectically reconfiguring the tradition in hope of solving the problems that now confront us.[50]

But how are judgments made about what is to be preserved and what demands revisioning and what direction creative bricolage should take among the options before us? According to what norms is immanent criticism carried out? As Stout answers these questions he seeks to carve out for himself a distinctive position that affirms the possibility of making moral claims while maintaining historicist commitments. By so doing he seeks to avoid both the traditional forms of foundationalism and the skepticism, nihilism, and relativism foundationalism's demise has engendered in some thinkers. Moreover, while claiming for himself the appellation of modest pragmatism, he wants to distinguish his position from certain "vulgar" forms of pragmatism, especially pragmatism's identification with a consequentialism interested only in ends, not means, that takes on the vocabulary of marketplace cost analysis.[51] A major way Stout attempts to carry out this task is by distinguishing between justification and truth.

A moral claim, or indeed any belief, is deemed justified according to Stout, to the degree to which it meets the standards of judgment indigenous to a particular context or practice. We have, as Stout states, no ability as historical beings to "somehow leap out of culture and history altogether and gaze directly into the Moral Law."[52] Therefore, for Stout, like many of the other historicists in this volume, all justification and justificatory practices are context located and dependent upon the norms that have historically developed within specific locales. Justification, for Stout, is, thus, defined as warranted assertability and such assertability is always relative to context, time, and place. As such, justification can only be explicated through the analysis of specific contexts and their norms, practices, and institutions; norms cannot be set forth for all times and places and justified beliefs cannot claim an absolute or unchanging status. Warranted belief always implies warranted for here and now, not for everywhere and always.

The relativity of justification to context does not signal, for Stout, subjectivism. Justified belief refers to standards "relative to one's epistemic circumstances, including reasons and evidence available at the current stage of inquiry, not to the arbitrary choice of individuals."[53] To recognize the historical and hence contingent and relative character of judgments is not to equate all normative assertions with the mere preference of individuals but with the standards developed in a particular context in reference to a specific practice.

Nor does Stout equate justification, interpreted as warranted assertability, with the invocation of arbitrary public opinion. Such a move reduces moral decision making to a merely sociological phenomenon in which epistemic argument is really sociological description in disguise and in which accountability disappears and the status quo is unavoidably reconfirmed. Instead, Stout, appealing to his assumptions that traditions are rich with critical resources and capable of hermeneutical innovation, argues that the process of justification is both thoroughly historical and critical. The moral decision maker can point to inconsistencies and incoherences in the positions that seek justification, deploying the standards already available. He or she can also appeal to other, perhaps counter-resources, in a tradition using the pluralistic character internal to a context to develop critical angles on issues and claims. And as always according to Stout, our capacity to understand that which is alien to us provides both the impetus and resources for reconfiguring our own tradition and the standards of our contexts.[54]

Thus, according to Stout, justification is a context-located process that is alive with all the critical potential of historical reflection. But while Stout identifies justified beliefs as those that we are warranted in asserting, he is insistent that these should be definitionally distinguished from claims to truth. Truth, according to Stout, is not relative to context in the same manner as justification; what is true is true not just here and now but always and everywhere.[55] How does Stout make such a claim given his historicist assumptions?

First, Stout denies that he is asserting a new form of foundational-ism or a revived correspondence theory of truth. Just as we can not decide which of our ideas or beliefs are justified by appealing to some object-in-itself, neither can we prove the truth of our assertions by com-paring them to an external, uninterpreted object. Instead Stout trades on Richard Rorty's argument that truth is a property of sentences and their interrelations.[56] Once one understands the internal workings of a lan-guage, then one can ascertain the "truth" of particular claims within the language. Stout's favorite example of a truth claim that transcends the contingency of social context is the claim that slavery is evil. Once we define slavery as "the coercive practice of buying, selling, and exercising complete power over other human beings against their will," then we can also see that such a practice is always morally problematic whatever the context in which it occurs.[57] Moreover, given that claims in one con-text can be translated into another language and context, assertions of truth can also be accurately rendered in languages and contexts that are different than their place of origin. There may be competing candidates for truth in those languages but that does not mean that the quality of truth associated with a claim is lost.

Now Stout acknowledges that in most circumstances what we take to be warranted in a given moment we also assume is true.[58] Thus, while there is a definitional distinction between truth claims and justified beliefs, in practice they coincide. To say they empirically coincide does not reduce, for Stout, to the assertion that the meaning of truth is war-ranted assertability.[59] For him, there are important reasons to maintain the distinction. One such reason is that it is a way to make sense of the fact that what we take to be warranted in one circumstance may at some later time turn out to have been wrong. Thus some people in America two hundred years ago or in ancient Athens may have, given their edu-cation, background, cultural norms, and so on, thought slavery was acceptable. Such a belief may not have been warranted but, indeed, unacceptable according to the canons of the day. But Stout's distinction leaves open the possibility that a belief such as this may in fact have been warranted in those circumstances but not thereby true. Or again, humans many centuries ago may have been warranted in thinking the earth was flat but we now know that claim was not true and never was true. There are, therefore, according to Stout, moral and scientific truths and falsehoods even if we do not always recognize them or even if we or others are justified, given the circumstances, in believing otherwise. Thus while justification is relative to context, truth is not. This distinction allows us finally to see others as morally wrong but not necessarily blameworthy, to build in a critical principle that recognizes the fallibility of our assertions, and to maintain truth beyond the clash of conflicting warranted claims.[60]

How are we to identify these candidates for truth or falsehood? Here Stout is reluctant to give his readers much substance. He steadfastly resists offering a new definition of truth that can be employed with every contested moral claim, eschewing this as a new foundational project. Instead he suggests for the historicist the best way to understand the notion of truth is to examine how it functions.[61] That is, we should engage in empirical and linguistic analysis; we should explore how people in fact use truth claims and what claims to truth particular languages make possible or rule out. When we undertake these forms of analysis we will find, Stout believes, that the historicizing of knowledge has not undermined our capacity to make truth claims, nor has it reduced us to a kind of epistemic behaviorism.[62]

Stout's analysis leads him to argue that the negative communitarian evaluation of our pluralistic society is more extreme than he believes the situation demands. Pluralism in itself is not an indication that meaningful moral debate cannot occur and that decisions cannot be rendered; indeed it provides rich resources to cope with our historical moment. Moreover, rather than having fallen into a new age of barbarism, we have creatively constructed a way of life that recognizes the undesirability of continuing to kill one another in order to secure agreement on our most cherished beliefs.[63] Liberal societies have thus configured themselves around what Stout refers to as a "thin or self-limiting conception of the good," a conception that relies on a stock of shared platitudes about the true and good—such as slavery is evil—and the tacit agreement that it is preferable not to push the need for consensus on the good too far.[64]

All this does not, however, lead Stout to too sanguine a view of liberal society. If MacIntyre and the communitarians are too negative for him, then Rorty with his best possible of all worlds fails to explore critically the costs contemporary liberal societies engender not only for their own citizens but also for other societies and peoples. Indeed, in a much stronger manner than does Rorty, Stout calls for what he terms stereoscopic social criticism that explores social practices and the internal goods related to them while linking such practices to the larger institutions that support and shape them. This critical practice will force us to call upon our diverse inheritances, to assess and criticize their possibilities, and to offer candidates for not only justified beliefs and practices but also ones for truth and falsehood.[65]

What roles does Stout, the ethicist and philosopher of religion, imagine religion and theology might play in this liberal society engaged in immanent and stereoscopic criticism? Stout does not simply dismiss religion or reduce it to a private project relegated to the private sphere. He acknowledges that contemporary persons are shaped by religious traditions as well as secular ones and argues that if we wish to understand the values and beliefs of our fellows "we had better develop the means for understanding the moral languages, including the theological ones, in which they occasionally address us and in which their deliberation is couched."[66] At least part of the reflexive ethnographer's or moral bricoleur's task is to give a thick and rich description of those languages along with the secular ones that have in our historical period so structured public moral discourse.

But if religious discourses are assumed to still carry weight, albeit in a diminished fashion, in contemporary liberal societies theology's role is far less apparent. According to Stout, theology, especially its academic form, has lost its voice, "its ability to command attention as a distinctive contributor to public discourse in our culture."[67] Stout's analysis of why this is the case revolves around his claim that academic theologians have sought a hearing in an arena that is fundamentally antithetical to classical theology and have done so by adopting or imitating the languages and perspectives of other disciplines. The result of this is that theologians have nothing distinctively "theological" to say and therefore end up repeating the "bromides of secular intellectuals in transparently figurative speech."[68] What would count as "distinctively theological" is not always clear, but it appears it would be akin to more classical forms of theological argument and expression. Thus, while religious languages and their beliefs and values will remain as an object of analysis for Stout, theology, at least in the contemporary forms Stout notes, will continue to loose its public force and to be discounted as a significant participant in the contemporary debates on morals.

Jeffrey Stout, like Richard Rorty, can be seen to share many of the assumptions and directions of thought taking shape in this volume. His form of historicism, with its clear cognizance of the traditioned character of human existence but its equally strong resistance to interpreting such historicity as static and impermeable; his emphasis upon the constructive, creative, and eclectic nature of human language and decision making; and his conviction that historicity and the pluralism it engenders do not lead ineluctably to the demise of a moral society but to the difficult, though not thereby unfruitful, task of debating the provisional goods we should pursue and the contingent values to which we should commit ourselves—these all resonate closely with positions articulated by pragmatic historicism. Moreover, Stout, in contrast to Rorty, offers a nondualistic rendering of public and private, a dynamic view of the innovative nature of traditions and an argument for internal criticism and the nonethnocentric relations among human communities. On these points he appears far closer to the position emerging in this work than does Richard Rorty. But as with Rorty, there are also points of difference between theological pragmatism and the mode of moral philosophy put forth by Stout. There are two areas of difference that are particularly relevant to the program undertaken here.

The first has to do with Stout's distinction between justified beliefs and truth. It must be acknowledged that Stout's position raises important questions for all historicists. In particular his concern to maintain a critical perspective that does not reduce truth to power or to sociological description is one that should not be dismissed lightly. His articulation of this distinction, however, often lends more confusion than light to the matter. Stout commentator Edmund Santurri has stated a number of criticisms of this, at least definitional, distinction. He claims that Stout's failure to offer an even provisional definition of truth so that one might recognize it if one encountered it, his lack of a clear analysis about how truth and the beliefs we hold as justified are linked, and his failure to recognize that the changing character of discourses and hence the instability of truth claims all raise questions about whether Stout's antirealist defense of truth is plausible.[69]

Importantly, to say that truth is a property of language rather than a relation of a proposition to an external reality does not necessarily get us very far. As more communitarian commentators Stanley Hauerwas and Philip D. Kenneson have argued even when we all concur that a given proposition or interpreted sentence is true the real debate is in the details; that is, we may gain agreement about the evil of slavery according to the linguistic conventions of a particular discourse and even in terms of the broadly based moral platitudes of a society. But this level of agreement does not resolve the contentious arguments about who counts as human or what is coercive, and so forth.[70] I would suggest that even the definition itself, when examined, turns out to be less obvious than we might have thought. It could never in fact be the case that anyone could exercise "complete power" or control over another person. We are always left with degrees of buying, selling, and exercising power over others, which in one degree or another we do all the time. Whether a degree of so doing is right or wrong, should count as slavery, as opposed to, say, the cultural arrangements of relations between men and women, is always going to be contextual. We might, on other grounds, be able to say that both then and now the enslavement of Africans was wrong without entailing that it was wrong because our linguistic conventions give us clear indication of its truth or falsity.

Stout's concern to avoid self-enclosed justificatory practices that merely reinscribe the power arrangements and the status quo of a context is certainly important. But perhaps his way out of this dilemma lies in his own dynamic view of traditions and languages. His portrayal of languages and traditions stresses the internal diversity and indeed instability of these historical productions in which there are always challenges and internal impetuses for change. Moreover, in his refusal to accept the notion of incommensurable traditions existing in isolation one from another he also lays the ground work for ongoing criticism and evaluation. Languages and cultures and communities are all open-ended and in this openness lies the possibility of ongoing revision. Here Richard Rorty's claim that the gap between truth and justification is really the distance between "the actual good and the possible better" suggests that we should not see truth as something always and ever fixed but as the possibility for always improving what we believe, reevaluating and criticizing our claims and transforming what we once thought was justifiable.[71] As Rorty states it, "From a pragmatist point of view, to say that what is rational for us now to believe may not be *true*, is simply to say that somebody may come up with a better idea. It is to say that there is always room for improved belief, since new evidence or new hypotheses, or a whole new vocabulary, may come along."[72]

Theological pragmatist Gordon Kaufman also offers something of an alternative to Stout's definitional understanding of truth. Kaufman stresses that especially when we are dealing with comprehensive interpretive frameworks and their symbolic resources we have to do with historical products that have developed in different places in quite different ways and without any transhistorical way of assessing their value. Thus he suggests that we need to begin with a notion of the truth as pluralistic, recognizing that "there are a number of (quite dissimilar) patterns of religious understanding and religious truth, each of them intelligible and persuasive in its own terms but, on certain fundamental issues, standing in tension (or even contradiction) with others."[73] On this level Kaufman's pluralistic conception of truth mirrors Stout's assertion that different frameworks yield varied candidates for truth. But Kaufman adds to this insight the further argument that because differing traditions are distinctive but not closed to one another we can also speak of truth being emergent. That is, out of the creative internal processes of traditions and the critical encounters with those who are different from ourselves, new and unexpected possibilities emerge. Thus, Kaufman argues that we should not see truth as an unchanging given or as a possession but rather as "a process of becoming, a reality that emerges (quite unexpectedly) in the course of conversation."[74] Truth as emergent does not, I think, suggest inevitable historical progress or that any new claim developing out of encounter with the other is better than its predecessor. What it implies is that historical processes, including those through which our claims to truth come into being, always entail the undoing and redoing of our claims to truth; it is not some unchanging given—be it in language or reality—that undermines our self-justificatory tendencies but the dynamic, unstable, internally contested, and externally challenged character of historical existence itself. The quest for truth, in this historicist mode, is certainly not a search for certitude or absoluteness. Nor is it an exploration of our linguistic systems to see what claims escape the vicissitudes of arguments about warrantability. Instead it combines a strong fallibilism with an openness to the challenges and changes that historical encounters engender with the hope that more adequate interpretations, Rorty's better ideas, might emerge.

Another area of Stout's work that evidences both overlap with but also a clear difference from pragmatic historicism relates to Stout's rendering of theology. Stout finally presents an unresolvable double bind for theologians.[75] First, he adopts a classical interpretation of theology. Second, he claims that public debates are structured in languages antithetical to such religiously based theological discourse. Third, he notes that theologians have indeed sought to converse in the cultural languages of the day, especially those found in the university, as a means of securing a voice for their discipline. But in so doing they speak in a register not their own and hence have nothing of distinctive value to offer the public debate. The unenviable choice for theologians appears to be a retreat to the distinctive languages of their traditions hence gaining uniqueness but at the price of being ignored by their secular cohorts, or losing their distinctive voice, thus also courting irrelevance. Pragmatic theologians, while affirming so much of Stout's work, cannot help but suggest that he has ruled us out as legitimate conversation partners not by argument but by definition. The view of theology articulated earlier in this volume suggested that there are alternative interpretations of theology that are neither concerned with ahistorical claims to truth, be they based upon appeal to metaphysics, revelation, or experience, nor with historicist but tradition-confined options such as postliberalism. Rather, the approach articulated herein proposes an interpretation of theology remarkably akin to Stout's own notion of moral philosophy as reflexive ethnography and bricolage. Pragmatic historicism, as an academic discipline, undertakes what Delwin Brown calls an ethnography of belief, that is, the task of identifying the religious beliefs of particular communities, including general assumptions about humanity and the cosmos, and tracing their interconnection with other cultural beliefs, institutions, and practices such as economic realities, political configurations, and the distribution and deployment of power.[76] Carrying out this task is never purely descriptive, but is a process in which the theologian also renders judgment of these systems of belief and practice, analyzing the varied purposes they serve and critically assessing their effects for both the communities that hold them and those with whom they interact. Finally, the pragmatic theologian also contributes to the reconstruction and creative envisionment of new possibilities, eclectically utilizing the plural resources of internally diverse traditions and being open to the input of other traditions and communities. In this view, all humans live out of interpretive traditions that are historical through and through, internally plural, and ever changing through the creative reconfiguration of their own histories and the appropriation of the resources of others. This interpretation blurs the distinction between religious and secular communities of interpretation and asserts rather that such ethnography of belief can fruitfully be carried out for atheists and humanists no less than for Christians, Buddhists, Muslims, or Jews. In all this, theologians, including shall we say "secular theologians," may well regain a distinctive voice and function but not through retreat to earlier theological languages; instead that voice will be a thoroughly historicist and pragmatist one, as much at home in the university and the public realm as any moral bricoleur.

CORNEL WEST

Cornel West is a pragmatist and historicist philosopher of religion who has been a resource referenced in earlier sections of this book. His nuanced understanding of the status and function of theory and his call for a thick historicism and a more materialist interpretation of culture were seen to parallel and support pragmatic historicism. But as a philosopher of religion, and not explicitly a theologian, his voice brings its own distinctive set of issues that it is important to examine in a systematic manner.

West has articulated a historicism that concurs with Rorty's and Stout's rejection of realist ontologies and foundationalist epistemologies. The recognition of human finitude and conditionedness bears with it the relinquishment of the quest for certainty and unchanging, ahistorical grounds for claims to knowledge and truth. It also, as with Stout and Rorty, leads away from essentialist and ahistorical interpretations of human nature. However these disavowals of realism, foundationalism, and essentialist anthropologies do not result, for West, in quite the theoretical reticence evidenced by Stout and Rorty.

First, West has set forth a clearer and fuller anthropology than either Stout or Rorty, an anthropology that challenges and seeks to replace the essentialist and transcendental notions of the human that pragmatists dismiss. For West, humans are historical and social beings, not isolated or atomistic individuals who can be understood outside of the networks of cultural meanings, institutions, and practices. But if humans are thoroughly embedded in cultures and their distinctive discourses, and emergent out of particular histories, West also asserts that we are agents who create both culture and history. Importantly, for West, there is not an unresolvable tension between human agency and traditionedness, as there seems often to be for Rorty and for other postmodern thinkers, but a reciprocal relatedness between the two. Human agency does not rule out historicity or traditionedness or vice versa. Rather they depend upon one another.

Humans are, for West, immersed in and dependent upon traditions and contexts, but these are not prisons to be escaped; they provide the material out of which human agency is wrought. As such neither humans nor their traditions are static or unchanging but are always undergoing alteration, taking on new shapes and possibilities. Thus West states: "All that human beings basically have are traditions—those institutions and practices, values and sensibilities, stories and symbols, ideas and metaphors that shape human identities, attitudes, outlooks and dispositions. These traditions are dynamic, malleable, and revisable, yet all changes in a tradition are done in light of some old or newly emerging tradition. Innovation presupposes some tradition and inaugurates another tradition."[77]

This historicist interpretation of human nature certainly displaces quests for certitude. It does not, however, replace them with skepticism about knowledge but with a reorientation toward the historical and social realms and to the myriad ways in which truth and knowledge are produced there. West states that eschewing foundationalist epistemologies means that "human inquiry into truths and knowledge shifts to the social and communal circumstances under which persons can communicate and cooperate in the process of acquiring knowledge."[78] In particular, the historicizing of human nature and human knowledge requires a "thickening" of analysis through genealogical exploration that offers "detailed accounts of the emergence, development, sustenance, and decline of vocabularies, discourses, and (nondiscursive) practices in the natural and human sciences against the background of dynamic changes in specific (and often coexisting) modes of production, political conflicts, cultural configurations, and personal turmoil."[79] To historicize knowledge without simultaneously politicizing it and tracing its formation in material culture is to offer, West asserts, a truncated historicism that refuses to be accountable for its own position and function; it leads, as in the case of Rorty, to assaults on "epistemological privilege" and relative silence about "forms of political, economic, racial, and sexual privilege."[80]

For West, as for Rorty and Stout, philosophy must forego its ancient role as arbitrator of final truth. Instead West suggests that philosophy be interpreted as the "historically circumscribed quest for wisdom."[81] But this quest for wisdom takes on a particular character in light of West's thick historicism. It requires, as indicated above, not only traditional philosophical reflection but also social analysis and cultural criticism. To carry out such analysis the philosopher must avail herself or himself of the most helpful historiographic, social, cultural, and political theories on the current scene, evaluating their fruitfulness in terms of how well they allow us comprehensively to contend with the complex relations among beliefs, practices, institutions, and identities. Once more, for West, theoretical reticence leads not to a better capacity to deal with concrete existence but to a blindness about our own assumptions and a lack of critical awareness.

But if, for West, philosophy becomes a species of cultural criticism, historical and social analysis is not sufficient. Instead philosophy must self-consciously engage in the articulation of normative visions that "regulate" social analysis and indicate the direction a particular society should pursue. Not only must philosophy venture theoretical positions but also normative ones. And because we are historical beings our normative visions do not emerge from whole cloth or from an essentialist nature of things but from historical communities and traditions. Thus West persistently argues that pragmatism should fully utilize the resources of those traditions, seeking the most adequate norms for today "from the best of available religious and secular traditions bequeathed to us from the past."[82]

West's view does not assume an uncritical stance toward either tradition or contemporary theory. Instead, it urges a dialectical relation between social analysis guided by moral norms and secular and religious worldviews scrutinized for how they are implicated in the situation and for their capacity to change it.[83] This dialectic, furthermore, takes place for the most practical of purposes, because the wisdom we seek is the wisdom not to discover eternal truths but to choose among the competing "social practices, contingent cultural descriptions and revisable scientific theories by which to live."[84] These choices will always be historical and as such fallible and conditioned but West argues that the kind of pragmatic analysis he urges will allow us to be more responsible historical agents better able to shape those decisions.

Truth thus takes on, for West, a thoroughly pragmatic character as that which "enhances the flourishing of human progress."[85] What counts as flourishing depends, as West contends repeatedly, on the normative vision that persons espouse; thus the bringing to light of such valuative assumptions and their relations to concrete institutions and practices is an imperative task. And West has not been reluctant to set forth his own normative vision, what he terms prophetic pragmatism.

Prophetic pragmatism brings together, extends, and transforms the historical lineages of prophetic Christianity, especially as this strand of Christianity has been expressed in African American liberation movements and thought, American pragmatic philosophy, and political and social analysis shaped by Gramscian Marxism. These resources carry compelling weight because in this time in history they are particularly illuminating of our western historical genealogies and our current situation and contain, as well, the capacity to encourage historical agency in the service of the alleviation of suffering and oppression. Out of this configuration of resources prophetic pragmatism espouses a vision shaped by "a universal consciousness that promotes an all-embracing democratic and libertarian moral vision, a historical consciousness that acknowledges human finitude and conditionedness, and a critical consciousness which encourages relentless critique and self-criticism for the aims of social change and personal humility."[86]

West, thus, pushes historicism and pragmatism beyond merely epistemological concerns to the concrete realm of cultural practices, institutions, and identities. In so doing he criticizes what he takes to be the fainthearted and truncated historicism of Rorty and gives much fuller articulation to Stout's call for stereoscopic criticism now driven by a self-consciously normative vision. Religious traditions appear not as atavistic holdovers from a bygone era but, along with their secular counterparts, as rich historical and contemporary resources demanding critical attention. And while West does not formally analyze theology's function, his own view of philosophy, especially of prophetic pragmatism, resonates strongly with the theological mode of pragmatism taking shape here. Perhaps West, true to his commitment to pragmatic experimentation, is less concerned than Stout with maintaining disciplinary boundaries and more concerned to foster an eclectic and inclusive debate among many perspectives.

Rorty and Stout, each in his own way, supported and challenged the position of pragmatic historicism. As such they have helped sharpen the questions with which pragmatic historicism must contend. West, with his sense of the importance of encompassing theories, his material rendering of culture and discourse, his dialectic between social analysis and ethical visions, and his blurring of religious and secular traditions has both furthered the debate within philosophical pragmatism and created a bridge between these forms of pragmatism and the explicitly theological mode being given expression in this volume. But more immediately and perhaps most importantly his willingness to give content to his norms and to put on the table a substantive vision both encourages and challenges a parallel effort from theological pragmatism. What contribution can theology make to the task of choosing "wisely" among West's "transient social practices, contingent cultural descriptions and revisable scientific theories"? It is to this final challenge that we now turn.

CHAPTER 6

Conclusion:
Beyond Luck and Weapons

THE MOVE TO NORMATIVE JUDGMENTS

Final chapters of books are curious things. Sometimes they summarize earlier arguments, pulling the threads together into a neatly formatted position. Other times they are the culmination of all that has gone before, saving the best for last. And often they are disappointing afterthoughts, anticlimactic finishes to the promise of what preceded. This final chapter has its own peculiar character. I do not know if the best has been saved for the end. But it is clear that what this chapter deals with are the most difficult and tenacious problems that face historicism and especially that theological form of pragmatic historicism I have been advocating. It is also abundantly apparent to me that not all of these difficulties will be resolved in the reflections that follow. In many ways this is neither surprising nor reason for professional despair. The very mode of historicism that is argued for in this volume admits from the outset the partial, incomplete, and essentially experimental nature of all of our proposals; it, too, therefore needs to be questioned and not only by those who find it lacking but by its very proponents. This chapter will turn, then, to the difficult questions that are still before us, seeking to articulate pragmatic historicism's understanding of norms and normative judgments as effectively as possible while simultaneously interrogating its own adequacy.

This book has claimed that many current proposals on the contemporary theological scene reflect widespread cultural and intellectual changes resulting from the deepening sense of the historical character of human life. It has surveyed several of these options, including postliberalism and revisionist theology. In both cases the analysis has concluded that these theological perspectives, while evidencing certain historicist sensibilities and commitments, nonetheless failed to express a full or consistent historicism or to carry through their positions to fully historicist conclusions.

The major intention of this work has not been, however, the critical one of discounting other positions. Instead, its central project has been to propose that there are emerging on the theological scene proposals by a number of different theologians that, when explored in relation to one another, suggest an alternative historicist model for theological reflection. This model has built on an expansive historicism that has sought, through broad conversations with a variety of scholarly disciplines, to set forth a view of nature, the cosmos, and human existence in historicist terms. In particular, it has sought to locate human life within the thick matrices of natural and human history and to reflect, from that perspective, upon the character of the theological task.

The argument that has emerged has been a complex one that cannot now be reiterated but only alluded to in the most general terms. It began with the assumption that, as historical creatures, humans exist within and out of the resources of particular natural and cultural contexts and strands of historical inheritances. These contexts and lineages are themselves historical, the product of intricate conscious and unconscious processes whereby the diverse elements of a given past and the contending dimensions of a current setting together result in distinctive configurations of historical existence. Human beings are both the product and fabricators of these historical processes, depending upon and contributing to both natural and human history.

One of the significant ways humans are not only constituted by but also agents of history has to do with our human capacity to construct interpretations of reality and attendant practices that organize, give direction to, and locate humanity within the larger world within which we exist. This human capacity for world creating has been especially associated with what we heuristically call religious traditions or encompassing worldviews. As with all other human cultural creations, religious interpretations of reality are contingent, tied to place and time, funded by the past and reflective of and contributors to present material and social relations including the power interests that inhere in them. As such, religious traditions of belief and practice are internally pluralistic, composed of multiple contending and contested elements, never reducible to settled meanings or singular sets of value. They form, thus, part of the cultural resources through which humans negotiate their historical existence and for which we struggle as we seek identity and place in a given context.

Theological reflection upon religious traditions, beliefs, symbols, and practices likewise becomes a cultural exercise shorn of ahistorical elements. Its task no longer entails the search for absolute truth, the depths of human subjectivity or the unchanging essence of a historical tradition. Instead it turns to the concrete and practical project of engaging particular religious or secular traditions to evaluate how they function in the larger cultural context, assessing their viability, tracing their interrelation with other social realities, and articulating new proposals for the orientation and direction of life. As such theology is a mode of cultural analysis and assessment and its task is critical, constructive, pragmatic, and normative.

Earlier chapters of this book have led to this strong assertion of the practical character of theological reflection. For not only do religious beliefs and practices emerge as strategies for human survival and flourishing but so, too, do theologians engage in reflections about these beliefs and practices in order to contribute to human cultural and natural viability. Thus, the criteria we invoke for assessing our various efforts to interpret reality and our human place within it must be the concrete and practical ones of how they function within, contribute to, and provide for the enhancement of historical existence.

The position developed here interprets theology, thus, as both a practice of critical analysis and of construction whose norms and criteria are pragmatic in character. Locating normative judgments in the present and interpreting them in pragmatic terms immediately, however, open a panorama of questions. What is the character of these norms that guide our decision making? Does pragmatic historicism have any content to its norms beside the maddeningly vague and general assertion that our interpretations and practices must be tested in concrete situations? If historicism points to the assertion that evaluations are always in the present then how do the criteria we invoke to make judgments or choose among options relate to the norms of the historical traditions out of which they, at least in part, emerged? If historicism leads to pragmatism is it also the case that pragmatism derives from historicism some content and direction? In this historicist perspective does the notion of truth carry any freight or is it to be replaced by more humble claims to adequacy? What does it mean to say our judgments should be proffered in the public realm in an age when at least the modern understanding of public is under severe challenge? What are the arenas in which we test our claims to truth or adequacy and whose voices are included and excluded in the process? Is pragmatic historicism finally efficacious and if so for whom?

These are some of the questions that face any pragmatic historicist. The rest of this chapter will explore a number, though not all, of these concerns, building toward a statement concerning the character and content of pragmatic norms. I will begin this discussion by a return to the question that has been present throughout this text, the question of the relation of the past and present in theological construction. It is here, once more, that pragmatic historicism differs from its historicist competitors and here also that it needs to clarify its own position.[1]

REVISITING THE RELATION OF PAST AND PRESENT

This work has attempted to set forth a view of historicity that attends both to the ways in which the past, in all its multiplicity, continues to fund the present and how humans, in every present, are the creators of new historical reality. The view articulated here has led us away from essentialist readings of religious traditions and resisted the tendency arbitrarily to bestow authority on some element in the past. Simultaneously it sought to avoid the proclivity of many contemporary theologians, including pragmatic historicists, to neglect how the past constitutes the present in concrete and powerful ways. Now as we enter the discussion of norms, those standards, ideals, and values that we invoke to guide our decision making and utilize to evaluate our proposals, the question of the status of the past in relation to the present comes to the fore once again.

It is important to begin once more by emphasizing that our norms, like all other human realities, have histories, that they emerge out of the complex processes that we inherit. Norms or standards of judgment do not simply appear, unrelated to and unentangled from the past. In large part what we take to be normative in any present era is a product of our dense histories, significantly shaped by the past out of which we and our traditions have come. For pragmatic historicism, then, even the most novel portrayal of reality and the most audaciously innovative criteria for judgment are situated and as such indebted to what has gone before and to their current environment. Our normative imaginings and judgments, as all other dimensions of human life, are traditioned.

To acknowledge the traditioned character of norms does not, however, mean that the present receives from the past self-evident or uncontested norms that we can simply appropriate or to which we can or should conform. Nor does the historical character of norms imply that the past or certain elements within it have some presumptive authoritative weight by virtue of being past. As this book has tirelessly argued, religious traditions and their pasts, like other cultural forms, come to us as multiple, cumulative, and full of contesting possibilities. Even when history appears to have weighted some options more than others, to have favored certain values over competing ones, there are always other alternatives, counter-ideals contending for our attention and demanding consideration. Moreover, what we even name as part of traditions, their content, boundaries, and normative orientations, are, at least in part, the result of contemporary struggles and decisions. Finally, as this work has also advocated, many contemporary persons interact not with single traditions but with multiple ones that compete for our loyalties and that we are forced to integrate in novel ways. Thus the values we raise up as having continuing viability in some form or those we declare now irrelevant or dangerous may all have their origins in the past but judgment about their current validity or lack thereof is a distinctly contemporary decision and responsibility.

Pragmatic historicism suggests, therefore, that while we must be mindful of the historicity of all of our norms, we must also resist pretending we have made sufficient arguments for the legitimacy of our values when we have displayed their historical lineage. As South African pragmatist theologian Simon Maimela has so strongly asserted, appealing to elements in our traditions may help us map our identities but "it does not establish the 'truth' of our theological claims."[2] To assert, for example, that something is biblical does not end debate about whether it should be espoused today. And while tracing the ways in which values and visions operated in the past contributes to historical wisdom those insights alone do not settle whether something should command our commitment in the present. These questions of truth, whatever notion of truth we employ, and of adequacy and continued vitality depend upon contemporary judgments and responsibility that cannot be foresworn by citation of historical precedence.

An illuminating way of approaching these issues is to play on philosopher of science Sandra Harding's distinction between causes and reasons. Tracing the causes of our beliefs and practices locate them within the rich strands of inheritance and contemporary contexts that influence both the possibilities and constraints of historical beings. Importantly, it allows us, according to Harding, to uncover the often covert factors that shape our positions.[3] Thus analysis of causal factors might help us to understand the varied roles gender or race or class or ethnicity or religious heritage have played in forming both our interpretations of reality and our critical norms for assessing them. Moreover, for Harding, there are no uncaused beliefs and practices; nothing human exists outside of the historical web of mutually constituting relations. Even, as Harding puts it, "a culture's best beliefs—what it calls knowledge—are socially situated."[4] Hence to speak of causes is not to deny the value of a belief or to dismiss it as merely "caused." It is to acknowledge that all of our claims and practices are located and to assert that the analysis of the varied factors that have influenced them is an indispensable, though not sufficient, moment in the process of evaluation.

Harding, while admitting the importance of tracing causes, adamantly refuses merely to reduce reasons to such causes. Detailing the causes of our beliefs and practices helps us understand, for Harding as for Maimela, their lineage. What it does not do is end the debate about whether we are justified in holding these positions now. We are still called upon to give reasons in our appropriate contexts, making our case for the validity of our positions. These arguments on behalf of a position will certainly be situated and have histories and may even appeal to how something functioned in the past as part of the rationale for its continued relevance. Thus the process of evaluation, while located in the present, cannot be disassociated from the past. Nonetheless, we are required to give good reasons for our proposals relevant to the purposes they serve and according to the canons of accountability accepted in our varied contexts.

Following Harding on this point we can then propose that while causes and reasons are connected and while each are contingent and located they are not simply collapsible into one another. And taking Maimela's point we can indicate that because a current belief or practice resonates with or is faithful to some dimension of a tradition's history tells us about historical connectedness but does not settle issues of validity. Tracing the complex historical factors that shape us crucially contributes to our understanding of why certain values, practices, and visions of human life carry weight for us. But such tracing does not exhaust our responsibility to present rationales on behalf of our claims today.

These arguments for reason-giving are further bolstered by the claim, developed in earlier chapters of this book, that humans, as historical, are not only constituted but that we are also historical agents contributing, through our actions and decisions, to the movement of history itself. For pragmatic historicism this recognition of human creative responsibility contributes as well to the argument that the site for normative judgment is the present and the criteria we invoke, although having histories, have a distinctive contemporary articulation.

Applying these assertions to our constructive proposals we might, for example, argue, as does Sallie McFague, that a vision of inclusive love and solidarity with the least powerful among us, including the earth, demands our loyalty today. Moreover we might also trace the historical precedents to this claim, referencing its resonance with certain versions of the Jesus story and prophetic traditions of the Hebrew scriptures. But what we cannot do is appeal to this vision's association with Jesus or the Bible or the Christian paradigm as sufficient reasons for a contemporary espousal of this stance. In some fundamental way, Jesus or the Bible, or whatever, may be the source or cause of this vision, but not its justification. For pragmatic historicism that case will need to be made on other grounds.

This approach is suggestive about the purposes we pursue when we attend to our pasts. Many theological perspectives turn to their tradition's histories, especially the originating events or texts of those histories, in order to identify presumed to be authoritative elements that can be cited to legitimate present claims. Thus, there are arguments over biblical texts or creedal statements and who gets their interpretation right. But pragmatic historicism turns back to the dense, pluralistic, and conflict-filled histories, not to isolate authorities to settle disputes but to identify resources to be engaged, struggled with, reconceived, and transfigured to help us today.

Certainly the norms we invoke to assess our claims, including our assertions about what values or standards from the past should continue to guide our judgment in whatever continued or transmuted form, will emerge out of ongoing engagement with individual and multiple traditions. Pragmatic historicism in no way disputes that what we invoke today has been shaped by what has gone before. But this reality of inheritance should not obscure the critical responsibility we bear for deciding what is of value from the past, what we will embrace, reject, transmute, or defend in our current context. Such responsibility points to the fact that not only does the past shape the present but so does our interpretation of the present and, very importantly, our expectations, hopes, and imaginative openness to the future. We are constituted by what has been but also by the not yet; the unsettled future as well as the contested past drives our decisions.

In all this pragmatic historicism contends that such critical and constructive argumentation should take place not only within the confines of specific religious traditions but also in conversation and negotiation with other traditions and within the varied and complex public sphere of contemporary life. If eschewing appeal to an authoritative past distinguishes this mode of theology from other historicisms like postliberalism, so too, does the move to the public arena. It is to a discussion of this move and to the procedural pragmatism it entails that we now turn.

PROCEDURAL PRAGMATISM: REENTERING THE PUBLIC ARENA

Pragmatic historicism has, thus far, located our normative evaluations in the present and has argued that, while our beliefs and practices and the norms we invoke to bolster them all have histories, they also require contemporary justification. These moves have not, and, as we shall see, will not tell us ahead of time what content these norms might have in every setting. This work will conclude that the content of our norms and criteria of assessment take shape in particular contexts and cannot, except generally and vaguely, be articulated outside those situations. However, I want to argue that pragmatic historicism does suggest that what can be specified are *procedures* that enhance and further the evaluative process. Moreover, I want to acknowledge at the outset that the procedural pragmatism developed below is not neutral, but comes with its own normative orientation, proposing values to pursue and loyalties to claim. Our means for exploring procedural pragmatism will be to examine first the widespread contention on the part of pragmatic historicists that theology must plead its case in the public arena and, then, to discuss more explicitly what might be the appropriate fields within which to develop our normative positions and in relation to which we should test our claims today.

It must be stated that for pragmatic historicists various beliefs and practices have differing purposes. While all human languages, symbol systems, and social and personal actions may well develop for the general purpose of aiding in our survival and flourishing, they do so in very different ways and for specific functions. All human cultural creations may be tools for negotiating our way through existence but they allow us to do different things, in different ways and out of quite distinctive needs and aims. Just as a hammer fulfills certain functions and a table saw others, so, too, do theology, science, poetry, legal argument, bureaucratic instructions, ritualistic worship, or sporting competitions; each provides particular vehicles for making our way through life with different tests by which to evaluate them. Criteria for assessment and judgment are, therefore, context specific, dependent upon the purposes to be served by proposals and the problems they seek to solve.

The combination of this recognition of the varied uses of our cultural creations and the acknowledgment of the historical and situated character of these human constructions has led certain thinkers to retreat to the confines of their traditions or to separate various cultural spheres off from one another. Some, such as postliberals, have located themselves within the boundaries of the Christian tradition, arguing for the validity of their claims solely in terms they believe emerge from that tradition and subordinating the claims of other arenas to the assumed mandates of Christianity. And Richard Rorty, with his assumptions that different languages play different games and that the public and private can stand at a distance from one another, positions his "strong poet" in an isolated private province unbeholden to the criteria of those who toil for the public good. For pragmatic historicists neither of these solutions work.

There are a number of reasons that pragmatic historicists decline the communitarian retreat, on the one hand, and the private nominalism of much postmodernism, on the other hand. In the first instance these reasons grow out of the assumptions about reality held by many pragmatic historicists. The social ontology, cosmology, and anthropology that were articulated in chapter 3 all entail the assertion that while historical existence is always concrete and particular, it is not thereby isolated and disconnected. Indeed, pragmatic historicists claim the very opposite. It is out of the intricate interconnections and interdependencies of historical existence that natural and human life gains the distinctiveness of its individual and communal expressions. Relationality and social connectedness do not vitiate particularity but fund it.

Moreover, the material view of culture and language that has been argued for has supported this claim that the various spheres of culture and experience cannot be cut off from one another. Religious communities or academic institutions, for example, come into being and function within the complex sets of social, political and cultural relations that structure human existence. To assume that they can be treated in isolation or that somehow they yield sets of internal norms disconnected from other social realities is fundamentally to misconstrue the nature of historicity. More pertinently, pragmatic historicist theologians are moved by these insights to inquire not only how our claims and practices are reflective of the broad social field within which they take shape but also how they might contribute to the social and cultural fabric that is continually in the making.

The historicist notion of tradition that has emerged in this work has in particular pointed pragmatic historicists to a more public arena of conversation and debate. If traditions of practice and thought, be they religious or political or intellectual, were self-contained or impermeable, then concluding that our justificatory practices were purely or even primarily internal affairs might make sense. But the view of historical traditions that has emerged here suggests something quite different. Traditions, including religious and academic ones, have porous, temporary, and continually reconfigured boundaries. Though particular, traditions are not self-enclosed; they emerge out of historical interactions and continually take different shapes through new interactions. In an interdependent world what occurs within the confines of any particular tradition reverberates across the natural and human world. Religious traditions and theologies thus have, whether they like it or not, a public status for which they are responsible.

Moreover, this work has also argued that as historical not only are humans traditioned beings but that we are multitraditioned. Hence in our individual and communal lives we are forced to contend with not one set of influences or one communal context but many. One central example of this can be seen in the claim by a number of pragmatic historicists that persons in the present historical context live in a world in which certain scientific assumptions have gained widespread credence and shape many arenas of present-day life and do so not only within the industrialized nations of the northern hemisphere but more globally.

Contemporary persons cannot just retreat to supposedly isolated religious traditions without also dealing with these other traditions, including scientific ones, that frame our world. Or again, many persons in the world today struggle for the basic requirements of existence and for self-determination. For pragmatic historicists, to propose that the religious sphere is disconnected for these persons from the concrete economic and political struggles in which they engage is to fail to see the interconnection of various forms of social relations and to neglect the ways in which traditions of interpretations and practice influence one another and intermingle to create intellectually and functionally coherent ways of thinking and acting.

These assumptions of interconnectedness, the multiple directionality of influence in a social cosmos, the functional intermingling of varied particularities are ones that would orient any pragmatic historicist toward a more public stance. But there are further reasons for this that are connected with interpretation of religious traditions in particular and with a specifically pragmatic historicist sense of the theological task. As was noted earlier in this work, pragmatic historicists, such as Gordon Kaufman, have suggested that religious traditions and their secular analogues are most helpfully conceived as comprehensive or synoptic interpretive networks within which humans are given, at least implicitly, a cosmic setting and in which, through belief, symbol, and practice, humans gain a sense of their role and purpose in life. Theology critically reflects upon this cultural practice and seeks to contribute to it. Precisely because religious traditions have this comprehensive thrust theology continually needs to test its evaluations, claims, and proposals in relation to an inclusive agenda. It needs to inquire about its adequacy in relation to the broadest range of material if in fact it is to contribute to making life meaningful and workable for those whose world consists of such myriad realities.[5]

These broad concerns would be, I think, incumbent upon thinkers working out of pragmatic historicist assumptions in any religious tradition. But pragmatic historicists who are related significantly to theistic traditions, especially Christianity, have augmented this argument with another, explicitly theistic reason for locating any discussion of validity in relation to the broadest range of data and in open arenas of debate. A primary focus of much theistic theological reflection includes the symbol of God. For pragmatic historicists the idea of God is the symbolic personification of theistic communities' understanding of the ultimate in terms of which human life is to be led. It has, as such, what Linell Cady calls "universal implications" that push us to consider our positions in relation to the widest panorama of existence.[6] Hence, arenas seemingly beyond the borders of our own community become relevant in theistic frameworks; theological concerns can never be merely local. Cady asserts, thus, that "devotion to God is not compatible either with a retreat from the public realm or, as importantly, with indifference as to its configuration."[7]

Kaufman offers a parallel argument for not only having concern for the broader realm of existence but for testing our claims in the arena of public debate. He asserts that the symbol God, as he interprets it, has within it a self-critical dimension that mandates that we continually assess our interpretations against the fullest range of material and in conversation with others, including those outside our traditions. This critical dimension flows from two factors. First, all our notions of God are human constructions, and hence, like all other human creations, are open to question. Their theological character does not remove them from the possibility of assessment in the public sphere.[8] But second, this symbol intends to give expression to what is ultimate in life in the face of the mystery of existence; as such it critically functions to undercut all human tendencies toward self-absolutizing and moves those who utilize it to a stance of continual reevaluation.[9] These two combine, for Kaufman, to level "all human cognitive elites and all religious hierarchies"[10] and suggest that "the most desirable overall context, therefore, for dealing with our deepest religious and theological issues would be unrestricted interchange among all interested parties."[11] Other traditions may have other warrants within their inheritance mandating these broad conversations. But for Kaufman it is not only the dictates of a historicist interpretation of reality that push theology in this direction but also the influence of a specific part of his theistic inheritance—the symbol of God.

These arguments demonstrate why pragmatic historicists in general and theistic pragmatic historicists in particular insist on considering a broad array of data as they assess the relevance and validity of our claims. Moreover, these same arguments press the theological consideration of such validity beyond the borders of local communities to conversation and debate in a more public realm. But what does it mean to have broad and open discussions when we admit the historically particular nature of our claims? What does public really mean here? Most often pragmatic historicists have invoked the notion of public as a contrast to hierarchical and authoritarian and noncritical modes of theological argumentation. Hence, it has primarily functioned as a disqualifier of other options rather than as a thoroughly articulated idea on its own. It is imperative, however, for pragmatic historicists to offer more positive interpretations of the public, ones that simultaneously keep in view the historical and particular character of our claims while also articulating how those claims should be vetted in arenas of open debate.

Linell Cady has made one such effort. In her work *Religion, Theology, and American Public Life*, she seeks to set forth a historicist interpretation of the public sphere and to redefine theology's relation to it. As background to her argument Cady sets forth a familiar portrayal of the decline of the medieval world, the rise of sectarian warfare, and the response to that in the emergence of liberalism and the modern liberal state. In this modern liberal state, associated initially with emerging western democracy, the particularities of concrete communities, identities, and experiences become the province of a private sphere while the public arena becomes the space of open inquiry untainted by tradition, the sphere in which shared criteria for judgment are formulated by "objective" reason, and the place of formal equality among persons in which differences are rendered invisible. Cady notes that this Enlightenment-inspired vision of the public had both emancipatory and irenic aims. It sought to free humans from the strictures of heteronomous authorities while simultaneously arbitrating conflicts without resort to warfare and the rule of power. Where conflicts arose they were to be resolved not by appeals to the authorities of the dominant group but by reference to those criteria upon which all rational persons could agree.[12]

But modern liberalism also has had deleterious effects, giving rise to a rampant individualism and its partner, consumer capitalism. Moreover, it failed to account adequately for the historical and traditioned character of all human life, replacing the particularities of competing traditions with the false universalism of a supposedly neutral public sphere. Liberalism offered what Cady terms a receptacle notion of the public, an image of the public as an empty container that holds its members shorn of their particularity.[13] While liberalism has given rise to ideals of universal human rights and equal treatment under the law it has also failed to recognize the conditioned, nonneutral character of all our human constructions including "public" norms and "objective knowledge" and to account for or provide nurture of the connections between its members and the communities that compose its larger context.

As this work has demonstrated, across wide expanses of the contemporary landscape these assumptions about the nature of public and private, objective knowledge, autonomous individuality, and so on have all been under attack by historicists. A number of these critical stances have issued forth in more communitarian approaches unconvinced of the possibilities for public discourse. Cady, for her part, seeks to offer a historicist interpretation of the public that counters the parochial conclusions of approaches like those of many communitarians or postliberals.[14] She does so by acknowledging that the modern assumptions of objectivity and unconditioned knowledge and truth have indeed been critically undermined. But, for Cady, recognizing the situated and concrete nature of human knowledge and experience does not remove from us the responsibility for reflecting upon issues that are broader than our small enclaves of religious tradition, academic specialization, and private interest. Nor are we released from the necessity of debating the value of our proposals for addressing these issues and their repercussions upon the wider social network of which we are a part.

Cady suggests that when we reflect upon those more inclusive issues we will do so from our particular perspectives; she is not proposing there is a new view from nowhere. But we can and must ask in the presence of those others with whom we share our social universe how our claims contribute to that interconnected web of being. Cady contends that although we may not have a notion of the common good shared by all humans we do inhabit a common, interconnected world upon which we depend. Hence we are obligated to inquire how our individual and communal beliefs and practices contribute to the common life and to do so in conversation with others who are part of this interconnected web and who, through their own beliefs and practices, contribute to it.

Cady, thus, argues for the reconception of "the public realm as the whole fabric of interrelated beings whose specificity is not outside public life but the substantive texture of it."[15] And the public task of theologians is not to leave one's particularity behind in some atavistic claim of universalism or neutrality but, precisely out of those particularities, to attend to the interconnected natural and human sphere that makes historical existence possible at all. Thus, according to Cady, "The task of a public theology is to elicit a recognition of and commitment to the common life within which we exist. In and through the appropriation of religious symbolism, public theology seeks to nurture, deepen, and transform our common life that, while obscured and damaged, is never totally eroded."[16]

If Linell Cady has called for interpreting the public as the interwoven fabric of particularities and has urged the nurture of the common life out of which such particularities emerge and upon which they depend, Delwin Brown has focused upon the nature of reason-giving and justificatory practices within this public sphere. Brown assumes our criteria for assessment are always historical and contingent, lacking timeless or universal character. However, this recognition does not entail the conclusion, made by so many communitarians, that "all criteria are always strictly local, entirely intrasystematic."[17] Though there may be no norms or criteria common to every historical setting, criteria often are common to more than one setting or tradition. And even where distinctive criteria or norms come into play, such particularity, as Jeffrey Stout also argues, does not rule out translation or explanation to others in different locales. "Criteria," according to Brown, "overlap some standpoints—disciplines, cultures, religions, and so forth—even if no criterion overlaps them all."[18] Our theologies may not be able to be tested in all contexts and against every element of historical data. However, Brown asserts, "No theology is entitled even tentatively to the claim of credibility if it is not tested in relation to at least some alternative perspectives."[19] Thus, for Brown, theology, like all other forms of human inquiry, carries a "cross-contextual obligation."[20]

These analyses suggest that "public" functions in several, interconnected ways. First, it refers to those arenas and sets of data that we must take into consideration as we assess the value of our theological claims and make arguments for their validity. The public, in this sense, refers to the inclusive fabric of all those interconnected particularities that make up historical reality, the vast web of local worlds—both natural and human.

But public also refers to the character and locale of our justificatory processes. For pragmatic historicists, theology is a public enterprise not only because its concerns are broad but because theology, to be relevant and legitimate, must be prepared to argue for its claims in debate and conversation with those beyond its locale of origin, in a variety of particular communities. Thus theology constructs its positions not only in light of the public, that is, the interconnected web of particular worlds, but also argues on behalf of those claims in public contexts where a plurality of local considerations and argumentations hold sway.

Recognizing that our public world is really the conglomeration of multiple, interrelated particular worlds also affects how we should view such public argumentation. While in principle public conceived as the interconnected whole encompasses every aspect of historical existence and form of argumentation, in practice, public, as the forum for open argumentation, never refers to a context in which every possible voice or perspective can be effectively present. Instead, most often we have multiple sites of adjudication in which varying sets of regionally shared or overlapping assumptions hold significance and in which certain realities or worlds demand particular attention and a critical say because of the ways in which they are affected by our proposals. Thus while theology is called to the table of public debate, there are, in reality, many tables; the public is always plural, neither singular nor uniform.

These two uses of public, as the inclusive web of local worlds and as the plural context of argumentation and reason giving, together serve to keep us alert to the elements mandated by pragmatic historicism. The latter reminds us that even our most public mode of argumentation is historical, situated in the context of particular, intersecting locales and reflective of the contingent and fallible values and convictions of those engaged in theological debate. It keeps us from moving too quickly to false universals or assuming we have carried out debate in a totally open sphere when in reality we have engaged only our most immediate neighbors.

But the former pushes us continually to widen the field of theological consideration and debate; it compels us to ask again and again who is not at this particular theological table, who is affected by our proposals but has no say in their evaluation, who gains and who loses because of our beliefs and practices. It, thus, mandates that we assess the adequacy of our visions not solely by recourse to the adept or experts within a tradition or merely according to dominant local perspectives. We must inquire, in light of this understanding of public, not only concerning the consequences of a worldview for those who benefit from it but also those who are its victims; we must ask our questions not only at the centers of traditions but at their margins, not only in terms of one tradition but also in terms of other traditions, not only for practitioners but also for all—believers or not—who experience its impact daily. In an interconnected world composed of many particular worlds it will no longer do to ask only what a version of Christianity means to its Christian adherents unless we also interrogate its implications for Jews and Buddhists and Muslims. Nor will it suffice to assay the value of a religious vision according to the privileged elite within its ranks without also hearing from those who are ruled deviant, heretical, unclean, and sinful.

The position articulated in this volume contends, thus, that while we can never get outside of natural and human history to decide whose picture of the way things are most closely corresponds to reality, what we can do is come together with our fellow humans and in the face of the vast array of natural realities with whom we share existence and ask the questions of how our local visions contribute to historical life. We can ask what difference it makes to espouse one set of values or practices or mode of interaction rather than another, what ideas, projects, and practices should we at this historical moment espouse and to which we should commit our lives. When we do so we will not come into one vast arena of conversation in which everyone shares the same principles but to varied and changing tables or contexts of public debate in which we as historical beings will have to make, time and time again, fallible determinations about these matters.

The above sections argue that the place for such critical reflection is the present and the arenas within which we should carry out our work are the varied public spheres within which we evaluate the repercussions of our positions both in terms of their local significance and against the ever widening horizon of an inclusive historical reality. What these assertions do not suggest is that the present is ontologically privileged over the past, that somehow here and not there authoritative truth resides. Instead the claims of the present have the same historical character as those of past. Hence, the real issue is not where we find some still point of ageless truth or presumed authority. It is, rather, where we locate accountability. And for pragmatic historicists these sites of responsibility are in the present and in the context of our relevant publics, the array of persons, communities, and natural realities before and with whom we must explore the causes, reasons, and repercussions of our ideas and actions.

All these considerations lead pragmatic historicists to a commitment to radically inclusionary strategies and democratic practices. If individuals, communities, and traditions can interact because of their overlapping criteria and ability to explain themselves to others, and if these also continually in fact do interact through processes of mutual influence, then it is imperative that the best conditions prevail to enhance these exchanges and evaluative deliberations. Further, pragmatic historicists have asserted that to create conditions supportive of real exchange and not just struggle requires the recognition, analysis, and redress of those dynamics of power that invest some perspectives with great legitimacy while dismissing others. It does little good to advocate a position that calls for open debate, inclusive of multiple voices, while ignoring the mechanisms by which many are rendered invisible, denied legitimacy, or so thoroughly located at the bottom of a hierarchy of values that their reality counts for little in the evaluative equation.

Thus when historicism is linked to pragmatism in the manner advocated in this volume there emerges, not a narrow utilitarian tool of the powerful but a mandate to work on behalf of those who have been systematically denied power. Thus the pragmatism advocated by thinkers particularly concerned with questions of liberation such as Simon Maimela, Cornel West, Rebecca Chopp, as well as myself, calls for attention to those whose views and very existence have not been considered heretofore and indeed suggests that in the face of longstanding inequalities our claims must continually be tested in terms of how they support or hinder the historical existence of those without power.[21]

Such preferential testing does not endow any group or individual with permanent or ontological legitimacy or virtue that is denied others. Instead, it is a strategic attempt to further the ideal of democratic interaction and to transform the dynamics of the unequal and unjust distribution of power that undermine open and public consideration of projects and beliefs. Hence, the commitment to inclusionary processes entails the corollary commitment to an ongoing critical process of asking who is excluded and why, who benefits and why, and to the attempt to create a more just world.

What is the goal of this inclusionary orientation? Do pragmatic historicists think that even when multiple voices are raised that somehow conflicts or power struggles or irreconcilable interpretations will not still abound? If religious traditions and worldviews are historical and particular, invested with interests and structured by diverse purposes, are we left inevitably with a panorama of possibilities without a means for finally deciding among them? There is clearly a sense in which this remains the case. For pragmatic historicists, while negotiation will change positions and open new possibilities, there will remain a plurality of worldviews, symbol systems, ritualistic practices, ways of being, and ethical orientations toward reality. If the point of our inclusionary practice is to overcome such pluralism and ongoing negotiation, it is clearly wrong-headed. We may live in one interconnected world, but we do so in a dazzling and dizzying multiplicity of ways.

But several important goals may be pursued through pragmatic historicism's commitment to inclusionary practices. Importantly, it moves the evaluative process beyond the alternatives of isolated self-justification and superficial show and tell. It assumes that our views and practices do indeed matter to more than those who hold them or live them out and, further, that the consequences of our claims for others need to be part of our own self-critical evaluation. While such a process will not tell us whose complex theoretical symbols have captured the nature of cosmic reality correctly or what practice will be relevant in another era, it will enable us to explore its repercussions for those who live in relation to it or who are affected by it. By so doing, it will focus our attention on what might be termed a historicized soteriology as we seek to respond to the concrete dilemmas and possibilities of human existence.

If pragmatic historicism moves us to a historically oriented soteriological focus for our justificatory practices and advocates that multiple voices should offer both possibilities for us to pursue and critical responses to our claims (as we do to them) then we need to ask whether we can ever hope for or see as a good the pursuit of at least localized consensus concerning matters of theological evaluation and judgment. On one level, this does not appear to be a goal to be sought. The proliferation of interpretive frameworks, symbol systems, and practices is an expression of our historicity and indeed provides ever emergent resources for confronting the exigencies of historical existence; it is through our plural and changing traditions that new historical possibilities take shape. Thus, neither within nor across religious and theological traditions can we expect nor should we want uniformity of belief or practice. Orthodoxies, be they liberal or conservative, progressive or reactionary, belie the pluralism and dynamism of historicity.

What of consensus as a goal on the level of evaluating the consequences, the soteriological ramifications, of our varied claims and proposals? Can I only hope that I will listen to others and they to me as we seek to make judgments about what paths of human action and thought should claim our intellectual and moral loyalty? Such consideration of the other as a legitimate voice in our own evaluative process is indeed a positive value for pragmatic historicism. I would also suggest that for pragmatic historicism temporary, localized, and revisable consensus, concerning the value of possible consequences of our interpretations, practices, and symbols, is an ideal to be pursued.

To suggest that not only should evaluative and justificatory processes include the voices of those who are affected by our claims but that we should also seek consensus about what are positive and negative ramifications resulting from those claims is not an easy position to maintain in our contemporary context, which recognizes and often seems to celebrate the conflictual nature of historical existence. Not only is historical existence pluralistic in nature but also characterized by the circulation of and struggle for power. For many Richard Rorty is correct when he says most everything finally comes down to a matter of luck or weapons.[22] But such a position is, from the perspective of this work, a self-defeating and sometimes self-indulgent orientation that excuses us all from the hard task of continually working to forge just agreements and compromises. To forego this work is to leave us all with the specter of endless battle in which the possibilities for a humane historicity are undermined. And while cynicism concerning the possibility for consensus on the part of those who have been denied power is more than understandable, the current easy retreat of so many who are content with luck and guns, including academics, into the safe haven of difference and incommensurability smacks of one more way to maintain the privilege and disparity of power that is ours.

It is, however, not only the privileged and powerful who disdain the search for consensus; this search is also opposed by many of those for whom such a call has been the mask for imposing dominant or majoritarian rule upon the minority, the heterodox, or the invisible. For many, consensus has entailed coercion and has functioned as a thin euphemism for shrewdly imposed conformity. But the perspective of pragmatic historicism envisioned here calls not for a simplistic recourse to majority rule or a consensus imposed by the guardians of orthodoxy but for a goal in which new forms of agreements are continually, if temporarily, reached by all relevant participants, or barring such agreement, that the majority comes to use its rule to work continually with others to forge ways to enlarge the range of interests met. The range of resolution achieved by a majority is not, then, an end, but a starting point from which to expand the resolution toward the inclusion of all in a true, if temporary, consensus.

Feminist philosopher Charlene Haddock Seigfried, in her work *Pragmatism and Feminism*, argues precisely for processes whereby we seek not only to include all relevant voices but also to pursue, as an ideal, a consensus in which temporary agreement is reached. She contends that we require such consensus because the problems we seek to address and the consequences we must assess are not private but social and concrete requiring, as she puts it, "concerted action to be solved equitably and efficaciously."[23] Thus she calls for a consensus in which, "the majority can be no less than every single participant."[24] This consensus will not occur often, Seigfried cautions us, and what counts as all relevant participants will vary from context to context. Moreover, when it does occur, it will always be "temporary, revisable, strategic, and directed toward specific ends-in-view."[25] Nonetheless, as an ideal, it gives shape to democratic practices and to the creation of "social, institutional, educational, political, and cultural" mechanisms that can enhance the possibilities for participation in evaluative processes.[26]

But, as Seigfried also notes, the achievement of consensus is difficult, not always possible, and even when it occurs, only temporary. Thus while our actions may be guided by this principle we are also forced to make decisions when no consensus is reached, when disagreements remain. And we are forced to do so knowing that not all needs will be met, that not all goods can or will be actualized simultaneously, not all individuals or groups will equally benefit or suffer from our decisions or their outcomes. Pragmatic historicism does not offer a way out of this dilemma. What it does is insist that when we evaluate our theological proposals that we do so with the fullest cognizance possible of their consequences and with a multiplicity of voices and perspectives as legitimate partners in the process of assessment. Such inclusion will mitigate, though certainly not eliminate, unjust or tragic outcomes. Perhaps most importantly of all, the pursuit of consensus will keep ever before us the cost of our failure to achieve it.

In the face of our tragic failure to achieve consensus how should we make decisions? There are two further suggestions that can be made from the perspective of pragmatic historicism. One plays with the suggestion by Francis Schüssler Fiorenza that we should seek a "wide reflective equilibrium."[27] Though similar to consensus, such an equilibrium is different in important ways. Equilibrium takes shape in the interplay of the various criteria that come with the multiple voices in theological conversation, balancing one off against another. Its goal, like that of consensus, is not to have one voice trump all the others. But those who seek an equilibrium also are cognizant that agreement is not always possible. Thus, in contrast to the dominance of one perspective or to absolute agreement among all perspectives, the goal of equilibrium is to build, through multilayered considerations, a cumulative case, the best case possible given our choices and the competing values we seek to accommodate.

If consensus is our ideal pragmatic goal and failing that a "wide reflective equilibrium" that balances but also, if necessary, chooses among competing values and voices, how do we decide what or who should have priority? The second suggestion pragmatic historicism makes is that precisely as a perspective concerned with the resolution of concrete problems and the enhancement of concrete life we need to prioritize according to the urgency of our problems. We will not always be able to wait for consensus. Nor can we simply remain motionless, paralyzed by our sense of tragic failure. We must act and we can only do so as we decide, in conversation with the broadest range of testimonies, what are the most pressing and consequential concerns of our time. Thus pragmatic historicism will be guided by inclusionary commitments, the critical principle of an ideal consensus and the living reality of the necessity of balancing competing values in the face of urgent needs. In all this pragmatic historicists search not for a new hegemony in which our views hold sway but a tentative, temporary, and continually revisable place to stand that responds to the needs at hand and contributes to the wider possibilities of life. It is to such a self-critical, vulnerable, and constructive task to which pragmatic historicism commits itself.

IN THE FACE OF MULTIPLE VOICES

There is an adage that says the devil is in the details. That is certainly the case with theological proposals including the ones under consideration here. If it is the task of the present to diagnose the problems to which we must attend, to articulate the norms and criteria for evaluating our responses, and to identify, criticize, and reconstruct elements of our inheritance so as to forge new interpretations of reality, then it is imperative to inquire what voices and perspectives should be part of this theological process. What are the multiple voices to which theologians must attend and who should have a say? What could consensus or even equilibrium mean and how could either be reached?

One way to state pragmatic historicism's position is to assert that all those who are affected, potentially or actually, by a theological claim or practice have a claim to participate in the evaluative process. Concretely, different perspectives, individuals, and communities will emerge as particularly relevant to specific situations but in a social universe this pragmatist commitment to inclusion could, in principle, entail everything that exists or might come to exist. While this assertion certainly demonstrates the daunting character of the task, I want to focus on the equally difficult exploration of more concrete specifics by pointing to three arenas or sets of voices that in this historical moment, especially for theology of the sort envisioned here, demand particular inclusion. Other historical moments and other locations in this era will call for different emphases. But these are among the voices that I believe it is important to have as interlocutors in the contemporary theological debate both because the principle of urgency indicates that if we do not include these voices we court disaster and, equally importantly, because the assumptions that shape pragmatic historicism compel such inclusion. The naturalized and social ontology and anthropology espoused by pragmatic historicism, the dynamic and pluralistic theory of religious traditions, and assertions concerning the multitraditioned experience of much contemporary life all push us to attend to these perspectives if we are to meet the needs of the day.

The Nonperson

The first voice is that of those human individuals and groups who are denied power, voice, the means for sustainable and meaningful life and often whose very existence is threatened. In his work, *The Power of the Poor in History*, Gustavo Gutiérrez strongly argued that contemporary theology in Europe and the United States was driven by the modern project of making sense of theological claims in the face of the relentless erosion of traditional religious beliefs and the spread of a secular scientific worldview. Thus, he said, much theology was responding to the question of the "nonbeliever." Over against this modernist project of the powerful, Gutiérrez called for a theology of liberation carried out in the face of and in response to the "nonperson," a theological project not only different from that of the dominant European and American theologies but in opposition to them.[28]

One of the questions that needs to be asked of the perspective espoused in this work is whether it continues, albeit in new guise, the concerns and projects that so shaped its liberal theological predecessors and that failed to include or provide the means of contributing to the struggles of the world's nonpersons. There is a sense in which pragmatic historicism does continue certain concerns of liberal theology. This work has suggested that theology must seek intellectual coherence with those contemporary interpretations of the world, generated within the natural and humanistic sciences, that have widespread credence if it is to make sense for many persons today. It has argued that we cannot separate the manifold worlds in which we live and that our only choice is whether we live out of anachronistic interpretations of reality or ones that have gained currency in the world we inhabit. This is the case not only for the bourgeois theologian hoping to fit into the intellectual world of his or her day but also for Gutiérrez's nonperson who likewise is shaped and influenced by assumptions about reality and the practical projects that flow from them. And it entails not only the cosmological hypotheses of contemporary speculative science but consideration of the picture of human social and cultural reality that is taking shape on the current scene.

When these latter assumptions are focused upon pragmatic historicism leads not away from Gutiérrez's nonperson but precisely to consideration of the profound interconnection of the human community and of humanity and nature and to the historically specific ways in which that interconnection has taken shape. In this view it is impossible to see the conditions and fortunes of the "nonbeliever" and the "nonperson" as disconnected. Both positively and negatively the possibilities for one intersect with the other. In particular, the social ontology of pragmatic historicism and its resultant commitment to inclusionary practices push pragmatic historicist theologians not only to include the fate of the dispossessed as part of the data for theological reflection but insist these voices must be theological speakers for themselves and participants in the ongoing process by which theological claims are constructed and assessed. This is not to say on every issue, every person has the exact same amount of say. It is to argue that persons who are or may be adversely affected by theological assertions and practices, who have been or may be rendered "nonpersons," have a claim to be heard and have their experience and interpretations as part of the data to be considered in any assessment process. And for that to take place clearly the conditions that result from the disparity of power must be addressed and continually remedied. Open consideration and debate are the byproducts of justice and equality; without them there is only struggle.

Thus this work has suggested that part of the theological task is to ask in the construction and evaluation of theological claims not only how those claims positively function to give individuals and groups orientation in thought and practice but who becomes the "nonperson," both within and outside our religious traditions. Gutiérrez utilizes the term nonperson to refer primarily to the poor. Without denying the significance of that definition, I would like to broaden the designation to indicate those groups or individuals who in a given context are rendered invisible or denied access to the means of self-determination. The content of the category would continually shift and no group or perspective would be exempt from the critical practice of evaluating itself in light of whom it deliberately or inadvertently not only leaves out but endows with negativity or nonbeing.[29] Furthermore the adoption of this critical theological stance would entail the acknowledgment that many persons, though not all, in fact occupy dual locations rendering others invisible and simultaneously being excluded themselves.

A few concrete examples might help to demonstrate what is entailed by this commitment to a process of interrogation by which the excluded continually place a critical claim upon those who make theological proposals and judgments. The poor who Gutiérrez argued should occupy the central place of concern for theologians present an obvious case. When liberal theology only assessed its value in relation to the goals of the nonpoor first world, assuming that those goals were everyone's, it not only failed to see those who suffered from poverty and oppression but also was blind to the connections of its own convictions and practices to the inhumane conditions of much of the rest of the world. Pragmatic historicism calls for the interconnection between the fate and condition of the "nonbeliever" and the "nonperson" to be traced and to be a central factor in analyzing the validity of our various claims.

Or again, when certain forms of contemporary Christian theology argue for notions of the image of God that positively include both men and women as the expression of God's nature, it must be asked who gets left out of this paradigm. When that is the question what comes to light is the heterosexist and humanocentric character of many of these claims. While they positively include women and make sociality central to our understanding of God, they often leave out all of nature and, on the human front, reflect implicit assumptions about the complementarity of male and female, excluding those whose identities are not so constructed. Lesbians and gays become the non-normative, the deviant, less than human, and nature continues to be represented as that which exists for human ends and needs. Pragmatic historicism calls for the inclusion of the so-called deviant and the non-normative at the theological table.[30]

Again, in one of the most obvious cases on the contemporary theological scene today, when feminist theology was interrogated by women of color it turned out not to be nearly so inclusive as it claimed but systematically to render the experiences of women of color invisible. While white feminists rightly called male theology into question for its false universalism and collusion in the oppression of women, it often failed to see its own implication in the racist and classist structures from which it benefited.[31] Pragmatic historicism calls for theological debate that continually asks who benefits from our claims, whose power is safeguarded and enhanced, and what must be done to make the theological equation more equitable.

In each of the examples pragmatic historicism suggests the same critical stance. It argues for a process of questioning that not only acknowledges the positive contributions of our constructions but seeks to uncover and challenge the exclusions that are also inherent in them. It recognizes that in any claim some things, persons, realities are left out; particular claims or groups or identities do not include all possibilities. Sometimes such omission is neutral, at other times it is disadvantageous to some but on balance may be justified, and at other points particular exclusions and their repercussions must be judged detrimental. What pragmatic historicism enjoins us to do in the face of this complexity is to inquire about how our interpretations of reality, our communal practices, symbol systems do not only lend us identity and purpose but also how they are detrimental to others. Moreover, pragmatic historicism contends that the way that should be determined is to create processes in which those persons who are negatively excluded have their own voice in the evaluative process, while simultaneously recognizing that those voices are continually changing and that they may have a privilege resulting from historical circumstance, but are, like other finite voices, fallible and contingent.

This way of speaking helps us keep in mind the exclusionary dimensions of all claims and the very negative consequences these can have. But it can also be misleading. For the process of inclusion is not just a critical process of asking who is rendered invisible, as though these persons or realities were blank ciphers, nonentities. The process of inclusion is also the positive process by which new voices contribute to the construction of theological interpretations for today. Gustavo Gutiérrez argued not only that we live in a world in which many persons bear the status of nonperson but that these persons struggle to gain and maintain humanness out of their own manifold resources; thus they are not empty vessels that those with more power now magnanimously fill with humanness. They are not, in the words of poet Adrienne Rich, "merely the sum of damages done to them."[32] Nor are they interested in what feminist theory has called the additive approach in which previously excluded individuals and groups are added to a category without that category being changed or altered. Those that are excluded always stand as challenges to the very understandings of what it means to be human that stripped them of their personhood. To say that theological processes of evaluation must always ask about who is excluded means, therefore, saying more than that a permanent place should be set at the theological table for the nonperson; it says instead that our theological tables must always be undergoing design changes and that more than the theological elite, magnanimous as they might be, must have a say in who sits where and what the topic of conversation will be. It asserts that theological conversations are not between "we" who have power and personhood and those who do not, but entail a continual process of renegotiating the multiple "we's" that compose the world.

The Voice of Religious Traditions

A second set of voices in the face of which our theological evaluative processes must take place today is that of other than our own religious traditions, practitioners, and thinkers. As we saw earlier, for some historicists such as postliberals the recognition of our historical particularity has led to the call for a return to religious communities and to a focus on the internal community; relations with other religious groups and individuals are relegated to the realm of occasional and ad hoc cooperation around concerns that are shared across traditions.

The position I am developing in this work suggests a quite different approach to the issue of pluralism and to the question of what theological relations should pertain among various groups. First, there is a clear sense in which pragmatic historicists tend to agree with postliberals; religious traditions, interpreted as encompassing networks of interpretation, practice, and values, are distinctive and do not lend themselves to any easy test whereby we can adjudicate between the highly complex and imaginative pictures that have developed over time, stating one gets reality "right" rather than another. If much historicism has generally foregone the correspondence theory of truth, certainly historicist theologians have argued that theological claims can no longer be tested in this manner. But as this chapter has argued, pragmatists have not concluded that therefore no tests of adequacy can be applied to our claims, nor that those evaluative judgments can only be rendered in terms of faithfulness to the givens of an enclosed community. For pragmatic historicism, our judgments pertain to how our claims contribute to the practical organization and interpretation of human life, and the arena for such critical assessments includes, in a social universe, more than our intimate associates. Therefore, pragmatic historicists resist the reduction of the relations among religious traditions to superficial exhibition of our "religious wares," isolation or ad hoc cooperation that leaves aside precisely those elements that make a tradition distinctive. Instead it has called for a renewal of conversations among religious traditions not in spite of our historical particularity but because of it.

Gordon Kaufman, in his recent work, *God, Mystery, Diversity*, has argued strenuously that the recognition of our historicity mandates this wider arena of debate. In this volume, Kaufman focuses on two important elements that characterize our historical existence. One is plurality. Human beings have fashioned themselves in response to their natural and human historical condition in a wide variety of ways. These ways do not share the kind of commonalities presupposed by perennialists who assume a common core across religious traditions. They represent distintive theoretical construals of the world and modes of being and practice. Thus Kaufman concludes that historicists must acknowledge the plurality of religious truths and ways of living and being. Religious claims to adequacy or truth are, therefore for Kaufman, really always plural, never singular.[33]

But if Kaufman begins with the assumption of plurality he is not content with the postliberal response to that. He assumes, with his pragmatic historicist cohorts, that historicity does not rule out communication and understanding but only makes it a painstaking historical task. Religious traditions do not exist in isolation from one another; they overlap, bump into each other, challenge each other and generally interact. Even more importantly, Kaufman argues, with a profound sense of urgency, our recognition of the historicity of our religious traditions and theological schemas must entail an acknowledgment of their partiality, contingency, fallibility, and need for correction and revision. This understanding of historicity should lead not to the safety of our local enclaves but to openness to the challenge and input of others. As Kaufman states, "To acknowledge forthrightly and regularly that our theological statements and claims are simply *ours*—they are the product of our human study and reflection, and of the spontaneity and creativity of our human powers imaginatively to envision a world and our human place within that world—is to set us free from these all too easy but false moves toward authoritarianism, which have characterized so much Christian theology in the past."[34]

Now for Kaufman, consciousness of the historicity of our claims should always issue forth in openness to critical revision. But in this work, Kaufman has elaborated what that openness means in a very distinctive way. He suggests that our current historical situation dictates that not only must we be willing to revise our traditions and interpretive schemas and practices out of the resources of our own traditions but that the religious traditions of humanity need to forge new and more-adequate-to-our-time interpretations from the resources of the many religious and secular traditions available to us. These visions will, no doubt, still be plural but that plurality will emerge from a more self-conscious openness to other perspectives. In his words, "The problems with which modernity confronts us—extending even to the possibility that we may obliterate humankind completely in a nuclear holocaust or total ecological collapse—demand that we bring together all the wisdom, devotion, and insight that humanity has accumulated in its long history, as we attempt to find orientation in today's world."[35]

In this view not only do others stand before us as challenges to the adequacy of our positions, but also as potential resources (as we are to them) for the construction of new visions. In this sense Kaufman proposes that not only are religious and theological truths *plural* but also that they are *emergent*. If we are to respond to the urgent needs of the historical moment every tool, resource, human possibility, both within and across traditions, must be seen as a potential resource. We must be open to the insights and wisdom from within and without our traditions, recognizing that creative possibilities, or emergent truths, come out of ongoing and open interchange among equals, all of whom are transformed by the encounter and whose interpretive schemas, values, and practices take on new shape and content through the process. When this occurs interreligious dialogue loses its superficial quality and instead becomes a disciplined practice of critical challenge, exchange, and reconstruction.

The overall direction of the argument of this book supports Kaufman's twin contentions of the multiple and emergent character of theological claims. The historical character of all theological assertions, the pluralism endemic within traditions, the porous boundaries between religious communities and the multitraditioned nature of individual and communal identities all bolster Kaufman's proposal. However, there are also questions that emerge from within pragmatic historicism that at the very least sound notes of caution here. I will indicate several. The first has to do with whether this approach really takes seriously enough the locatedness of human life. Is this one more version of modern "man" who picks and chooses from wherever he might like without full cognizance of his own situatedness and with even less sense that the traditions and resources of others are not his for the taking? Is this model really what Delwin Brown calls the "bee and nectar" model of theological construction in which a theological elite flits from flower to flower borrowing indiscriminately?[36]

When this is coupled with the second concern, the criticism takes on more ominous tones. That second area of concern relates to the unequal distribution of power and the question of whether Kaufman's model of conversation is really adequate for the struggles that go on between and within religious traditions. Who gains from the process of borrowing and whose traditions are raided for the benefit of the powerful? One needs only to look at the current appropriation of Native American sacred traditions and practices by whites or the western usurpation of eastern religions to realize that often the interchange among religious groups has not always been equitable but a process of dispossession and even cultural plundering. In addition, religious thinkers and practitioners often have sought not critical dialogue with others, in which all are open to the possibility of transformation, but victory and control over others and the ascendancy of their own religious tradition as the only legitimate one. Linked, these concerns lead to the query of whether Kaufman's proposal of creative exchange is not one more vehicle, albeit

unwittingly, for the creation of new hegemonies or at least the oblitera-
tion of valuable diversities.

I think these are real cautions that need to be continually applied by
pragmatic historicists to our own work. Still, I would argue that an
approach that leaves open the possibility for creatively envisioning
emergent traditions out of the resources of multiple traditions is not
only consistent with the version of pragmatic historicism articulated in
this volume but also one of the sources of hope for our time. Human
beings and their communities do not stay so neatly put within the
boundaries erected for and even by them. Both conceptually and functionally, persons and communities all over the world construct ways of
living in the world that are less concerned with purity of lineage and
more with how varied traditions that influence them can be resources in
the face of the ongoing and changing challenges of life. To admit this as
theologians and to engage in this practice self-consciously and critically
is not automatically to be perpetrators of cultural or religious imperialism and theft but can be a profoundly humble practice of acknowledging that no group or thought or value system is fully adequate on its
own but requires the wisdom and insight of others both as a corrective
and a resource. But to engage in this kind of practice, as the above section argued, is always to be embedded in social relations shaped by disparity of power and must, therefore, continually entail the redress of
such inequity if "conversations" among the religious and secular traditions of humanity are not to be covert mechanisms of control, plunder,
and domination.

There is also a third issue that the notion of theological construction
out of the resources of multiple traditions rather than singular, though
internally pluralistic, traditions poses. And that is the question of efficacy. There is a sense in which this question of what is the most efficacious manner in which to proceed can only be answered concretely and
empirically. My own suspicion is that such empirical evidence is very
mixed, yielding simultaneous confirmation that effective religious and
theological reconstruction has taken place by means of the creative reappropriation and transformation of the resources internal to a tradition
but also through the intermingling and cross-fertilization of diverse traditions. Or again, I think much evidence can be amassed to point to the
fact that humans often borrow from each other by reinterpreting the
materials of another tradition under the guise of their own or resist the
loss of their own inheritance by hiding it in a more dominant one as so
many of the indigenous persons of the Americas did in the face of colo-
nial expansion. Thus given the diverse evidence, there is probably no
one pragmatic historicist position to be defended on this issue. Nonetheless it is important to note that there are pragmatic historicists who,

while committed to evaluating their position in ever widening arenas or publics, do not conclude from that stance that the most effective way to develop religious or theological visions is through a Kaufmanesque synthetic process.

Delwin Brown has made perhaps the strongest arguments against this approach. He has not argued that people who reside in different religious traditions and communities cannot understand each other, nor has he argued that we are not accountable to one another to explain, give reasons for, and bear the responsibilities for the outcomes of our interpretations of reality and our ways of life. Nor has he denied that we borrow, sometimes quite substantially, from each other. What he has maintained is that to be historical is to be canalized. That is, he asserts, human beings tend to organize and interpret their lives under the rubric of specific traditions and therefore change is most effectively wrought and maintained through the self-conscious and creative reconstruction of particular traditions' heritages. Moreover, the appropriation of external material from other traditions is most successfully carried out, Brown contends, by integrating those resources within the categories and practices of one's dominant framework. Thus Brown has pled his case for theologians to attend to their own inheritances and the creative possibilities that inhere there not because religious traditions are pure or adequate or isolatable or incommensurable but because the pragmatic possibilities for making a concrete difference in persons' lives generally lie more in this direction than in the broader search for meaning and value.[37]

My own position mediates the difference between the approaches posed by Kaufman and Brown. With Brown, I confirm the need to work the internal possibilities of various traditions; a central task of theology is the creative extension of the resources found within particular traditions. As stated in chapter 4, Kaufman's tendency to ignore the concrete historical inheritance of Christianity has often rendered his position less than compelling to those who continue to live their lives within specificities of that tradition. But as I have argued earlier in this text, it is not clear at all that humans interpret their lives and define their identities within singular or even dominant traditions but are in fact multitraditioned. This is not only the case for the multiplicity of influences that emerge from religion, gender, race, class, and so on, but numerous humans also affirm and live out of explicitly multiple religious perspectives. While for many in our North American context it is inconceivable to claim multiple religious affiliations, that is not the case everywhere. Not only have religious traditions emerged out of the intermingling of sources but individuals also affirm simultaneously that, for example, they are Buddhist and Shinto, practitioners of the Mayan cosmo-vision and Catholics, and so forth.[38] Moreover, there are also persons who do not embrace traditions side by side, if you will, but make something new out of the influences and possibilities that impinge on their lives.

These varied ways humans construct meaning and value suggest that there is not one way that theologians should proceed but that our approaches must be as varied as those we seek to serve. Some theologians will certainly continue primarily to engage in the creative reconstruction of one tradition; others may well see their imaginative work, while situated, not so cleanly or clearly located within the borders of a singular community. For my own part, the issue of efficacy appears most fundamentally in our urgent need for new interpretive models and frameworks to meet the complex needs of our world. It is not evident to me, as it is not for Kaufman, that the inheritances of any single tradition, however internally pluralistic, can meet the needs of the moment. On this issue I side with those pragmatists who aver that only together can we adequately respond to our world and that in the pursuit of survival and the flourishing of historical existence we must be open to any instrument that might guide us safely not to our homes of yesterday but to new homes that we have yet to build or even envision.

The Voice of Nature

Pragmatic historicism's commitment to an inclusive field of evaluation for assessing our claims is also embodied in the turn to a third arena—nature. William Dean, Sallie McFague and Gordon Kaufman have all argued that as we seek to identify the problems that confront us and to evaluate the validity of our attempts to respond to the complexities of our times we must attend not only to humanity but also to the natural sphere out of which we have emerged, upon which we depend.[39] Their reasons for asserting this range from Kaufman's sense that human existence depends upon nature to survive to William Dean's arguments calling for a naturalized historicism and historicized naturalism to Sallie McFague's assertion that the nonhuman realm exerts a claim upon humans that is not reducible to its utility for us. My own position has followed these thinkers in arguing that there is no human history that can be attended to outside the constraints and possibilities of the nonhuman world. It has, further, resisted the radical separation between nature and history, space and time, contending that temporality and consciousness are material and embodied and that bodies, places, and spaces are historical. The form of expansive historicism that has emerged herein has, hence, indicated the importance of including all provinces constituting the interconnected and interdependent network of historical existence within our considerations as we seek to determine the value and limits of our theological proposals.

The inclusion of nature as a testing site for our theological proposals expresses pragmatic historicism's distinctive agenda, differentiating it both from other theological historicisms and from many forms of non-theological pragmatism. But this inclusionary agenda also demonstrates, once again, how difficult it is to carry out the programs of an expansive historicism. The democratic and just inclusion of our fellow humans is, as we all know, enormously challenging in practice. How much more so when we turn to the nonhuman world. What does it mean to see the vast world of nature as a sphere that demands our accountability, how would we know what that entails and what happens when we are, as is inevitably the case, forced to decide among competing values and claims?

It has been Sallie McFague's work that presents us with the strongest vision of what the turn to this wider realm involves and, that, in the process, presents us with its most complex questions. McFague's book *The Body of God: An Ecological Theology* is a provocative attempt to rethink Christian theology in light of what she has termed the common creation story that is widely accepted as the interpretation of reality for our time. Her reinterpretation of nature and of humanity's place within the cosmic context is, thus, developed from two directions—out of the picture of reality emerging from contemporary science and from her interpretation of the claims of Christianity reinterpreted now in relation to this new understanding of the universe.

For McFague, the common creation story details a picture of reality as a dynamic, interconnected process of immense proportions extending over enormous expanses of time and space. In this story humans appear neither at the center of the drama, its main show, nor as a special kind of reality separable from other creatures and natural phenomena. As McFague states it, "according to contemporary science, the religious/secular/modern picture of human reality is a lie, a very large and dangerous lie. According to the common creation story, we are not the center of things by any stretch of the imagination."[40] Rather we are one part, albeit a potentially dangerous part, of "a vast community of individuals within the ecosystem, each of which is related in intricate ways to all others in the community of life."[41] For McFague, if we begin with the assumptions of this portrayal of reality, then we are required to think holistically, to move beyond even the democratic vision articulated above to what she calls a "biocracy" and to move our loyalties not only beyond our enclaves of family, nation, religious tradition, but also species to become accountable to the web of existence itself and to all others who share this cosmos and especially the planet earth with us.[42]

The dual moves of portraying reality as interdependent and inter-connected and simultaneously decentering humanity hold several impor-tant repercussions for pragmatic historicists. First, they indicate that we humans cannot fully understand the implications of our values, prac-tices, or interpretations even for ourselves unless we take into consider-ation their impact on the wider ecological context of which we are a part. But when human beings are decentered, only part of the cosmic historical process, not its focus or end, then other questions press in upon our evaluative process. Other than human realities emerge as hav-ing significance for themselves and for the larger realm of existence that are not reducible to the solely utilitarian value of how they benefit humans. We are compelled, in this perspective, to recognize that value and to inquire how our claims and actions impact the well-being of all those with whom we share existence, to test, as William Dean states, our claims not only before our fellow humans but before "the bar of an interpreted natural history."[43]

McFague and thinkers like Dean, thus, urge us to widen what counts as relevant data through attending to nature itself or to those humans whose knowledge exceeds that of theologians on these issues. But Sallie McFague takes her vision of our human relation to the natu-ral, material, and bodily dimensions of existence in an even more radi-cal direction. For she develops her stance not only through elaborating the implications for theology of the common creation story but by rein-terpreting and then reapplying what she takes to be a version of the Christian story to these matters. McFague argues for a portrayal of the Christian story shaped by a vision of inclusive love and a radical com-mitment to the outcast, the other, the oppressed. When this vision is brought to bear upon the question of the significance of nature for how we judge our human actions and beliefs, then more is mandated than including the nonhuman world as an element in our consideration. We are rather compelled to live and act in solidarity not only with the non-persons of the world but nature as well. In particular, because of humanity's historical misuse and mistreatment of nature, McFague sug-gests that we are currently called to prioritize its claims upon us; thus nature becomes, in this schema, the "new poor," the outcast, the vul-nerable on behalf of whose liberation we are called to struggle and with whom we are called to suffer.[44]

McFague, thus, appeals to two trajectories—contemporary scien-tific pictures of reality and her version of compelling elements within the Christian tradition—to refocus our attention on nature. Importantly, McFague also acknowledges that while these two lines of influence sup-port each other in forcing a new interest in nature, they nonetheless challenge one another, highlighting the difficulty of determining what values will shape our evaluative processes. They support each other, she claims, because the picture emerging from science includes not only an evolutionary tale of survival of the fittest and development via arbitrary chance but is, as well, a story of evolution that has now become conscious and that can contribute to the next stages of evolutionary development by means other than ruthless struggle; self-conscious concern for the other is now an evolutionary possibility. But she suggests her Christian story also stands in defiance of her common creation story, finally always siding with, as naturalist Loren Eiseley once put it, "the lost ones, the failures of the world."[45] Her Christian vision, she suggests, is in very important respects, counter-evolutionary and incompatible with the story emerging from modern science.[46]

And, finally, for McFague, this Christian set of values and commitments also outruns the more inclusive stories made possible by cultural evolution, for these always are constructed for our own benefit and do not issue forth in radical commitment to the well-being of the other.[47] Thus the Christian story is not only counterevolutionary for McFague but also countercultural, calling for solidarity with the vulnerable, even unto death. In McFague's words "Neither biological nor cultural evolution includes this radical next step of identification with the vulnerable and needy through the death of the self."[48]

McFague's position shares a good deal in common with what is being argued for in this book but also departs from it as well. First, it is not clear that there is not more room than McFague imagines in the scientific picture of reality for forms of evolution not reducible to a species-against-species version of evolution. But there are more salient points of tension to be considered. Earlier it was stated that McFague has a tendency to elevate her vision of inclusive love as normative by virtue of its association with Jesus or the Christic paradigm rather than through argumentation about its continued viability. The critical response was that for pragmatic historicists the question is not whether Jesus lived this way but whether we should. This tendency to drift toward theology by citation is further problematized when McFague now suggests that the Christian story is countercultural, that it stands over against human cultural possibilities. But what could this claim mean? Is the Christian story a unitary vision? Is it somehow not a human vision, but one that has its origins outside of the historical constraints and possibilities she has gone to such trouble to establish? Are everyone else's visions human stories but somehow the story of inclusive love comes from outside and does not share the same status? Such claims are not plausible, but even if they were, why should we follow a vision from "outside" of history?

According to the position articulated in this book McFague's way of arguing for a vision of inclusive love is misguided. The Christian story or McFague's version of that is not countercultural in the sense that it is somehow not a cultural story, developed in history and competitive with other stories and traditions that have the same human character. It may certainly challenge other interpretations of reality and ways of being, including quite dominant ones. But that fact does not remove this set of claims from their historical setting or alter their character as a human interpretation of reality. They, like all other interpretations of reality and normative visions of how we should live, are human products developed through our human historical existence within a wider natural history. The call for inclusive love is one such human possibility that has emerged among the welter of other alternatives.

For the pragmatic historicism advocated in this book both the common creation story and the story of inclusive love are equally human cultural products. They need to be assessed in terms of the reasons they offer for themselves, the roles they play and the needs they meet. Certainly the historical traditions out of which these stories emerged will proffer their own reasons for following their dictates that will be part of that assessment process. But, for those who espouse the tenets of pragmatic historicism, the claims of religious traditions, no less than other traditions, must not be defended merely by the citation of authorities or the hint that their source and character is somehow different from those of other cultural artifacts or other religious communities; these, too, must enter the realm of historical evaluation.

The pragmatic historicism argued for here has attempted to set forth reasons for widening the arena of evaluation that do not depend upon a new appeal to authority or suggestions that certain visions are countercultural and thereby noncultural. It has done so by advancing an expansive historicism that places human historicity within and as part of a wider historical context of connectedness and reciprocal dependencies. This all suggests that humanity is only part of the great cosmic process, not its only point or sole valuable element. When this is the location of human history, then it is imperative not only to ask questions concerning the possible ramifications for humans but also to inquire how the wider natural realm of which we are a part and upon which we depend is also affected by the interpretations and proposals for living that we commend. This means that while certainly humans will continue to make decisions that most likely will prioritize the human community, choosing say the value of human life over that of cancer cells, we should do so out of a far more complex sense of the interconnectedness of the world and out of the recognition that to choose one good over another is a tragic choice that entails real loss.

Finally, I would suggest that Sallie McFague offers another, much more pragmatically oriented, rationale for espousing her vision of inclusive love than what appears by saying Jesus lived this way or hinting that somehow this does not have the culture-bound character of other possibilities. And that is her suggestion that finally this vision of radical solidarity with all that exists is compelling because those who have adopted it have found it transformative and liberating. To say that our interpretations of reality are practical vehicles for helping us negotiate life does not ahead of time decide in concrete circumstances what that will mean. The best case for radical solidarity is not that Jesus proposed it but that it made possible for him and others a life worth living and commending.

While we have looked at the character of pragmatic criteria, their location, and the procedures for enacting them, it is also pertinent now to inquire whether we can say anything about their content. In a sense it is clear that the move to the public realm and the procedures of inclusion that move mandated contain values and norms already. They are not neutral or contentless. But they do not tell us in any particular moment of consideration what might give us normative direction for self-evaluation and for the conversation and negotiation among various perspectives. It is to this question that we now turn.

THE CONTENT OF PRAGMATIC NORMS

This work has proposed that an expansive historicism eventuates in pragmatism, in the sense that finally we need to evaluate and assess the validity of our claims and practices in terms of the ramifications they have for concrete lives, communities, and the natural world. Often pragmatists have been content to argue that it is only in concrete situations that these ramifications and the explicit norms for measuring them can be given content or body; while we can advocate a certain procedure to insure broad representation in our normative considerations, we are nonetheless pushed to specific moments for criteria to take shape. Two of the theologians I have designated pragmatic historicists have suggested that we can do more than that, that the kind of expansive historicism being articulated here harbors within it norms that should shape specific deliberations. As we will see, I consider both of these proposals suggestive but also problematic. They are important, however, for they raise for us, now close to the end of this work, significant questions concerning the nature of this project.

In chapter 3 it was noted that William Dean not only argued for historicism and pragmatism but that he added a third element to his analysis, that of radical empiricism. Dean's version of radical empiricism stressed that human beings not only traffick with the world through language but, as do all other living realities, encounter the world through nonlinguistic means.[49] There is a world, Dean was seen to posit, lying "beyond the linguistically-posited world," that is apprehended through feeling, through a kind of affectional sensibility. The world, so encountered, is heavy with significance and direction, but we are only aware of it from our particular locations in history, and we only sense it in the most nebulous fashion. For Dean, this version of radical empiricism keeps faith with historicism, for it asserts unequivocally that nothing that is experienced in this manner is outside of history and that this mode of awareness represents, on a nonlinguistic level, a form of interpretive process that is replicated on conscious and linguistically shaped levels of experience. Simultaneously, while not foresaking historicist insights, Dean and his fellow radical empiricists have sought to avoid a narrow linguisticism that overlooks the bodily dimensions of experience and that separates human experience from all other modes of experience.

But Dean wishes to offer more than a fuller account of experience than is set forth by most historicists. He also thinks radical empiricism suggests a way out of the dangers of subjectivism that he believes stalk historicism. On the one hand, Dean is wary of making very substantial claims for radical empiricism. This form of awareness does not yield clear or certain norms or criteria against which we can easily test our linguistic construals of reality and of humanity's place in the cosmos. Dean concurs, therefore, with other pragmatic historicists that the norms for evaluating the viability of our ideas, practices, and beliefs must finally be largely pragmatic ones and that these emerge in the midst of the historical process. Thus he asserts, with other pragmatists, that "history is both gatekeeper and judge, both stage of new variations and slaughterhouse of old ones."[50] Furthermore, as we have been maintaining in this work, the historical stage is not limited only to human history but to natural history as well.

Dean, however, is not content with only enlarging the sphere of evaluation to include the natural realm within the province of pragmatism. He is worried about how we go about making our pragmatic judgments both in relation to human history and natural history. How do we decide what counts as acceptable or as satisfactory? "On what grounds," Dean asks, "is something declared valuable or not?"[51] Many pragmatists would simply say that such decisions are the fallible efforts of historical creatures and that there are no grounds or sources beyond the ones we ourselves have devised. Dean sees in such answers the dangers of subjectivism, of mere preference. While he agrees that what counts as valuable, life enhancing, fruitful, and all the other terms pragmatists invoke is indeed delineated in historical contexts, he again proposes that this is not a full enough account of how our conceptions of value are justified. Instead he turns to radical empiricism and suggests that history, human and natural, is the bearer of both conscious and unconscious value. While we are, at best, only dimly and occasionally aware of this value, attention to this deeper context of value provides a fuller way to understand how history yields criteria, and perhaps a way to develop or at least argue for notions of what is satisfactory and valuable in less arbitrary ways.[52] That is to say, we know not only our local interests, but also, though vaguely, we are aware of the interests of broader segments of the world in which we exist.

This use of radical empiricism is a very interesting but, from the view of this work, problematic project. Even on Dean's own terms this use of radical empiricism is questionable. To begin with, Dean has thoroughly acknowledged the constructive human role in the creation of norms, ruling out any noninterpreted reception of data. He has also testified to the utter vagueness of our awareness of nonlinguistically transmitted value. It becomes difficult to see how appeal to this level of experience yields anything very concrete or how in fact it avoids the subjectivism that he fears elsewhere. Dean, himself, acknowledges as much when, in *History Making History*, he proposes that what is required is a historicist epistemology that would clarify how "history yields criteria" and how the dim, vaguely felt values referred to by radical empiricists become ingredient in our conscious forms of knowledge.[53] At this point such an epistemology still remains a future project whose repercussions for pragmatism remain unclear. I would suggest that we are not in a position to argue that the level of experience to which radical empiricism points gives us clear or usable norms by which to assess our competing conscious and linguistically formulated proposals. But even more fundamentally, to say history yields criteria, even if we could make them clear, does not solve our problems of judgment, for history yields *all* criteria, including conflicting ones. Explaining where criteria or values come from is not giving a justification (or indeed falsification) of them.

What Dean's radical empiricism does do is bolster the need to keep as wide open the arena for testing our proposals as we can and to be open to multiple voices, including the voices of bodies and material realities. That is to say, the best way to avoid subjectivism is through conversation and debate in which the widest range of input is considered. Dean's radical empiricism forces us always to be aware in our deliberations that we are more than conscious minds and that we must attend to such wider arenas of concern in our search for adequate ways of thinking and acting. Dean's position also reminds us that our judgments, though made in the present, are shaped by what we inherit; when we evaluate our claims pragmatically we ask not only what something might mean now but what it has meant, its role in history. To fail to do so is to court myopia, a historical shortsightedness. What Dean's position does not provide, however, is a way beyond the fallibility and partiality of the evaluative process and the values that shape it in any given moment.

Gordon Kaufman has recently proffered his own suggestion for filling out the content of pragmatic criteria. In the past Kaufman has argued that our norms are primarily pragmatic in nature but he has limited his proposals about the content of these norms to general claims that theological systems and religious worldviews have as their overarching concern humanization, the support and nurture of what we take to be the best possibilities for human becoming and development. The concrete content of humanization was always an open question for Kaufman to be decided upon in specific historical contexts. In his recent work, *In Face of Mystery*, Kaufman has sought to flesh out more fully the meaning of humanization and he does so by excavating what he understands to be the nature of historicity.[54]

Kaufman carries out this task by setting forth not only what he takes to be a description of the features of historicity but also what he proposes are the normative dimensions that can be discovered in historicity itself. Kaufman develops his notion of historicity in two connected ways. On one level he seeks to make general descriptive claims that accurately fit and account for all human ways of becoming; hence he traces a general movement from the biological to the biohistorical to the historical to multiple ways of being historical, that is, cultural. A major advantage of this descriptive key is that it accounts for the diverse ways in which human existence has fashioned itself.

But Kaufman also maintains that when human historicity is fully explicated it is seen to have a normative import: historicity entails a normative impulse, it is a moral enterprise. Kaufman articulates a detailed argument concerning the nature of action as implicitly moral in nature to sustain his position. But, in sum, he contends that humans are creatures who, through the advent of consciousness, are now capable of contributing to the maintenance and furtherance of the cosmic evolutionary process from which human life came forth and of responsible human life within that cosmic context. It is precisely this capacity for self-directing action that is at the heart of human historicity. Moreover, such historicity is only sustained and enhanced by its continued exercise in responsible freedom. Thus to begin with the notion of humans as historical beings leads Kaufman to a normative vision of humans as profoundly moral agents who, in order to maintain such historicity, must continually protect and enlarge their capacity for responsible and free action.[55]

Thus when historicity is excavated it yields norms that can be used to assess systems and behaviors both within cultural traditions and across them. Such norms, Kaufman suggests, relate to the exercise of historicity now interpreted in terms of responsible agency. Moreover, this agency can be seen to require a range of conditions, including a high level of self-awareness, the presence of alternatives, the capacity to control one's body and environment, and the resources of a rich symbolic and linguistic tradition.

Kaufman acknowledges that the notion of historicity, both as descriptive and normative, is historical itself and that it has emerged from within the western context and reflects especially the forms of life of certain individuals and groups within that context. And he knows that this presents particular dangers. He attempts to mitigate these dangers by being open about the origins of these ideas, by arguing that all humans have crossed the threshold of basic historicity, by contending that there is not a singular way responsible historicity can be deployed, and finally by calling for conversation about alternative notions that would modify or challenge his own.[56]

While these caveats are admirable, problems remain. The concern is not that Kaufman offers a normative picture that has particular, western origins and that inevitably this vision challenges other interpretations; all theoretical portrayals of reality are located within histories and all raise questions concerning alternatives. The western origins of Kaufman's ideas should no more rule them out than any other origins. The difficulty arises in that Kaufman appears to make a rather ahistorical appeal to the intrinsic nature of historicity and, in the process, privileges a particular development of that historicity over others. Thus, under the guise of unpacking historicity itself Kaufman elevates human history over natural history, the agential mind over a supposedly more passive body, and a view of human fulfillment predicated upon agency and conscious control.

The position argued for in this book is that Kaufman has foreshortened the debate about the direction human historicity should pursue. Kaufman's proposal is not an elucidation of the normative elements inherent in historicity itself but one assessment of the multiple concrete and possible directions historicity has developed and might unfold in the future. This particular rendition of the western version of historicity would then be required to make its case, as would all others, not by appeal to the intrinsic nature of historicity itself but according to the canons of pragmatic adjudication of what sort of life this normative vision entails in comparison with others. To see Kaufman's proposal as one possible direction for historicity to take leaves open the possibility that there are other, perhaps equally or more valid forms that historicity might take even in the West. Kaufman's formal and apriori collapse of the descriptive and the normative cut short precisely the fuller inquiry most of his position mandates, leaving us, for all its caveats, with the uneasy sense that here, in this particular strand of human history, free and responsible agency or at least the conditions for it have found their fullest manifestation. While all other humans have crossed some threshold and hence qualify as human, there lingers unmistakably the implication that somehow the vast rest of humanity has yet to enter the fullness of human existence. That may be a historical conclusion to be reached through analysis and debate, but it should not be one rendered by definition that leaves out alternatives from the start.

If these questions can be posed of Kaufman, it must also be asked whether the normative thrust of this text's proposals concerning expansive historicism do not evidence the same covert importation of particular, especially western, values of democracy, open and critical inquiry, and so on, under the guise of unpacking the procedural implications of an expansive historicism. There is a sense in which this is the case; no description, even the most self-critical and open ended, is without normative implications. These are hypotheses whose attendant values are to be continually uncovered and scrutinized. Yet at the same time I think they have a different character than do Kaufman's proposals. The values inherent in the pragmatic procedures espoused above leave a great deal open; they flow from our lack of certitude about any universal norms and therefore they attempt to safeguard the place of negotiation and debate. They embody a great sense of fallibilism and therefore the conviction that we should create procedures that proliferate proposals rather than rule them out before the conversation takes place. Moreover, it is freely acknowledged that these proposals are themselves fallible suggestions about how to proceed and what direction historicity might take; it is never asserted or assumed that they, rather than other positions, are the only possibilities to be inferred from the nature of historicity. In this view Kaufman's proposals become one possible way historicity might fashion itself, not the one way mandated by historicity itself. They, too, would have to contend in specific circumstances and concrete debate for their validity.

The analysis of Dean's and Kaufman's attempts to fill in the blanks of a pragmatist's view of truth and validity suggests that in fact we are left with multiple proposals that can only be assessed by virtue of norms hammered out in concrete circumstances for particular purposes. For many people this will appear to leave us with precious little and will not meet the urge for directionality and certitude concerning what is the best or most humane or what most enhances our historicity. What this book has urged is not a content given ahead of time that answers those questions but instead a procedural pragmatism that seeks to ensure that as many voices as are relevant and possible are part of the process of framing the questions, setting forth alternatives, and assessing them. To wish for norms that will apply everywhere or have the same basic content is finally to hope for an escape from the historical task of asking what it means to believe this or that, to live in this manner or that one, and then deciding with our fellow humans and in light of the claims of the nonhuman world what we will venture and what we will not. Pragmatic historicism calls us to embrace that historical task, engaging in the construction of truth for our times, open always to the emergent possibilities that are both our judge and our hope for the future.

In all this the notion of truth has a dual role. On the one hand it points to those claims that in any moment we take to be warranted, that are defensible in light of what we know at the moment and are the result of open and free encounters with all relevant participants. These truths are fragile and fallible, often plural, the outcomes of our varied attempts to achieve a consensus about what is best in a given circumstance. Pragmatic historicism calls us to forego the notions of timeless or absolute truth and to accept the seemingly oxymoronic claim of fallible and frequently multiple truths upon which we are nonetheless willing to stake our lives.

But invoking the notion of truth also serves for pragmatic historicists a critical function, indicating that our present claims are always temporary, never achieve perfect or fully just consensus, and are always open to revision, criticism, and replacement. Thus Richard Rorty refers to the difference between truth and justification as the distinction between the good we have and the better that might be achieved at some future moment.[57] Gordon Kaufman asserts that truths are not only plural and contingent but emergent, the continually changing product of a dynamic and open historical process.[58] And Linell Cady appeals to a regulative notion of truth as that which is the product of an ideal social consensus; such an ideal consensus is never achieved in reality but precisely as an ideal it critically calls our present efforts into question and elicits from us a commitment to pursue more just and adequate interpretations and practices.[59]

Pragmatic historicism leaves us, then, not with a new means to achieve certitude or even with a clear calculus by which we might, in every circumstance, measure our human efforts. It leaves us rather with the hard task of venturing claims and practices, testing them, and continually revising them in light of the forms of life they make possible. Our truths will always be fallible truths but they are, nonetheless, ones by which we can and do live meaningful lives.

Pragmatic historicism also leaves us with concrete problems to solve and real dilemmas to address. Much of this book has been concerned with methodological and procedural issues. In this sense, it only points to a particular kind of substantive theology that it does not itself deliver. But as these methodological and procedural issues have been played out it has become clear that much more than method is at stake. Procedurally pragmatic historicism was seen to commit itself to broad and inclusive deliberations. But to do so has also entailed inquiring about who and what are currently left out of much theological consideration. And when we asked that question several areas came to the fore as demanding urgent response on the part of a theology whose task is the creation of visions of reality that can contribute to the nurture of historical existence. Thus, through our procedural interrogation, issues concerning the acute condition of the earth and of those who suffer in poverty and oppression and of a pluralistic world in which religious difference is interpreted not as a resource but a cause for violence and hate all presented themselves to us as concerns to which pragmatic historicism must attend if it is to be efficacious in our world.

This process also brings us full circle again, back once more to the inheritance bequeathed us by our traditions. If our task is to respond to the needs of our day, the identification of those problems also guides us as we face that vast panorama that makes up our past and as we seek the resources to confront the challenges of the era. As this book has argued, our historical traditions do not come to us in neat packages, with clearly marked essences; they come to us as multiple and contending conglomerations. It is we who must decide what should be extended, as Cady puts it, what must be jettisoned or opposed or transformed. And it is we who must, in light of the urgent dilemmas we seek to redress, and our hopes for an imagined future, discern possibilities for novel resources both in and at the juncture of traditions.

There will surely be different answers about what should be extended and what new possibilities should be ventured. Theologians working primarily within Christianity might, for example, appropriate and reconstruct ideas of creation as the body of God in light of the ecological crisis or of God as Sophia in response to feminists or of a Christ no longer tied to Jesus in an exclusive manner given the radical religious pluralism of our world. Other traditions will radically reconstruct their own heritage. And the bold advocates of syncretism will intermingle multiple pasts as they create new traditions.

In all these modes, pragmatic, historicist theologians, whether committed participants in or interested reflectors upon particular traditions, will self-consciously and unapologetically contribute to the reconstruction and, for some, forging of novel networks of belief and practice we have called religions. Not only analysis of traditions is called for; the theological task demands substantive and concrete proposals for belief and practice today. And it requires, as we have been contending, that we articulate these proposals both within traditions but also in conversation, argument, and negotiation with those with whom we share our social and natural world. It is by such internal and external processes that we are best equipped to measure our contribution to the fabric of historical existence and to our fragile hopes for the future.[60]

TRAGEDY AND HOPE

This work has sought to trace historicist sensibilities as they have come to be articulated within and have an impact upon theology. It has done so by first exploring two major theological options currently on the scene, postliberalism and revisionism, and arguing that for all of their promise as historicist forms of theology, they nonetheless are problematic at very important junctures. The major intention of the book has been to contend that there is emerging another historicist trajectory that is suggestive of a different direction—pragmatic historicism—that theology might pursue. The major effort of this volume has been to set forth pragmatic historicism, to examine its presuppositions and detail its parameters.

Pragmatic historicism is a theological perspective that has emerged at a very particular juncture in history. We are in a historical moment when many of the traditional resources for interpreting life, deciding what was good or true, sensing our place in the universe, determining what should claim our human loyalty have been seriously undermined. For some this situation points to a nihilism that foregoes all judgment; for others a confessional isolationism that seeks a new certainty in the return to the past; and for still others the search for new universals. Pragmatic historicism finds in this moment another direction to pursue. Pragmatic historicism, in linking an expansive historicism with pragmatism, has sought to return us to the messiness of history, to the task of taking responsibility for how we use our complex, rich, and ever so ambivalent inheritances and to the possibility that out of encounter with others we may determine new options not yet imagined. All our theological efforts, like all other human efforts, will be fallible and limited; they will not gain us a new certitude, promise of moral rightness, or guarantee of positive outcomes. They will, without doubt, be criticized and left behind by some future generation.

This pragmatic historicists' picture of historical existence and of the theologian's role within it is, I would suggest, both tragic and hopeful in character. The original American pragmatists were often accused of being overly optimistic about human historical possibilities. They exhibited an American can-do spirit contending that humans should identify their concrete problems and then set about finding ways to solve these problems. There certainly was some of that spirit in thinkers such as Dewey but as Sidney Hook argued in a famous article, "Pragmatism and the Tragic Sense of Life," there was also a profound sense of the fallibility and limitation of historical existence in pragmatism.[61] I believe pragmatic historicism, as a theological perspective, shares that tragic sense.

As Hook points out, tragedy is not just the triumph of evil over good or the inability for the good and true to triumph in a final sense; it is also the necessity of continually choosing some goods over others, actualizing some values at the cost of denying or postponing other things of worth. In this sense, pragmatic historicism—both as an historicism and as a pragmatism—is in part a tragic perspective.

As a historicism, the position developed in this volume concedes that the options concretely offered up by history are never as inclusive as they could be. History grants to each people and place the option of addressing some dilemmas, but not others. The decisions made by earlier communities result in some possibilities while closing off others for those that come later. The limitations of mind and imagination, of heart and conscience, of physical ability and natural resources all contribute to the limited possibilities that are available in any concrete historical moment, giving us options but constricting them as well. Future generations will certainly wonder, as we have done concerning our forebears, whether we could have done better. And of course we always could have to some degree. But a tragic historicism knows that while history is open and malleable it can also be stingy.

As a pragmatism, too, this position acknowledges tragedy, the tragedy of possibilities given but not given simultaneously. We are presented with goods, genuine goods, but we must choose among them. We know that we frequently excuse our neglect of some values over others by saying that they are mutually exclusive. But it is also the case that in every circumstance we are, in fact, confronted with the need to choose among goods and values and possibilities. We address one group's needs and allow another group to suffer, we solve one set of problems and leave another to fester, we affirm one complex of values and let others languish—truly, because we must if we are to address any needs at all, solve any problems at all, affirm any values at all. Pragmatism means that we must choose and in choosing evaluate our options according to their consequences. But, almost always, in choosing to actualize some possibilities we choose to sacrifice others that also make a rightful claim upon us, that portend benefits of their own deserving of realization. If history can be stingy, it can also be cruel.

But these lamentations must also be accompanied by a sense of hope, even joy. History does not present at any one time all the options that are imaginatively relevant, but it does present us with options, possibilities that are real goods to be embraced and pursued. If the historical process does not yield carefully calibrated goods, capable of mutual and simultaneous realization, it does offer us possibilities that can enrich and liberate, rescue and sustain. Moreover, it is a gift of our subjectivity that we can imagine ideals, new possibilities, new ways of interacting, and new, heretofore never considered, values to be pursued and in light of which we might live better lives. Much is certainly denied us, both by the constraints of history and by our own failures. And both our losses and our failures are reason to grieve. But such tragedy should not diminish our joy in the possibilities that do come into view, that are realizable, that are realized. Nor should it lessen our commitment to widen the arena of possibilities for ourselves and for others.

Pragmatic historicism, thus, is a hard doctrine. It calls us to choose without perfect choices, to justify them when finality is impossible, in terms of consequences that are never fully clear. But it is an appreciative doctrine, for it acknowledges that our power to choose comes from resources that we have been given by all that proceeds us. It is a positive doctrine, for it continually affirms the margin of creativity that we do have. It is a hopeful doctrine for it wagers on, not a promise of victory in or beyond history, but history's openness and generosity. Yet it is a modest doctrine, for it realizes that it too will be superseded some day. And, finally, it is a responsible doctrine, for it holds that we are in part creators of the future and it calls us to create that future with care.

NOTES

CHAPTER 1. HISTORIES AND CONTEXTS

1. David Tracy, *Plurality and Ambiguity: Hermeneutics, Religion, Hope* (San Francisco: Harper & Row, 1987), 67. For background on the development of various senses of historicity, see Georg G. Iggers, *The German Conception of History: The National Tradition of Historical Thought from Herder to the Present* (Middletown, Conn.: Wesleyan University Press, 1983); Georg G. Iggers, "Historicism," in *The Dictionary of the History of Ideas*, ed. Philip P. Wiener (New York: Scribner, 1973–74); Van A. Harvey, *The Historian and the Believer: The Morality of Historical Knowledge and Christian Belief* (New York: Macmillan, 1966). For recent developments in other fields, see *The New Historicism*, ed. H. Aram Vesser (New York: Routledge, 1989); *The New Historicism Reader*, ed. H. Aram Vesser (New York: Routledge, 1994); and *New Historicism and Cultural Materialism: A Reader*, ed. Kiernan Ryan (London: Arnold, 1996).

2. I am grateful to Meredith Underwood, a student in the University of Denver–Iliff School of Theology Ph.D. program, for pointing out the ways current language about "interruptions" in and "the fissures" of history can obscure the fact that the horrors of history have historical causes that we need to trace and for which we must be accountable.

3. Peter Novick, *That Noble Dream: The "Objectivity Question" and the American Historical Profession* (Cambridge: Cambridge University Press, 1988), 16.

4. There is a sense in which this analysis stands over against the position articulated by William Dean, a theologian who plays a significant role in the rest of this volume. Dean has gone to great effort to recover the American philosophical and theological traditions that preceded contemporary historicism and pragmatism but that have so often been ignored by present-day theologians and philosophers. I applaud such an effort, but Dean also tends to ignore Continental developments that have also funded today's historicism. This work argues that our heritage is more pluralistic and complex than Dean's analysis suggests. See William Dean, *History Making History: The New Historicism in American Religious Thought* (Albany: State University of New York Press, 1988), esp. chs. 2, 3.

5. For a variety of explorations of the rise of modernity see Susan Bordo, *The Flight to Objectivity: Essays on Cartesianism and Culture* (Albany: State University of New York Press, 1987); Jeffrey Stout, *Flight from Authority: Religion, Morality and the Quest for Autonomy* (Notre Dame: University of Notre

Dame Press, 1981); and Stephen Toulmin, *Cosmopolis: The Hidden Agenda of Modernity* (New York: Free Press, 1990).

6. Donald N. Levine, *The Flight from Ambiguity: Essays in Social and Cultural Theory* (Chicago: University of Chicago Press, 1985), 3.

7. Wayne Proudfoot, *Religious Experience* (Berkeley: University of California Press, 1985), 3ff.

8. Ibid., 199ff.

9. See J. Samuel Preus: *Explaining Religion: Criticism and Theory from Bodin to Freud* (New Haven: Yale University Press, 1987) for a history of the rise of naturalistic interpretations of religion.

10. It would be inaccurate to identify the assertion that religion escaped the explanatory gaze of human inquiry only with theologians and the stance that religion was open to critical analysis with nontheologians. Nonetheless, these differing trajectories set in motion developments that continue to vex us today, including the issue of whether theology is part of the study of religion or a confessional alternative and whether one can be a theologian or even a student of religion as a nonbeliever or again whether explanations of religious beliefs or practices have to be acceptable to their adherents. Theology especially has had to struggle with this legacy as it has sought to establish itself as a legitimate discipline in the academy. And, as we will see, one of the prominent theological responses on the contemporary scene has been for theologians to distance themselves from the Schleiermachian solution and to introduce interpretations of religion that locate religion as a cultural phenomenon in such a way as to bring theology and other aspects of the study of religion in closer relation. For a helpful rereading of the development of the sciences of religion and their relation to theology, see *Religion in the Making: The Emergence of the Sciences of Religion*, ed. Arie L. Molendijk and Peter Pels (Leiden: Brill, 1998).

11. Thelma Lavine, "The Case for a New American Pragmatism," *Free Inquiry* 11.3 (Summer 1991): 46.

12. Shirley Jackson Case, "Wither Historicism in Theology," *The Process of Religions: Essays in Honor of Dean Shailer Mathews*, ed. M. H. Krumbine (New York: Macmillan, 1933), 68.

13. Ibid., 67.

14. It might well be pointed out that for all this talk about the plural character of modernity, that this is still primarily a western project (though one with widespread effects). This is certainly the case and an important issue that will emerge as this work unfolds concerns what happens to theology when our traditions are not only internally pluralistic but when we stand at the crossroads of multiple traditions.

15. See Cornel West, *The American Evasion of Philosophy: A Genealogy of Pragmatism* (Madison: University of Wisconsin Press, 1989).

16. See Robert Cummings Neville, *The Highroad around Modernism* (Albany: State University of New York Press, 1992) for the argument that postmodernisms that treat modernity as more or less identified with the Enlightenment are historically inaccurate and fail to note that the American philosophical and theological traditions offered historicist alternatives. Hence, for Neville to repudiate the Enlightenment agenda is decidedly *not* to reject all of modernity.

17. Peter C. Hodgson, *Revisioning the Church: Ecclesial Freedom in the New Paradigm* (Philadelphia: Westminster Press, 1988), 13.

18. See Gordon D. Kaufman, *Theology for a Nuclear Age* (Philadelphia: Westminster Press, 1985); and Sallie McFague, *The Body of God: An Ecological Theology* (Minneapolis: Augsburg Fortress, 1994).

19. See Langdon Gilkey, *Society and the Sacred: Toward a Theology of Culture in Decline* (New York: The Crossroad Publishing Company, 1981); and Hodgson, *Revisioning the Church*.

20. This book is arguing that a sense of historicity is widespread. There are, however, forms of postmodernism that while sharing the sense of contingency, particularity, and relativity stressed by the historicim developed in this volume also exhibit a rather ahistorical bent and a cavalier indifference to how the past shapes the present. This work insists both that the past—in all its contentious multiplicity—affects the present and that it is important for us to trace the intricate legacies we have inherited. Moreover, as this book will argue, to do so in no way assumes a naive sense of historical uniformity or continuity but insists on real but complex relations between past and present and among the multiple factors that constitute the present. For an important work tracing the "non free-floating" character of postmodernism, see David Harvey, *The Condition of Postmodernity* (Oxford: Blackwell Publishers, 1989).

CHAPTER 2. THEOLOGICAL ROADS NOT TAKEN

1. There are other theological approaches that might also have claimed attention here. One such perspective is deconstructionism as it has been articulated most fully by Mark C. Taylor. Taylor has argued that the central and unifying ideas of western thought—God, self, history, and the Book—have all become suspect. Each is part of the "ontotheological" tradition that fails to acknowledge the contingency, arbitrariness, and particularity (irreducible otherness) of finite existence. As such, Taylor's position embodies a rejection, especially, of the ahistorical assumptions of Enlightenment modernity, as well as a resistance to the pseudo, or at least truncated historicism of Hegel. Nonetheless, this orientation also exhibits a definite ahistorical bent of its own, a failure of historicist nerve that leaves its proponents outside the fray of concrete, temporal, truly ambiguous history. Deconstructionism places enormous weight on the constructive and seemingly agential character of the historicized subject, with little attention to how that subject is constituted by relations with others. The social, political and economic conditions that constitute subjects are rarely analyzed while personal and psychological processes are focused upon. Moreover, how past history shapes and influences subjectivity undergoes little analysis. And finally, while otherness is often referred to, that other seems most often to be the other "within," the alien within ourselves and not the other—live and concrete—who challenges us as different by virtue of gender, race, religion, culture, or class. See Mark C. Taylor, *Erring: A Postmodern A/Theology* (Chicago: University of Chicago Press, 1984); and *Altarity* (Chicago: University of Chicago Press, 1987).

2. George A. Lindbeck, *The Nature of Doctrine: Religion and Theology in a Postliberal Age* (Philadelphia: The Westminster Press, 1984). *The Nature of Doctrine* has been the most influential statement of Lindbeck's position and will hence receive the most attention in this work. See also "Scripture, Consensus, and Community," in *Biblical Interpretation in Crisis: The Ratzinger Conference on Bible and Church*, ed. Richard John Neuhaus (Grand Rapids, Mich.: William B. Eerdmans Publishing Company, 1989), 74–101; "The Story-Shaped Church: Critical Exegesis and Theological Interpretation," in *Scriptural Authority and Narrative Interpretation*, ed. Garrett Green (Philadelphia: Fortress Press, 1987), 161–78; and "The Church's Mission to a Postmodern Culture," in *Postmodern Theology: Christian Faith in a Pluralistic World*, ed. Frederick B. Burnham (New York: Harper & Row, 1989), 37–55. For a series of articles from a variety of perspectives on Lindbeck see *Modern Theology* 4.2 (October 1987) and *Theology and Dialogue: Essays in Conversation with George Lindbeck*, ed. Bruce D. Marshall (Notre Dame, Ind.: University of Notre Dame Press, 1990).

3. Lindbeck, *The Nature of Doctrine*, 21.

4. Ibid., 38.

5. Lindbeck, "Scripture, Consensus, and Community," 94. Also see *The Nature of Doctrine*, 34.

6. Ibid., esp. ch. 2.

7. Ibid., 32f.

8. Ibid., 35.

9. Ibid., 37.

10. Ibid., 83.

11. Ibid., 81.

12. Ibid., 35.

13. Ibid., 80.

14. Lindbeck, "Scripture, Consensus, and Community," 75. Lindbeck not only argues that Christianity is centered by the Bible and that the Bible, to be scripture and not just a collection of texts, must be read Christologically and through a Trinitarian hermeneutic. He also asserts that it is best read as a narrative of God and God's people rather than as a historical account or mythological expression of timeless truth or the depiction of religious experience. Thus his theory, when played out in relation to Christianity, combines a view of Christianity focused on the Bible, understood as narrative, and interpreted through a Christological and Trinitarian unifying hermeneutic. For essays that follow Lindbeck's lead concerning a Trinitarian hermeneutic, see *Reclaiming the Bible for the Church*, ed. Carl E. Braaten and Robert W. Jenson (Grand Rapids, Mich.: William B. Eerdmans Publishing Company, 1995).

15. Lindbeck, *The Nature of Doctrine*, 113ff.

16. Ibid., 118.

17. Ibid., 94.

18. Ibid., 83. See also, "Scripture, Consensus, and Community," 88f. for how these directives provide unity and the means for dealing with communal conflict.

19. Lindbeck, *The Nature of Doctrine*, 62.

20. Ibid., 79.

21. Ibid.

22. Ibid., 100. Lindbeck's orientation toward the "orthodox" and "ecumenical" derive from his deep concern for communities that can sustain identity and provide direction in life and for the unity he believes is required for the flourishing of these communities. See "Scripture, Consensus, and Community," 90f.

23. Lindbeck, *The Nature of Doctrine*, 51.

24. Ibid.

25. Ibid., 41.

26. Ibid.

27. William Werpekowski, "Ad Hoc Apologetics," *Journal of Religion* 66 (1986): 282–301; and William C. Placher, *Unapologetic Theology* (Louisville, Ky.: Westminster/John Knox Press, 1984), esp. ch. 7.

28. Delwin Brown, *Boundaries of Our Habitations: Tradition and Theological Construction* (Albany: State University of New York Press, 1994), 125. Kathryn Tanner, once closely identified with postliberalism, has also questioned the stability of Lindbeck's rules: "They are susceptible to change in the historical course of decisions by the human actors involved. Appeal to communal norms will not guarantee, then, as postliberals want it to, stability underneath the changing forms of history." See Tanner, *Theories of Culture: A New Agenda for Theology* (Minneapolis: Fortress Press, 1997), 141. William C. Placher, for his part, stresses the dynamic and diverse character of the "core" of Christianity. See Placher, "Gospels' Ends: Plurality and Ambiguity in Biblical Narratives," *Modern Theology* 10.2 (April 1994): 143–63.

29. Lindbeck, *The Nature of Doctrine*, 83. Lindbeck seems to think that as the world of the reader is absorbed into the world of the Christian story the former is changed while the latter remains intact, at least in its essentials. Thus, he can state that "Platonism and Aristotelianism . . . were assimilated into the scriptural framework and thus Christianized" without assuming that Christianity was significantly "Platonized" or remade or significantly altered by its interaction with Aristotelian thought. Lindbeck, "Scripture, Consensus, and Community," 86.

30. Linell E. Cady, *Religion, Theology, and American Public Life* (Albany: State University of New York Press, 1993), 49.

31. The analysis in this chapter will focus primarily upon Tracy's *The Analogical Imagination: Christian Theology and the Culture of Pluralism* (New York: Crossroad, 1981); and *Plurality and Ambiguity: Hermeneutics, Religion, Hope* (San Francisco: Harper & Row, 1987).

32. Tracy, *Plurality and Ambiguity*, 28–29.

33. See especially, Tracy, *The Analogical Imagination*, 99–154.

34. Ibid., 154; and Tracy, *Plurality and Ambiguity*, 12, 14.

35. Tracy, *The Analogical Imagination*, 110.

36. Ibid., 157–58.

37. Ibid., 163.

38. Ibid., 99.

39. Ibid., 177.

40. Ibid., esp. ch. 3.

41. Ibid., 115, 362.

42. Tracy, *Plurality and Ambiguity*, 36f.

43. Ibid., 36.

44. Ibid., 36–37.

45. Ibid., 104.

46. Ibid., 96.

47. Richard Bernstein, "Radical Plurality, Fearful Ambiguity, and Engaged Hope," *Journal of Religion* 69 (January 1989): 82.

48. Tracy, *Plurality and Ambiguity*, 27, 81.

49. David Tracy, "Lindbeck and the New Program for Theology: A Reflection," *The Thomist* 49 (1985): 470.

50. Tracy, *Plurality and Ambiguity*, 29.

CHAPTER 3. HISTORICISM AND HUMAN WORLDVIEWS

1. While I have designated the theologians to be explored in this work as pragmatic historicists, they have, heretofore, been given or have given themselves other designations. Hence, Gordon Kaufman is known as a constructivist, William Dean a new historicist, Delwin Brown a constructive historicist; Sallie McFague has been called a revisionist and has recently seemed even to forsake the use of history as a central interpretive category. She is included under the rubric of pragmatic historicism because: (a) she fits well with the expansive historicism advocated for here; (b) she is very much an historicist in her conception of theology as metaphorical; and (c) her exploration of normative judgment is centrally, if not totally, pragmatic in character. See note 30 for further discussion of McFague's misgivings about history.

2. For discussions for and against theory, see W. J. T. Mitchell, ed., *Against Theory: Literary Studies and the New Pragmatism* (Chicago: University of Chicago Press, 1985); and Jonathan Arac and Barbara Johnson, eds., *Consequences of Theory* (Baltimore: Johns Hopkins University Press, 1991).

3. See Mark C. Taylor, *Erring: A Postmodern A/Theology* (Chicago: University of Chicago Press, 1984); *Deconstructing Theology* (New York: Crossroad Publishing Co., 1982); and *Altarity* (Chicago: University of Chicago Press, 1987).

4. See Sidney Hook, *Metaphysics of Pragmatism* (Amherst, N.Y.: Prometheus Books, 1997 [1927]) for an early defense of a historicized metaphysics and its relation to pragmatic commitments. Hook asserts that without a particular view of the world it is impossible to respond to the problems that confront an era and that, therefore, pragmatism requires *some* working interpretation of reality.

5. Frank Lentricchia, *Criticism and Social Change* (Chicago: University of Chicago Press, 1983), 12.

6. Alasdair MacIntyre, *Whose Justice? Which Rationality?* (Notre Dame, Ind.: University of Notre Dame Press, 1988), 7. Gordon Kaufman asserts that "[q]uestions about the fundamental meaning and usefulness of the principal categories of a world-view do not arise when those categories are working prop-

erly, that is when they succeed in organizing experience and life into a relatively intelligible whole." When these begin to "crack apart," we have, Kaufman suggests, two choices: retrenchment or critical reconstruction. See "Mystery, Critical Consciousness, and Faith," in *The Rationality of Religious Belief: Essays in Honor of Basil Mitchell*, ed. William J. Abraham and Steven W. Holtzer (Oxford: Clarendon Press, 1987), 59–60.

7. Gordon D. Kaufman, *The Theological Imagination: Constructing the Concept of God* (Philadelphia: The Westminster Press, 1981), 14.

8. Sallie McFague, *Models of God: Theology for an Ecological, Nuclear Age* (Philadelphia: Fortress Press, 1987), 14.

9. Giles Gunn, *Thinking across the American Grain: Ideology, Intellect, and the New Pragmatism* (Chicago: The University of Chicago Press, 1992), 70.

10. Ibid., 38.

11. Francis Schüssler Fiorenza, "The Crisis of Hermeneutics and Christian Theology," in *Theology at the End of Modernity*, ed. Sheila Greeve Davaney (Philadelphia: Trinity Press International, 1991), 117–140.

12. Jeffrey Stout, *Ethics after Babel: The Languages of Morals and Their Discontents* (Boston: Beacon Press, 1988), 178.

13. For examples of thinkers of the early Chicago School of Theology who espoused a conversation between theology and the sciences, both natural and social, see (especially) Gerald Birney Smith, "Theology and Scientific Method," *The Biblical World* 39 (1912): 236–47; "Theology and the Doctrine of Evolution," *The Biblical World* 45 (1915): 37–44; and "Some Conditions to Be Observed in the Attempt to Correlate Science and Religion," *Religious Education* 23 (1928): 304–10. Also see Shalier Mathews, *The Social Teachings of Jesus* (New York: Hodder and Stoughton, 1897); and Henry Nelson Wieman, *Religious Experience and the Scientific Method* (New York: Macmillan, 1926). For an account of the Chicago School, see Delwin Brown, "The Fall of '26: Gerald Birney Smith and the Collapse of Socio-Historical Theology," *American Journal of Theology and Philosophy* 11.3 (September 1990): 183–201; William Dean, *History Making History: The New Historicism in American Religious Thought* (Albany: State University of New York Press, 1988), ch. 3. For more readings from the Chicago School, see *The Chicago School of Theology: Pioneers in Religious Inquiry*, 2 vols., ed. W. Creighton Peden and Jerome A. Stone (Lewiston: N.Y.: The Edwin Mellen Press, 1996).

14. Thomas Kuhn, *The Structure of Scientific Revolutions* (Chicago: The University of Chicago Press, 1962); and Paul Feyerabend, *Against Method: Outline of an Anarchistic Theory of Knowledge* (London: Verso, 1984); Stephen Toulmin, *The Return of Cosmology: Postmodern Science and the Theology of Nature* (Berkeley: University of California Press, 1982); Sandra Harding, *Whose Science? Whose Knowledge? Thinking from Women's Lives* (Ithaca, N.Y.: Cornell University Press, 1991); and Helen E. Longino, *Science as Social Knowledge: Values and Objectivity in Scientific Inquiry* (Princeton: Princeton University Press, 1990).

15. James M. Gustafson, "Theological Anthropology and the Human Sciences," in *Theology at the End of Modernity*, ed. Sheila Greeve Davaney (Philadelphia: Trinity Press International, 1991), 69.

16. Gordon D. Kaufman, *In Face of Mystery: A Constructive Theology* (Cambridge, Mass.: Harvard University Press, 1993), chs. 17, 6.

17. William Dean, "Humanistic Historicism and Naturalistic Historicism," in *Theology at the End of Modernity*, ed. Sheila Greeve Davaney (Philadelphia: Trinity Press International, 1991), 41–59.

18. Sallie McFague, "An Earthly Theological Agenda," *Christian Century* 108 (January 2–9, 1991): 12.

19. See Richard Rorty, "Solidarity or Objectivity?" in *Post-Analytic Philosophy*, ed. John Rajchman and Cornel West (New York: Columbia University Press, 1985), 12.

20. Clifford Geertz, "The Uses of Diversity," *Michigan Quarterly Review* 25.25 (Winter 1986): 117.

21. Ibid., 118.

22. Ibid., 119. It is important to note that while they resonate with Geertz's rejection of cultural incommensurability and his insistence that different cultures, for all their particularity, can enrich one another, pragmatic historicists do not necessarily agree with other Geertzian anthropological theories. While Kaufman borrows heavily from Geertz, Delwin Brown is much more attuned to post-Geertzian anthropology such as that of James Clifford. See Brown, *Boundaries of Our Habitations: Tradition and Theological Construction* (Albany: State University of New York Press, 1994), esp. ch. 3.

23. Cornel West, *The American Evasion of Philosophy: A Genealogy of Pragmatism* (Madison: The University of Wisconsin Press, 1989), 207.

24. Kaufman, *In Face of Mystery*, 6.

25. Sallie McFague, *The Body of God: An Ecological Theology* (Minneapolis: Fortress Press, 1993), 26.

26. For McFague's version of the "Common Creation Story," see the following: *The Body of God: An Ecological Theology*, esp. ch. 2; and "Cosmology and Christianity: Implications of the Common Creation Story for Theology," in *Theology at the End of Modernity*, ed. Sheila Greeve Davaney (Philadelphia: Trinity Press International, 1991), 19–40. As McFague herself notes, much of this construal of the world, and of the human in it, was anticipated by earlier process philosophy and theology.

27. McFague, "Cosmology and Christianity," 25.

28. Ibid., 31.

29. Ibid., 29.

30. Ibid., 32. This strong sense of the common connections between human reality and all other creaturely existence has even led McFague to suggest history is not the best entree into a contemporary interpretation of human existence. Instead, we should focus upon bodies, space, and material existence. This work suggests that historicity and embodiedness cannot be separated and that what is required is not a focus upon nature and bodies rather than history, but an embodied materialist historicity and a historized naturalism. McFague, in fact, provides us such an interpretation despite her cautions about history and therefore has been included as a pivotal historicist in this work. For McFague's misgivings about a focus upon history, see *The Body of God*, 99ff.

31. For William Dean's arguments, see *History Making History: The New Historicism in American Religious Thought*, esp. ch. 6; and "Humanistic Historicism and Naturalistic Historicism," 41–59.

32. William Dean, *American Religious Empiricism* (Albany: State University of New York Press, 1986), 51.

33. Ibid., 52. See also William Dean, *The Religious Critic in American Culture* (Albany: State University of New York Press, 1994), ch. 7.

34. Dean, "Humanistic Historicism," 42, 45.

35. Dean, *American Religious Empiricism*, 51.

36. Ibid., 52.

37. Ibid.

38. Gunn, *Thinking across the American Grain*, 69.

39. For Dean's account of radical empiricism, see *American Religious Empiricism*, x–xi, 19, 21–23, 83–84.

40. Dean, *History Making History*, 82ff.

41. Dean, "Humanistic Historicism," 44. I am supportive of the effort to articulate an embodied materialist historicity and a historicized naturalism. However, I am not convinced that Dean's use of the category of interpretation to describe processes within nature is legitimate or helpful. While anthropocentricism is always a lurking problem in our descriptions of the nonhuman world, the use of a term so thoroughly tied to human consciousness and linguistic activity requires a great deal of justification. Moreover, I think it oddly enough has the opposite effect to the one Dean desires, for rather than naturalizing human processes, it reinscribes the very linguistic focus that Dean seeks to undermine elsewhere. Although it is important to highlight continuities between human and nonhuman realities and to see human existence as located within and part of a larger natural context, there are, perhaps, better ways to articulate these points than appeal to the category of interpretation.

42. For Delwin Brown's account of radical empiricism see *Boundaries*, esp. chs. 2, 4. For another account of radical empiricism, see Nancy Frankenberry, *Religion and Radical Empiricism* (Albany: State University of New York Press, 1987), esp. chs. 3, 4, 5.

43. Brown, *Boundaries*, 49.

44. Ibid., 50.

45. Ibid., 51.

46. Ibid.

47. Ibid.

48. Brown, in contrast to some radical empiricists (e.g., Frankenberry), does not argue that we somehow experience the "whole" of reality. He states that "if there is a preconceptual mode of awareness, it does not follow that this awareness necessarily includes a 'sense of the whole,' or, if it does, that this sense of the whole has anything to do with religion." See "Marginalizing the Life of Language: Radical Empiricism as a Critique of Gadamer," in *New Essays in Religious Naturalism* ed. W. Creighton Peden and Larry E. Axel (Macon, Ga.: Mercer University Press, 1993), 31.

49. Brown, *Boundaries*, 52.

50. For a full account of Gordon Kaufman's position, see *In Face of Mystery*, part II.

51. Ibid., 14.
52. Ibid., 112.
53. Ibid., 32.
54. McFague, "An Earthly Theological Agenda."
55. Kaufman, *In Face of Mystery*, 33.
56. Ibid., 133.
57. Ibid., 105. See also part II.
58. Ibid., 266.
59. For positions that emphasize the productive character of power and the creative processes of cultural negotiation see the following: Michel Foucault, *Power/Knowledge: Selected Interviews and Other Writings, 1972–1977*, ed. C. Gordon, trans. C. Gordon et al. (New York: Pantheon, 1977); Roy Wagner, *The Invention of Culture* (Chicago: University of Chicago Press, 1981); James Clifford, *Predicament of Culture: Twentieth-Century Ethnography, Literature, and Art* (Cambridge, Mass.: Harvard University Press, 1988); Raymond Williams, *Marxism and Literature* (Oxford: Oxford University Press, 1977). For theological views that also move in these directions, see Brown, *Boundaries*, and Kathryn Tanner, "Theology and Popular Culture," in *Changing Conversations: Religious Reflection and Cultural Analysis*, ed. Dwight N. Hopkins and Sheila Greeve Davaney (New York: Routledge Press, 1997), 103–22, and *Theories of Culture: A New Agenda for Theology* (Minneapolis: Fortress Press, 1997).

CHAPTER 4. THEOLOGY IN A HISTORICIST PERSPECTIVE

1. For the fullest statements of Kaufman's positions, see Gordon D. Kaufman, *In Face of Mystery: A Constructive Theology* (Cambridge, Mass.: Harvard University Press, 1993), part II, and *God, Mystery, Diversity: Christian Theology in a Pluralistic World* (Minneapolis: Fortress Press, 1996), ch. 4.
2. In talking of religious traditions as encompassing interpretive networks of meaning, value, and practice, Kaufman and the other theologians discussed in this chapter are similar to many thinkers in the study of religion today. However, there are also important challenges to this way of portraying religions. Among those is the work of Terry F. Godlove Jr. Godlove argues, in *Religion, Interpretation and Diversity of Belief: The Framework Model from Kant to Durkheim to Davidson* (Macon, Ga.: Mercer University Press, 1997) against the widespread tendency in religious studies and cognate fields such as anthropology of religion, to understand religions as overarching conceptual schemes or interpretive grids that organize the raw and supposedly neutral data of experience. He asserts that this way of thinking derived from a relativistic misreading of Kant by Durkheim and has issued forth in our time in notions of radically incommensurate frameworks, differing "globally" from one another and resulting in a thoroughgoing relativism. Overagainst such ideas, Godlove resorts to a two-pronged argument. He invokes Donald Davidson's famous argument against conceptual schemes interpreted as incommensurable frameworks to assert that humans share a common store of beliefs and assumptions without which we would not be able to recognize or understand. Godlove then returns

to Kant to offer a Kantian transcendental argument concerning forms of receptivity and categories of understanding that are common to all human beings and that we cannot help but presuppose in all reflection about the world.

Over against this rejection of the so-called framework model, Godlove suggests that religious traditions are complex theoretical networks that do not rule out underlying commonality or unity but presuppose predominant agreement. Thus diversity of belief is located on the theoretical level and decreased on the level of what Godlove refers to as the "concrete."

Godlove's book is an interesting and important reflection on current theories of religion. It is not clear, however, that the criticisms Godlove sets forth apply to pragmatic historicists. Kaufman, whom Godlove highlights as a theologian utilizing the framework perspective, perhaps is most open to Godlove's attacks. Kaufman, in fact, does use the language of frameworks and conceptual alternatives. However, Godlove's reading of Kaufman is extremely superficial. Kaufman, and other pragmatic historicists, thoroughly reject precisely the notions of incommensurability and thoroughgoing relativism that trouble Godlove. Kaufman asserts that religious traditions are highly developed complex networks of meaning that are distinctive and difficult to reduce to one another on a theoretical level. But that does not lead him to claims of incommensurability or untranslatability but back to arenas of concrete repercussions where comparison and judgment are possible. Indeed pushing Kaufman may lead, as a number of his critics have suggested, back to the Kant Godlove so admires.

For a variety of discussions of the status of the term religion, see *Critical Terms for Religious Studies*, ed. Mark C. Taylor (Chicago: University of Chicago Press, 1998); Peter Harrison, *"Religion" and the Religions in the English Enlightenment* (Cambridge: Cambridge University Press, 1990); Nicholas Lash, *The Beginning and the End of "Religion"* (Cambridge: Cambridge University Press, 1996); *The Insider/Outsider Problem in the Study of Religion: A Reader*, ed. Russell T. McCutcheon (London: Cassell, 1999); and Russell T. McCutcheon, *The Manufacturing of Religion: The Discourse on Sui Generis Religion and the Politics of Nostalgia* (New York: Oxford University Press, 1997).

3. Kaufman, *In Face of Mystery*, 70.

4. Kaufman tends to assume the indispensability of "world construction," that is, the presence and necessity of at least implicit working assumptions about reality. Whether such assumptions are expendable is both an empirical and a "transcendental" question about the conditions of knowing and experiencing our world. On both levels, this issue continues to be vigorously disputed.

5. While Kaufman insists religious traditions or worldviews offer distinctive alternatives and should not be interpreted as cultural variations on common experiences or senses of reality, he, nonetheless, rejects the notion that they cannot engage one another. Indeed, he thinks such engagement should result in the emergence of new historical possibilities.

6. Gordon D. Kaufman, "Mystery, Critical Consciousness, and Faith," in *The Rationality of Religious Belief: Essays in Honor of Basil Mitchell*, ed. William J. Abraham and Steven W. Holtzer (Oxford: Clarendon Press, 1987), 59–60.

7. Kaufman, *In Face of Mystery*, 8.

8. Gordon D. Kaufman, *The Theological Imagination: Constructing the Concept of God* (Philadelphia: The Westminster Press, 1981), esp. ch. 4.

9. Ibid., 22.

10. Kaufman, *In Face of Mystery*, 27.

11. Ibid., 41.

12. Ibid., 28.

13. Ibid., 24ff.

14. Ibid., 30–31.

15. Ibid., 29.

16. Kaufman, *God, Mystery, Diversity*, esp. chs. 3, 11, and 12. In an interesting fashion, Godlove's arguments might well support the borrowing from and intermingling of traditions in a way that the incommensurable framework model rules out. See note 2.

17. Ibid., 296.

18. Sallie McFague, *Metaphorical Theology: Models of God in Religious Language* (Philadelphia: Fortress Press, 1982); and *Models of God: Theology for an Ecological, Nuclear Age* (Philadelphia: Fortress Press, 1987).

19. McFague, *Models of God*, 3.

20. McFague, *Metaphorical Theology*, 15.

21. McFague, *Models of God*, 193.

22. Ibid., 32, 40.

23. Ibid., 3.

24. Sallie McFague, *The Body of God: An Ecological Theology* (Minneapolis: Fortress Press, 1993).

25. McFague, *Models of God*, 36.

26. Ibid., 41.

27. McFague, *The Body of God*, 73–76.

28. McFague, *Models of God*, 41.

29. Ibid., 35.

30. Ibid., 42.

31. Ibid., 43.

32. Ibid., 45.

33. Ibid., x.

34. Ibid., 46.

35. Ibid., 36.

36. McFague explores the conflict between the evolutionary story and her Christian story most thoroughly in *The Body of God*, esp. ch. 6.

37. In *The Body of God*, McFague seems to leave behind the language of two poles and instead adopts Francis Schüssler Fiorenza's language of "wide reflective equilibrium," which invokes multiple sources and criteria to build a cumulative case for a position. However, she does not maintain this orientation, but as the book develops, reverts to the distinction between the Christian vision and the contemporary vision with the Christian model taking normative precedence without full explanation why. The perspective of this book is that Fiorenza's approach is more adequate to a historicist outlook. For McFague on Fiorenza, see *The Body of God*, 84–87, 239.

38. Ibid., 160f., 189f.

39. William Dean, *History Making History: The New Historicism in American Religious Thought* (Albany: State University of New York Press, 1988), 18.

40. William Dean, *American Religious Empiricism* (Albany: State University of New York Press, 1986), 114.

41. Ibid.

42. Ibid.

43. Ibid., 117.

44. Ibid., 115.

45. Dean, *History Making History*, 17.

46. Dean, *American Religious Empiricism*, 114. Dean, in an interesting parallel to this claim about locating one's self in a religious tradition, calls for us to locate ourselves within the context of particular nation-states instead of more globally. My counterclaim would be that just as limiting ourselves to the confines of one religious tradition can be problematic today, so is an overidentification with a nation-state. Perhaps both religious traditions and nation-states are growing obsolete in our interdependent world. See Dean, *The Religious Critic in American Culture* (Albany: State University of New York Press, 1994).

47. Linell E. Cady, *Religion, Theology and American Public Life* (Albany: State University of New York Press, 1993).

48. Ibid., 56.

49. Ibid., 41ff.

50. Ibid., 51.

51. Ibid.

52. Ibid.

53. I think Cady's examples of theologians setting forth portrayals of the "whole" of the tradition demonstrate how problematic her approach is. She turns, in particular, to the work of feminist theologians Rosemary Radford Ruether and Virginia Mollenkott as examples of theologians extending the Christian tradition by this strategy. But I would contend that they are not offering any notion of the whole of the tradition or the general thrust of the tradition but are pursuing what is known as a "canon within the canon" approach. Such a way of proceeding elevates a particular strand or point within a tradition and claims for it a normativity absent from the rest of the tradition. In Ruether's case this strand is the prophetic-liberating trajectory within Hebrew religion and Christianity. When examined, this approach also turns to "isolated elements" in the tradition, though it sometimes denies them the absolute status bestowed upon them by Cady's conventionalists such as postliberals. My point is that the difference between Cady's examples of conventionalists and her feminist extentionalists is *not* that one elevates "isolated elements" from the past, for both do; the differences lie in the status afforded those elements and the uses to which they are put.

53. Ibid., 195, no. 28.

54. Ibid., 61, 145.

55. Ibid., 143.

56. Ibid., 144.

57. Delwin Brown, "Beyond Boundaries: Toward a Radical Historicism in Theology," *American Journal of Theology and Philosophy* 18.2 (May 1997).

58. Ibid.

59. Delwin Brown, *Boundaries of Our Habitations: Tradition and Theological Construction* (Albany: State University of New York Press, 1994).

60. Ibid., 63.

61. Ibid., 67. Kathryn Tanner has also recently stressed a dynamic, unstable, and conflict-filled model of culture that resonates strongly with Brown. See Tanner, *Theories of Culture: A New Agenda for Theology* (Minneapolis: Fortress Press, 1997). It should also be noted that debates continue about whether the concept of culture has now become overused and encompasses so much that its organizing power and heuristic utility have been weakened. See Bernard McGrane, *Beyond Anthropology: Society and the Other* (New York: Columbia University Press, 1989) and Tomoko Masuzawa, "Culture," in *Critical Terms for Religious Studies*, ed. Mark C. Taylor (Chicago: University of Chicago Press, 1998).

62. Brown, *Boundaries of Our Habitations*, 4.

63. Ibid., 114.

64. Ibid., 113.

65. Ibid., 77–83.

66. Ibid., 116.

67. Ibid., 135–36.

68. George A. Lindbeck, *The Nature of Doctrine: Religion and Theology in a Postliberal Age* (Philadelphia: Westminster Press, 1984), 81.

69. Brown, *Boundaries of Our Habitations*, 92ff., 145ff.

70. Brown, "Beyond Boundaries."

71. Lawrence E. Sullivan, "'Seeking an End to the Primary Text' or 'Putting an End to the Text as Primary,'" in *Beyond the Classics: Essays in Religious Studies and Liberal Education*, ed. Frank E. Reynolds and Sheryl L. Burkhalter (Atlanta, Ga.: Scholars Press, 1990), 58.

72. Rosalind Shaw and Charles Stewart, "Introduction: Problematizing Syncretism," in *Syncretism/Anti-Syncretism: The Politics of Religious Synthesis*, ed. Charles Stewart and Rosalind Shaw (London and New York: Routledge, 1994), 10.

73. The question of whether identities are tied to single dominant traditions or emerge out of the intersection of varied traditions is in large part an empirical question. And the analysis of this book suggests that such exploration reveals no singular way human identity is wrought, but that the process of identity formation differs from time and place to time and place. However, in our time many accounts depict the progressive pluralization of identity. This work also suggests that such pluralization and multitraditionedness is not, contra the postliberals, necessarily a problem to overcome but may indeed have certain advantages in our age. It has asked further, what kind of theology might best take account of not only our traditionedness but also our multitraditionedness.

74. James Clifford, *The Predicament of Culture: Twentieth-Century Ethnography, Literature and Art* (Cambridge, Mass.: Harvard University Press, 1988), 14.

75. Ibid.

76. Ibid., 11.

77. Ibid., 4.

78. Delwin Brown, "Refashioning Self and Other: Theology, Academy and the New Ethnography," in *Converging On Culture: Theologians in Dialogue with Cultural Analysis and Criticism* ed. Delwin Brown, Sheila Greeve Davaney, and Kathryn Tanner (New York: Oxford University Press/AAR, 2001).

79. Sullivan, 45.

80. Richard Rorty, *Contingency, irony and solidarity* (Cambridge: Cambridge University Press, 1989), 91.

CHAPTER 5. PHILOSOPHICAL FELLOW TRAVELERS

1. Works by Richard Rorty that are especially pertinent to the issues explored in this book include *Philosophy and the Mirror of Nature* (Princeton: Princeton University Press, 1980); *Consequences of Pragmatism* (Minneapolis: University of Minnesota Press, 1982); *Contingency, irony, and solidarity* (Cambridge: Cambridge University Press, 1989); *Objectivity, Relativism, and Truth: Philosophical Papers I* (Cambridge: Cambridge University Press, 1991).

2. Cornel West, review of *Philosophy and the Mirror of Nature*, *Union Seminary Quarterly Review* 37 (Fall/Winter 1981–82): 179–85.

3. Rorty, *Contingency, irony and solidarity*, 5.

4. David L. Hall, *Richard Rorty: Prophet and Poet of the New Pragmatism* (Albany: State University of New York Press, 1994), 80ff.

5. Rorty, *Contingency, irony and solidarity*, 42.

6. Ibid., 7.

7. Rorty, *Consequences of Pragmatism*, xlii.

8. Ibid., *Contingency, irony and solidarity*, 50.

9. Ibid., 7, 11, 41; Rorty, *Consequences of Pragmatism*, xix.

10. Rorty, *Contingency, irony and solidarity*, 42.

11. Ibid., esp. part II.

12. Rorty, *Consequences of Pragmatism*, xix.

13. Rorty, *Philosophy and the Mirror of Nature*, ch. VIII.

14. Ibid., 266–67; and Rorty, *Contingency, irony and solidarity*, 8.

15. Rorty, "Trotsky and the Wild Orchids," in *Wild Orchids and Trotsky: Messages from American Universities*, ed. Mark Edmundson (New York: Penguin Books, 1993), 43.

16. Rorty, *Contingency, irony and solidarity*, 5.

17. Ibid.

18. Rorty, *Objectivity, Relativism and Truth*, 26; *Consequences of Pragmatism*, xxxvii.

19. Rorty, *Objectivity, Relativism and Truth*, 200–1.

20. Ibid., 23.

21. Rorty, "Trotsky and the Wild Orchids," 32.

22. See Thomas Haskell, "The Curious Persistence of Rights Talk in the Age of 'Interpretation,'" *The Journal of American History* 74.3 (December 1987): 984–1012, for a discussion of the debate about what happens to claims on behalf of human rights when their Enlightenment warrants are eroded.

23. Rorty, Contingency, irony and solidarity, 53.

24. For references to the public/private split, see ibid., xv, 83, 120, 197.

25. Rorty, "Trotsky and the Wild Orchids," 29–50.

26. Nancy Fraser. Unruly Practices: Power, Discourse and Gender in Contemporary Social Theory (Minneapolis: University of Minnesota Press), ch. 5; David Hall, Richard Rorty, esp. chs. 1–2.

27. Rorty, "Trotsky and the Wild Orchids," 36.

28. Rorty, Contingency, irony and solidarity, xiii.

29. Richard Rorty, "Religion as a Conversation Stopper," Common Knowledge 3 (Spring 1996): 2. Rorty most often speaks of the public/private split as one between the sphere of obligation and the arena wherein obligation does not pertain rather than invoking the contrast between communal and individual. However, his statements in relation to religion indicate the latter split between communal and individual also plays a part in the public/private distinction.

30. Richard Rorty, "Religious Faith, Intellectual Responsibility, and Romance," in Pragmatism, Neo-Pragmatism, and Religion: Conversations with Richard Rorty, ed. Charley D. Hardwick and Donald A. Crosby (New York: Peter Lang, 1997), 14.

31. Ibid., 1.

32. Hall, Richard Rorty, 107.

33. Linell E. Cady, Religion, Theology and American Public Life (Albany: State University of New York Press, 1993), 90.

34. Jeffrey Stout, Ethics after Babel: The Languages of Morals and Their Discontents (Boston: Beacon Press, 1988), ch. 12.

35. Henry S. Levinson, "Rorty, Diggins, and the Promise of Pragmatism," in Pragmatism, Neo-Pragmatism, and Religion: Conversations with Richard Rorty, ed. Charley D. Hardwick and Donald A. Crosby (New York: Peter Lang, 1997).

36. Gordon D. Kaufman. God, Mystery, Diversity: Christian Theology in a Pluralistic World (Minneapolis: Fortress Press, 1996), ch. 1.

37. Cady, Religion, Theology and American Public Life, 73–74, 81–83.

38. Jeffrey Stout, The Flight from Authority: Religion, Morality and the Quest for Autonomy (Notre Dame, Ind.: University of Notre Dame Press, 1981), 67.

39. Stout, Ethics after Babel.

40. Alasdair MacIntyre, After Virtue, 2nd edition (Notre Dame, Ind.: University of Notre Dame Press, 1984), 245.

41. Stout, Ethics after Babel, 120.

42. Ibid., 2.

43. Ibid., xi.

44. Ibid., 19f, 63f.

45. Ibid., 64–65.

46. Ibid.

47. Ibid., 142.

48. Delwin Brown, Boundaries of Our Habitations: Tradition and Theological Construction (Albany: State University of New York Press, 1994), chs. 1, 4.

49. Stout, *Ethics after Babel*, 73.

50. Ibid., 74–77, 78, 218, 240.

51. Ibid., 249f.

52. Ibid., 23. For a subsequent discussion of justification and truth see "On Having a Morality in Common," in *Prospects for a Common Morality*, ed. Gene Outka and John P. Reed (Princeton: Princeton University Press, 1993).

53. Stout, *Ethics after Babel*, 29–30.

54. Ibid., 27.

55. Ibid., 21ff.

56. Ibid., 54, 62–63.

57. Ibid., 21.

58. Ibid., 24.

59. Ibid., 26.

60. Ibid., 29ff.

61. Ibid., 28.

62. Ibid., 244.

63. Ibid., 214.

64. Ibid., 212.

65. Ibid., 282ff.

66. Ibid., 188.

67. Ibid., 163.

68. Ibid.

69. Edmund Santurri, "Nihilism Revisited," *The Journal of Religion* 71.1 (January 1991): 67–78.

70. Stanley Hauerwas and Philip D. Kenneson, "A Review Essay: Flight from Foundationalism or Things Aren't as Bad as They Seem," *Soundings* 71 (1988): 683–99.

71. Rorty, *Objectivity, Relativism and Truth*, 23.

72. Ibid.

73. Kaufman, *God, Mystery, Diversity*, 196.

74. Ibid., 198.

75. For similar criticisms, see Victor Anderson, "The Pragmatic Secularization of Theology," in *Pragmatism, Neo-Pragmatism, and Religion: Conversations with Richard Rorty*, ed. Charley D. Hardwick and Donald A. Crosby (New York: Peter Lang, 1997), 104ff.

76. Delwin Brown, "Refashioning Self and Other: Theology, Academy and the New Ethnography," in *Converging on Culture: Theologians in Dialogue with Cultural Analysis and Criticism*, ed. Delwin Brown, Sheila Greeve Davaney, and Kathryn Tanner (New York: Oxford University Press/AAR, 2001).

77. Cornel West, *The American Evasion of Philosophy: A Genealogy of Pragmatism* (Madison: The University of Wisconsin Press, 1989), 230.

78. Ibid., 213.

79. Ibid., 208.

80. Ibid.

81. Ibid., 230.

82. Cornel West, *Keeping Faith: Philosophy and Race in America* (New York: Routledge Publishing Co, 1993), 130.

83. Ibid., 132.

84. Ibid., 134.

85. Ibid., 46.

86. West, *The American Evasion of Philosophy*, 232.

CHAPTER 6. CONCLUSION

1. There is a sense in which this text overemphasizes the issue of the past. A pragmatic historicist might speak much more emphatically than is the case here of how the role of the imagined and hoped-for future critically shapes our decisions. The reasons for such elaboration on the question of the past are twofold: (1) pragmatic historicists have often been accused of failing to theorize the status and role of the past adequately, and (2) the status and role given to the past by pragmatic historicists is distinctive from that bestowed upon the past by other historicist theologians.

2. Simon Maimela, "Black Theology and the Quest for a God of Liberation," in *Theology at the End of Modernity*, ed. Sheila Greeve Davaney (Philadelphia: Trinity Press International, 1991), 157.

3. Sandra Harding, *Whose Science, Whose Knowledge? Thinking from Women's Lives* (Ithaca, N.Y.: Cornell University Press, 1991), 78.

4. Ibid., 119.

5. Gordon D. Kaufman, *In Face of Mystery: A Constructive Theology* (Cambridge, Mass.: Harvard University Press, 1993), 64f.

6. Linell Cady, *Religion, Theology and American Public Life* (Albany: State University of New York Press, 1993), 99.

7. Ibid., 116.

8. Kaufman, *In Face of Mystery*, 43.

9. Ibid., 43, 65f.

10. Ibid., 66.

11. Ibid.

12. Cady, *Religion, Theology and American Public Life*, 9ff.

13. Ibid., 68–69.

14. Ibid., esp. ch. 2, 31–33.

15. Ibid., 85.

16. Ibid., 92.

17. Delwin Brown, *Boundaries of Our Habitations: Tradition and Theological Construction* (Albany: State University of New York Press, 1994), 5.

18. Ibid., 5–6.

19. Ibid., 6.

20. Ibid.

21. See Maimela, "Black Theology and the Quest for a God of Liberation." Cornel West, *The American Evasion of Philosophy: A Genealogy of Pragmatism* (Madison: The University of Wisconsin Press, 1989), esp. ch. 6. Rebecca Chopp, "Emerging Issues and Theological Education," *Theological Education* (Spring 1990): 106–24, and "Feminism's Theological Pragmatics: A Social Naturalism of Women's Experience," *The Journal of Religion* 67 (April 1987):

239–56. For a thoughtful and powerful linking of a relational cosmology and a commitment to justice as solidarity, see Douglas Sturm, *Solidarity and Suffering: Essays Toward a Politics of Relationality* (Albany: State University of New York Press, 1998).

22. Richard Rorty, *Contingency, irony, and solidarity* (Cambridge: Cambridge University Press, 1989) 91.

23. Charlene Haddock Seigfried, *Pragmatism and Feminism: Reweaving the Social Fabric* (Chicago: The University of Chicago Press, 1996), 275. For some, the pursuit of consensus is counterproductive. Serene Jones, in a recent article, has argued for the efficacy of rhetorical devices that "demonize" our opponents; in the case she explores the administration of Yale University and its disputes with various labor unions at the university. The approach supported in this volume rules out such one-sided and un-self-critical moves. See Serene Jones, "Cultural Labor and Theological Critique," in *Converging on Culture: Theologians in Dialogue with Cultural Analysis and Criticism*, ed. Delwin Brown, Sheila Greeve Davaney, and Kathryn Tanner (New York: Oxford University/AAR Press, 2001).

24. Seigfried, *Pragmatism and Feminism*, 275.

25. Ibid.

26. Ibid.

27. Francis Schüssler Fiorenza, *Foundational Theology: Jesus and the Church* (New York: Crossroad, 1984), 302f.

28. Gustavo Gutiérrez, *The Power of the Poor in History* (Maryknoll, N.Y.: Orbis Books, 1983), 91f.

29. See Janet R. Jakobsen, "The Body Politic vs. Lesbian Bodies: Publics, Counter-Publics and the Uses of Norms," in *Horizons in Feminist Theology: Identity, Tradition, and Norms*, ed. Rebecca Chopp and Sheila Greeve Davaney (Minneapolis: Fortress Press, 1997) for a helpful depiction of our processes of creating "nonpersons" and the problematic status of the "public."

30. See Larry Kent Graham, *Discovering Images of God: Narratives of Care Among Lesbians and Gays* (Louisville, Ky.: Westminster/John Knox Press, 1997)

31. See Jacquelyn Grant, *White Women's Christ and Black Women's Jesus* (Atlanta: Scholars Press, 1989), esp. ch. 7.

32. Adrienne Rich, "Sources: XV," in *Your Native Land, Your Life* (New York: W. W. Norton, 1986), 17.

33. Gordon D. Kaufman, *God, Mystery, Diversity: Christian Theology in a Pluralistic World* (Minneapolis: Fortress Press, 1996), chs. 3, 12.

34. Ibid., 65.

35. Ibid.

36. Delwin Brown, "Knowing the Mystery of God: Neville and Apophatic Theology," in *Critical Studies in the Thought of Robert C. Neville*, ed. J. Harley Chapman and Nancy Frankenberry (Albany: State University of New York Press, 1999). I am appreciative of both Brown and Linell Cady who have raised this issue with great intensity to me.

37. Brown, *Boundaries of Our Habitations*, 116–19, 132, 137.

38. One very interesting question that is raised by the possibility that some persons live out of more than one religious tradition at once is whether that real-

ity does not challenge the notion of religions as encompassing networks of meaning and value that provide orientation for the multiple dimensions of life. This is a different question than whether we can intermingle traditions functionally or conceptually. That has to do with issues of incommensurability, translatability, and so forth. The claim that one can be, say, a Catholic and practitioner of the Mayan cosmo-vision raises the question of comprehensiveness of traditions and whether location within plural encompassing religions is intelligible at all.

39. See William Dean, "Humanistic Historicism and Naturalistic Historicism," in *Theology at the End of Modernity*, ed. Sheila Greeve Davaney (Philadelphia: Trinity Press International, 1991); Kaufman, *In Face of Mystery*; Sallie McFague, *The Body of God: An Ecological Nuclear Age* (Minneapolis: Fortress Press, 1994).

40. McFague, *The Body of God*, 108.

41. Ibid.

42. Ibid., 109.

43. Dean, "Humanistic Historicism," 44.

44. McFague, *The Body of God*, 165, 200–201.

45. Loren Eiseley, *The Unexpected Universe* (New York: Harcourt, Brace & World, 1964), 86.

46. McFague, *The Body of God*, 172.

47. Ibid., 173.

48. Ibid., 174.

49. For Dean on radical empiricism, see *American Religious Empiricism* (Albany: State University of New York Press, 1986), x–xi, 19, 21–23; *History Making History: The New Historicism in American Religious Thought* (Albany: State University of New York Press, 1988), xi, 21, 24, 101, 142; and "Empirical Theology: A Revisable Tradition," *Process Studies*, Summer 1990, 85–102.

50. Dean, *History Making History*, 105.

51. Ibid., 82.

52. In this, Dean seems less aware than he might be that these values come to us because of power and not only because they have "stood the test of time."

53. Dean, *History Making History*, 83.

54. Kaufman, *In Face of Mystery*, esp. chs. 10–14.

55. Ibid., esp. ch. 10.

56. Ibid., 129f, 139f.

57. Richard Rorty, *Objectivity, Relativism, and Truth: Philosophical Papers I* (Cambridge: Cambridge University Press, 1991), 23.

58. Kaufman, *God, Mystery, Diversity*, esp. ch. 12.

59. Cady, *Religion, Theology and American Public Life*, 79.

60. Such substantive theological work is already being articulated by many of those I have labeled pragmatic historicists. The reconstructive work on the idea of God by Kaufman and McFague stands out. Interestingly, little substantive proposals for reconstructing Christian doctrines and symbols have emerged from other historicist perspectives, most notably postliberalism.

61. Sidney Hook, "Pragmatism and the Tragic Sense of Life," *Contemporary American Philosophy*, ed. John E. Smith (London: George Allen & Unwin, 1970).

SELECT BIBLIOGRAPHY

Anderson, Victor, "The Pragmatic Secularization of Theology." In *Pragmatism, Neo-Pragmatism, and Religion: Conversations with Richard Rorty*. Edited by Charley D. Hardwick and Donald A. Crosby. New York: Peter Lang, 1997.

Brown, Delwin. "Refashioning Self and Other: Theology, Academy and the New Ethnography." In *Converging on Culture: Theologians in Dialogue with Cultural Analysis and Criticism*. Edited by Delwin Brown, Sheila Greeve Davaney, and Kathryn Tanner. New York: Oxford University Press/AAR, 2001.

———. "Knowing the Mystery of God: Neville and Apophatic Theology." In *Critical Studies in the Thought of Robert C. Neville*. Edited by J. Harley Chapman and Nancy Frankenberry. Albany: State University of New York Press, 1999.

———. "Beyond Boundaries: Toward a Radical Historicism in Theology." *American Journal of Theology and Philosophy* 18.2 (May 1997).

———. *Boundaries of Our Habitations: Tradition and Theological Construction*. Albany, New York: State University of New York Press, 1994.

———. "Marginalizing the Life of Language: Radical Empiricism as a Critique of Gadamer." In *New Essays in Religious Naturalism*. Edited by Creighton Peden and Larry Axel. Macon, Ga.: Mercer University Press, 1993.

———. "The Fall of '26: Gerald Birney Smith and the Collapse of Socio-Historical Theology." *American Journal of Theology and Philosophy* 11.3 (September 1990).

Cady, Linell E. *Religion, Theology, and American Public Life*. Albany: State University of New York Press, 1993.

Chopp, Rebecca, "Emerging Issues and Theological Education." *Theological Education* (Spring 1990).

———. "Feminism's Theological Pragmatics: A Social Naturalism of Women's Experience." *The Journal of Religion* 67 (April 1987).

Davaney, Sheila Greeve. "Theology and the Turn to Cultural Analysis." In *Converging on Culture: Theologians in Dialogue with Cultural Analysis and Criticism*. New York: Oxford University Press/AAR, 2001.

———. "Judging Theologies: Truth in an Historicist Perspective." In *Pragmatism, Neo-Pragmatism, and Religion: Conversations with Richard Rorty*. Edited by Charley D. Hardwick and Donald E. Crosby. New York: Peter Lang Publishing, 1997.

———. "Between the One and the Many: A Response to Delwin Brown's Theory of Tradition." *American Journal of Philosophy and Theology* 18.2 (May 1997).

——. "Mapping Theologies." In *Changing Conversations*. Edited by Dwight Hopkins and Sheila Greeve Davaney. New York: Routledge, 1996.

——. "Human Historicity, Cosmic Creativity and the Theological Imagination: Reflections on the Work of Gordon D. Kaufman." *Religious Studies Review* 20.3 (July 1994).

——, ed. *Theology at the End of Modernity*. Philadelphia: Trinity Press International, 1991.

——. "Directions in Historicism: Language, Experience and Pragmatic Adjudication." *Zygon: Journal of Religion and Science* 26.2 (June 1991).

Dean, William D. *The Religious Critic in American Culture*. Albany: State University of New York Press, 1994.

——. "Humanistic Historicism and Naturalistic Historicism." In *Theology at the End of Modernity*. Edited by Sheila Greeve Davaney. Philadelphia: Trinity Press International, 1991.

——. "Empirical Theology: A Revisable Tradition." *Process Studies*, Summer 1990.

——. *History Making History: The New Historicism in American Religious Thought*. Albany: State University of New York Press, 1988.

——. *American Religious Empiricism*. Albany: State University of New York Press, 1986.

Kaufman, Gordon D. *God, Mystery, Diversity: Christian Theology in a Pluralistic World*. Minneapolis: Fortress Press, 1996.

——. *In Face of Mystery: A Constructive Theology*. Cambridge, Mass.: Harvard University Press, 1993.

——. "Mystery, Critical Consciousness, and Faith." In *The Rationality of Religious Belief: Essays in Honor of Basil Mitchell*. Edited by William J. Abraham and Steven W. Holtzer. Oxford: Clarendon Press, 1987.

——. *Theology for a Nuclear Age*. Philadelphia: Westminster Press, 1985.

——. *The Theological Imagination: Constructing the Concept of God*. Philadelphia: The Westminster Press, 1981.

Lindbeck, George A. "Scripture, Consensus, and Community." In *Biblical Interpretation in Crisis: The Ratzinger Conference on Bible and Church*. Edited by Richard John Neuhaus, 74–101. Grand Rapids, Mich.: William B. Eerdmans, 1989.

——. "The Church's Mission to a Postmodern Culture." In *Postmodern Theology: Christian Faith in a Pluralistic World*. Edited by Frederic B. Burnham. New York: Harper & Row, 1989.

——. "The Story-Shaped Church: Critical Exegesis and Theological Interpretation." In *Scriptural Authority and Narrative Interpretation*. Edited by Garrett Green. Philadelphia: Fortress Press, 1987.

——. *The Nature of Doctrine: Religion and Theology in a Postliberal Age*. Philadelphia: The Westminster Press, 1984.

Maimela, Simon. "Black Theology and the Quest for a God of Liberation." In *Theology at the End of Modernity*. Edited by Sheila Greeve Davaney. Philadelphia: Trinity Press International, 1991.

McFague, Sallie. *The Body of God: An Ecological Theology*. Minneapolis: Fortress, 1994.

———. "An Earthly Theological Agenda." *Christian Century* 108 (January 2–9, 1991).

———. "Cosmology and Christianity: Implications of the Common Creation Story for Theology." In *Theology at the End of Modernity.* Edited by Sheila Greeve Davaney. Philadelphia: Trinity Press International, 1991.

———. *Models of God: Theology for an Ecological Nuclear Age.* Philadelphia: Fortress Press, 1987.

———. *Metaphorical Theology: Models of God in Religious Language.* Philadelphia: Fortress Press, 1982.

Rorty, Richard. *Objectivity, Relativism, and Truth: Philosophical Papers I.* Cambridge: Cambridge University Press, 1991.

———. *Contingency, irony and solidarity.* Cambridge: Cambridge University Press, 1989.

———. "Solidarity or Objectivity?" In *Post-Analytic Philosophy.* Edited by John Rajchman and Cornel West. New York: Columbia University Press, 1985.

———. *Consequences of Pragmatism.* Minneapolis: University of Minnesota Press, 1982.

———. *Philosophy and the Mirror of Nature.* Princeton, N.J.: Princeton University Press, 1980.

Stout, Jeffrey. *Ethics after Babel: The Languages of Morals and Their Discontents.* Boston: Beacon Press, 1988.

———. *Flight from Authority: Religion, Morality and the Quest for Autonomy.* Notre Dame, Ind.: University of Notre Dame Press, 1981.

Tanner, Kathryn. "Theology and Popular Culture." In *Changing Conversations: Religious Reflection and Cultural Analysis.* Edited by Dwight N. Hopkins and Sheila Greeve Davaney. New York: Routledge Press, 1997.

———. *Theories of Culture: A New Agenda for Theology.* Minneapolis: Fortress Press, 1997.

Tracy, David. *Plurality and Ambiguity: Hermeneutics, Religion, Hope.* San Francisco: Harper & Row, 1987.

———. *The Analogical Imagination: Christian Theology and the Culture of Pluralism.* New York: Crossroad, 1981.

———. "Lindbeck and the New Program for Theology: A Reflection." *The Thomist* 49, 1985.

West, Cornel. *The American Evasion of Philosophy: A Genealogy of Pragmatism.* Madison: University of Wisconsin Press, 1989.

———. Review of *Philosophy and the Mirror of Nature* by Richard Rorty, *Union Seminary Quarterly Review* 37 (Fall/Winter 1981–82).

INDEX

adjudication. *See* judgments, normative

agency: and tradition, 74–75, 104, 107, 142; as human responsibility, 25, 26, 75–76, 143, 144, 185, 189. *See also* pragmatic historicism: on agency

Altizer, Thomas J. J., 16, 20

anthropocentrism, 59, 67, 68–69

assumptions. *See* theories

authority: breakdown of, in modernity, 5–6, 11, 12, 158; location of, 13, 40, 43–44, 47, 94–95. *See also* pragmatic historicism: on authority

Barth, Karl, 14–15, 16, 57

Bernstein, Richard, 47

Bible, the, 33, 34, 39, 87, 95, 152, 196 n.14

bricolage, 109, 133, 137, 140, 141. *See also* syncretism

Brown, Delwin, 12, 39, 56, 72, 73, 76, 90, 99, 101, 113, 173, 198 n.1, 200 n.22, 201 n.48; on agency, 104, 107; on historicism, 104; on human existence, 70–71, 104, 107, 109, 175; on normative criteria and judgments, 71, 159–60; on reality, 70–71; on the nature and task of theology, 106, 108, 115, 140–41, 159–60, 175; on the relation between past and present, 104, 106–7; on tradition(s), 104–11, 132

Cady, Linell, 40, 99, 127, 129, 188; on God, 156–57; on normative

criteria and judgments, 102–3; on the nature and task of theology, 101–4, 159; on the public sphere, 158–59; on the relation between past and present, 102; on tradition(s), 102–3, 205 n.53; on truth, 158, 187

Case, Shirley Jackson, 12, 13

Chicago School, the, 12–13, 14, 57, 199 n.13

Chopp, Rebecca, 162

Christianity, 10, 11, 12–13, 16, 20–21, 112, 117, 144, 152, 196 n.14, 197 n.28, 197 n. 29. *See also* pragmatic historicism: on Christianity; theology, Christian

classics, 42–48, 89, 100, 106. *See also* Tracy, David

Clifford, James, 104, 110, 113, 200 n.22

"common creation story," 65, 97, 177, 178, 180

Cone, James, 17

correlation, method of, 42, 43–44, 94. *See also* McFague, Sallie; Tracy, David

cosmology. *See* reality

criteria, normative: as historical, 84, 123–24, 133–34, 143, 159, 182–83; as pragmatic, 48, 123–24, 133–34, 143–44, 182, 184; content of, 69, 84, 144–45, 182–85; location of, 5, 25, 34, 47–48, 71, 94–96, 97, 102–3, 129, 143–44, 158, 177–78, 182–85. *See also* pragmatic historicism: on normative criteria

Bishop Spong
Karen Armstrong